RICH CHRISTIANS IN AN AGE OF HUNGER

By the same author

Andreas Bodenstein Von Karlstadt 'Studies in Medieval and Reformation Thought'
The Chicago Declaration
Karlstadt's Battle with Luther: Documents in a Liberal-Radical Debate
Christ and Violence
Cry Justice: The Bible on Hunger and Poverty
Living More Simply
Evangelicals and Development: Toward a Theology of Social Change
Lifestyle in the Eighties: An Evangelical Commitment to Simple Lifestyle
Nuclear Holocaust and Christian Hope
Completely Pro-Life
Preaching About Life in a Threatening World
Nonviolence: The Invincible Weapon? (Exploring the Limits of Nonviolence)

RICH CHRISTIANS IN AN AGE OF HUNGER

Ronald J. Sider

HODDER AND STOUGHTON
LONDON SYDNEY AUCKLAND TORONTO

For Ted, Michael, and Sonya

NOTE TO UK EDITION

Many figures in this book which come from World Bank statistics etc. have been left in dollars. Other sums have been converted to pounds sterling. In May 1990, when the conversion work was done, the rate of exchange was 1.64 but this has risen to 1.9 at the time of going to press. As a rough guide, halve any dollar figure to get its equivalent value – e.g. $10 ⌒ £5.

British Library Cataloguing in Publication Data

Sider, Ronald J.
    Rich christians in an age of hunger. – New ed.
    1. Wealth – Christian viewpoints
    I. Title
    261.834

    ISBN 0-340-35468-2

Published by Hodder & Stoughton, a division of Hodder & Stoughton Ltd, Mill Road, Dunton Green, Sevenoaks, Kent TN13 2YA. Editorial Office: 47 Bedford Square, London WC1B 3DP. Photoset by Rowland Phototypesetting Ltd, Bury St Edmunds, Suffolk. Printed in Great Britain by Cox & Wyman Ltd, Reading, Berks.

Contents

Acknowledgments

Many wonderful friends have helped in a wide variety of ways during the writing, revising and typing of the several versions and editions. Without seeking to suggest their responsibility for what still remains inadequate, I want to acknowledge my appreciation for their invaluable help: Judy and John F. Alexander, Nancy Alexander, Anne Allen, Mary Beekley-Peacock, Robert Chase, Calvin DeWitt, Carl Gambs, Linwood Geiger, Donald Hay, Gil Heebner, Roland Hoksbergen, Larry Hollar, Carl Kreider, John Mason, Tom McDaniel, Naomi Miller, John Mitchell, Titus Peachey, Ketly Pierre, Grant Power, Bill Rau, Don Reeves, Harry Rempel, Debbie Reuman, Philip Shea, Joe Sheldon, Arthur Simon, Tom Sine, Stephen L. S. Smith, Robin Songer, Richard Taylor, John P. Tiemstra, Michael Trueblood, Carol and Merold Westphal.

Perhaps all books must be lived before they are written. That is certainly true of books like this one. I must immediately confess that I make no claim to be living out the full implications of this book. But I have begun the pilgrimage. The most important reason I am even a little way down the path is my wife, Arbutus Lichti Sider. Always enthusiastic about a simpler living standard, spontaneously generous and eager to experiment, she has slowly tugged me along. For her critical reading of the manuscript, for our life together without which this book would never have been possible and for her love, I express my deepest appreciation.

The British edition, like the American, is affectionately dedicated to our three children, Theodore Ronald, Michael Jay and Sonya Maria, who will have to live in the global village we are now creating.

Introduction

This book is about joy and self-fulfilment – that genuine joy and enduring happiness that flow from practising Jesus's paradoxical teaching that it is better to give than to receive.

Millions of North Americans and Western Europeans are in despair as they seek in vain for happiness through ever greater material abundance. The idolatrous materialism of the economic rat race creates alcoholics, ruined marriages and heart attacks. Jesus offers a better way of joy through sharing.

We cannot gain happiness by seeking it directly. It comes as a by-product as we give ourselves to others. I can personally witness to this truth. Many suppose that the lifestyle I have written about and sought to live is hard and painful. In truth, my life overflows with joy and fulfilment.

Did you know that for around £300 you can create a new job for a poor person and thus dramatically transform that person's whole family? In the process, you experience a joy that the self-centred never taste.

I do not mean to hide the fact that this book reports wrenching facts and calls for costly living. Millions of people die unnecessarily every year because rich folk like you and me have ignored the Bible's clear teaching that God measures the integrity of our faith by how we respond to the poor. So I report the tragic facts of hunger and starvation (Part 1) and explain the biblical teaching about God's special compassion for the poor and weak (Part 2).

But the book also shares exciting news (Part 3) about how you and I can assist the poor to help themselves – and in the process, also help ourselves. Joy and happiness do come from giving. By spending less on ourselves, we can transform the lives of neighbours who will die unless we care.

Part 1

Poor Lazarus
and Rich Christians

1

A BILLION HUNGRY NEIGHBOURS

> Sometimes I think, 'If I die, I won't have to see my children suffering as they are.' Sometimes I even think of killing myself. So often I see them crying, hungry; and there I am, without a cent to buy them some bread. I think, 'My God, I can't face it! I'll end my life. I don't want to look any more!'[1]
> (Iracema da Silva, resident of a slum in Brazil).

Hunger and starvation stalk the land. Famine is alive and well on planet earth. Thirty-five thousand children die every day of starvation and diseases related to malnutrition.

Can overfed, comfortably clothed and luxuriously housed persons understand poverty? Can we truly feel what it is like to be a nine-year-old boy playing outside a village school which he cannot attend because his father is unable to afford the necessary books? (The books would cost less than my wife and I spent on some entertainment one evening during the writing of this book.) Can we really feel what it means for poverty-stricken parents to watch with helpless grief as their baby daughter dies of a common childhood disease because, like at least one quarter of our global neighbours even today, they lack access to elementary health services?

One way to try and answer this question is to list what a typical family living in the industrialised Northern Hemisphere would need to give up if they were to adopt the lifestyle of a typical family living among our 1.375 billion neighbours who live in absolute poverty.[2] Economist Robert Heilbroner has itemised the abandoned 'luxuries'

in an American household, which could be any household
in the industrialised Northern Hemisphere.

We begin by invading the house of our imaginary
American family to strip it of its furniture. Everything
goes: beds, chairs, tables, television set, lamps. We will
leave the family with a few old blankets, a kitchen table,
a wooden chair. Along with the bureaus go the clothes.
Each member of the family may keep in his 'wardrobe'
his oldest suit or dress, a shirt or blouse. We will permit a
pair of shoes for the head of the family, but none for the
wife or children.

We move to the kitchen. The appliances have already
been taken out, so we turn to the cupboards. . . . The
box of matches may stay, a small bag of flour, some sugar
and salt. A few moldy potatoes, already in the garbage
can, must be hastily rescued, for they will provide much
of tonight's meal. We will leave a handful of onions, and
a dish of dried beans. All the rest we take away: the meat,
the fresh vegetables, the canned goods, the crackers, the
candy.

Now we have stripped the house: the bathroom has
been dismantled, the running water shut off, the electric
wires taken out. Next we take away the house. The
family can move to the toolshed. . . .

Communications must go next. No more newspapers,
magazines, books – not that they are missed, since we
must take away our family's literacy as well. Instead, in
our shantytown we will allow one radio. . . .

Now government services must go. No more postmen,
no more firemen. There is a school, but it is three miles
away and consists of two classrooms. . . . There are, of
course, no hospitals or doctors nearby. The nearest clinic
is ten miles away and is tended by a midwife. It can
be reached by bicycle, provided that the family has a
bicycle, which is unlikely. . . .

Finally, money. We will allow our family a cash hoard
of $5.00 [£3.00]. This will prevent our breadwinner from
experiencing the tragedy of an Iranian peasant who went

blind because he could not raise the $3.94 [£2.40] which he mistakenly thought he needed to receive admission to a hospital where he could have been cured.[3]

How many of our brothers and sisters confront that kind of grinding poverty today? Professor Michael Todaro, who writes one of the widely used texts in economic development, estimates that at least 1.375 billion people live in absolute poverty like this, although it is difficult to obtain precise statistics.[4] People living in absolute poverty lack the minimum income necessary to obtain the food, clothing and shelter required for mere survival.[5] More than 750 million of these desperately poor folk are malnourished. According to the 1988 World Bank Report, the number of people with inadequate diets in developing countries (excluding China) increased from 650 million to 730 million between 1970 and 1980. Tragically, according to the World Bank, 'since 1980 matters have turned from bad to worse'. Its figures show that, in twenty-one out of thirty-five low-income developing countries, the daily calorie supply per capita was lower in 1985 than in 1965.[6] The exact number of people lacking minimally adequate diets, clothing and shelter may not be available. And it varies depending on harvests, war and natural disasters. But the overall picture is indisputable and wrenching. Over a billion desperate neighbours live in absolute poverty.

New Economic Divisions in the Third World

Almost all of the 1.3 billion desperately poor people live in what used to be called the Third World. Until recently, all countries that were not a part of the developed world (whether capitalist or communist) were lumped together as 'Third World' nations. But changes in the last twenty years, especially since the fourfold increase of oil prices in 1973–4, require a new division. The World Bank's *World Development Report 1989* divides countries into: low-income countries, lower middle-income countries, and upper middle-income countries.[7]

India, China, Bangladesh, Pakistan and many African countries, including Ethiopia, Burundi, Chad, Tanzania and Somalia, belong to the low-income countries. Low-income countries have a population of 2.8 billion people. GNP per capita ranges from $130 to $450 per year.[8] Infant mortality rates are up to ten times higher than in the developed world, and population growth rates are higher (see tables 1 and 4). Typically, only one in two people is literate, though in Somalia literacy is 12 per cent and in Tanzania it is 85 per cent.[9] Unless major internal and external changes come, there is little prospect of a significant improvement in the appalling conditions for many of the people in these low-income countries. Hunger and related disease will continue to strike down millions every year.

Lower middle-income countries (600 million people) have an annual per capita GNP ranging from $520 to $1,930. This category includes many Latin American countries, a few of the richest African nations, such as Zimbabwe ($580), and some Asian nations, such as the Philippines ($590) at the bottom of the scale and Malaysia ($1,810) at the top. These countries have a somewhat brighter future although they still have large numbers of very poor people.

Upper middle-income countries (430 million people) include the richest Latin American nations (e.g., Brazil and Argentina) and rapidly developing nations like South Korea. Per capita GNP ranges from Brazil's $2,020 to Oman's $5,810.

Then there are the high-income nations with 780 million people. Per capita GNP ranges from Spain's $6,010 to Switzerland's $21,330. For the US, it is $18,530 and the UK, $10,420.[10]

Over the last few decades, many of the middle-income nations have experienced significant economic growth. In some cases, such as South Korea, the lot of the poor has improved somewhat. Too often, however, the poor have benefited very little. Brazil and Mexico are classic examples. In Brazil a military dictatorship, strongly supported by the United States, fostered real economic growth at the rate of 10 per cent per year from 1968 to 1974. Growth of about 9 per cent per year continued through to 1980, tapering off to 3.3 per cent from 1980 through to 1987.[11]

Who profited? Even Brazil's own minister of finance admitted in 1972 that only 5 per cent of the people had benefited from the fantastic growth of the Brazilian economy. The Brazilian government did not challenge a 1974 study that showed that the real purchasing power of the poorest two-thirds of the people had declined by more than a half in the preceding ten years. In 1989, two-thirds of Brazilian families tried to survive on less than $300 a month.[12] In 1975, 58 per cent of the Brazilian children under the age of eighteen were malnourished.[13] In 1980, 40 per cent of the total population suffered from malnutrition.[14] Today, two-thirds of the total population of 141 million people lack the minimum daily calories. More than 40 per cent of the children under five years of age still suffer from malnutrition. During the years 1980–7, 13 per cent of all children from 0–4 years old were moderately or severely underweight, and 31 per cent of all children between the ages of two and five suffered from moderate and severe stunting – the result of malnutrition.[15]

Today in Brazil the poorest 60 per cent of the population receive 16.4 per cent of the national income. The richest 20 per cent receive 66.6 per cent.[16] Tragically, Brazil's rapid economic growth has done far too little to help the people who need it most.

In Mexico where the average per capita income grew in real terms by 2.7 per cent a year between 1960 and 1978, the richest 20 per cent managed to edge their share of income up from 56.5 per cent to 57.7 per cent. Meanwhile, the poor got a smaller share. In 1968 the bottom 40 per cent got 12.2 per cent of the income pie; by 1977 it was below 10 per cent. The poorest 20 per cent saw their share cut from 3.6 per cent to below 3 per cent. This is not to say that the poor actually had lower incomes. Figures show that the per capita income of the poorest 20 per cent of the people stayed about the same, rising from £112 to about £114 per year. The wealthy 20 per cent, on the other hand, saw their incomes rise from £1,748 to £2,270. Thus the average poor person saw his or her meagre income rise by £2.00 over a period of eighteen years, while the average rich person added £520 in the same period.[17]

The tears and agony of all these people are captured in the words of Mrs Alarin from the Philippines, when the president of World Vision visited her home a few years ago. Cooking utensils were the family's only furniture. Mr Alarin made forty pence on good days as an ice vendor. Several nights a month Mrs Alarin stayed up all night to make a coconut sweet which she sold on the street. Total income for her midnight toil: twenty-five pence. The family had not tasted meat for a month when the World Vision official visited Mrs Alarin:

> Tears washed her dark, sunken eye sockets as she spoke: 'I feel so sad when my children cry at night because they have no food. I know my life will never change. What can I do to solve my problems? I am so worried about the future of my children. I want them to go to school, but how can we afford it? I am sick most of the time, but I can't go to the doctor because each visit costs two pesos [fifteen pence] and the medicine is extra. What can I do?' She broke down into quiet sobbing. I admit without shame that I wept with her.[18]

World poverty is a hundred million mothers weeping, like Mrs Alarin, because they cannot feed their children.

What has led to our tragic situation?

The Background

In the late 1960s the Green Revolution created widespread optimism. Agricultural specialists produced new strains of rice and wheat. As a result, poor countries such as Mexico and India were almost self-sufficient in cereals by the early

1970s. Better strains of grain, increased irrigation, expanding acreage, and more fertiliser enabled world food production to outpace population growth for several decades. To be sure, there were local famines and short-term problems caused by things like the quadrupling of oil prices in 1973–4. Always, of course, the very poor starved in the midst of enough. Overall, however, the food picture looked good through to 1984. World grain production actually increased 260 per cent between 1950 and 1984.

The last five years, however, present a more disturbing picture. There has been only a 1 per cent increase in grain production since 1984. But the population continues to grow at the rate of 88 million additional people to feed every year. As a result, the per capita grain output has declined by 7 per cent. In the short run, stocks of grain stored from the previous years made up two-thirds of the deficiency. But the number of hungry people has also increased dramatically. Carry-over stocks are down to little more than pipeline supplies – a very dangerous situation.

During 1988, the hottest year in the twentieth century, the grain harvest in the US breadbasket suffered devastation. For the first time in decades, the US grain harvest fell below US domestic consumption. People expected the good weather of 1989 plus cultivation of idle US cropland to rebuild depleted grain stocks. That did not happen and food experts are worried.

The US normally exports grain to more than one hundred countries. If the US and other major grain-growing areas experience another year like 1988 before grain stocks are replenished, widespread famine will result.[19]

Even if that does not happen, however, millions will continue to starve.

Famine Redefined

Lester Brown, one of the most prominent specialists on food and environmental issues today, has pointed out that we must redefine famine.

One reason it is possible for the world's affluent to ignore such tragedies is that changes have occurred in the way that famine manifests itself. In earlier historical periods . . . whole nations . . . experienced widespread starvation and death. Today the advancement in both national and international distribution systems has concentrated the effects of food scarcity among the world's poor, wherever they are.[20]

People with money can always buy food; famine affects only the poor. When food scarcity triples the price of grain imports, as it did in 1972 to 1974, middle- and upper-income people in developing countries continue to eat. But people who are already devoting 50 per cent of their incomes to food simply eat less and die sooner. Death usually results from diseases their underfed bodies could not resist.

Children are the first victims. In developing countries, the infant mortality rate is up to ten times higher than that in developed countries. Malnutrition is a contributory cause in the death of many children. In 1990, UNICEF reported that in 1988, 151 million children under five in the developing world were malnourished. The same report stated that more than 250,000 small children die every week from malnutrition and illnesses that can be easily prevented. At the current rate, 'more than 100 million children will die from illness and malnutrition in the 1990s'.[21]

Carolina Maria de Jesus helps one feel the terror and anguish endured by the poor in a land where they could have enough food. The feelings faithfully recorded daily on scraps of paper by this uneducated, brilliant woman who struggled to survive in the slums of Brazil's second largest city, Sâo Paulo, were published in a gripping diary called *Child of the Dark*.

Today I'm sad. I'm nervous. I don't know if I should start crying or start running until I fall unconscious. At dawn it was raining. I couldn't go out to get any money [she gathered junk each day to earn money for food] . . . I have a few tin cans and a little scrap that I'm going to sell to Senhor Manuel. When Joâo came home from school, I sent him to sell the scrap. He got thirteen cruzeiros. He bought a glass of mineral water: two cruzeiros. I was furious with him. . . .

The children eat a lot of bread. They like soft bread but when they don't have it, they eat hard bread. . . .

Oh Sâo Paulo! A queen that vainly shows her sky-scrapers that are her crown of gold. All dressed up in velvet and silk but with cheap stockings underneath – the favela [the slum].

The money didn't stretch far enough to buy meat, so I cooked macaroni with a carrot. I didn't have any grease, it was horrible. Vera was the only one who complained yet asked for more.

'Mama, sell me to Dona Julita, because she has delicious food.'[22]

Stan Mooneyham tells of a heart-rending visit to the home of Sebastian and Maria Nascimento, a poor Brazilian couple. The one-room, thatched lean-to had a sand floor. One stool, a charcoal hibachi, and four cots covered with sacks partly filled with a bit of straw were the only furniture.

My emotions could scarcely take in what I saw and heard. The three-year-old twins, lying naked and unmoving on a small cot, were in the last act of their personal drama. Mercifully, the curtain was coming down on their brief appearance. Malnutrition was the villain. The two-year-old played a silent role, his brain already vegetating from marasmus, a severe form of malnourishment.

The father is without work. Both he and Maria are anguished over their existence, but they are too proud to beg. He tries to shine shoes. Maria cannot talk about their condition. She tries, but the words just will not come. Her mother's love is deep and tender, and the daily deterioration of her children is more than she can bear. Tears must be the vocabulary of the anguished soul.[23]

Carolina's little girl need not have begged to be sold to a rich neighbour. While Sebastian and Maria's twins lay dying, there was an abundance of food in the world. But it was not divided fairly. The well-to-do in Brazil had plenty to eat. Two hundred and ten million US citizens were consuming enough food (partly because of high consumption of grain-fed livestock) to feed over one billion people in the poor countries. Oxford economist Donald Hay has recently pointed out that a mere 2 per cent of the world's grain harvest would be enough, if shared, to erase the problem of hunger and malnutrition around the world![24]

This is how famine has been redefined, or rather, redistributed! It no longer inconveniences the rich and powerful. It strikes only the poor and powerless. Since the poor usually die quietly in relative obscurity, the rich of all nations comfortably ignore this kind of famine. But famine – redefined and redistributed – is alive and well. Even in good times, millions and millions of people go to bed hungry. Their children's brains vegetate and their bodies succumb prematurely to disease.

Poverty means illiteracy, inadequate medical care, disease, brain damage.

Only 44 per cent of India's 800.3 million people could read in 1987. Indeed, in 1987 only 61 per cent of all the 3.86 billion people in the developing world were literate. This represents an increase over the 1960 rate of *40 per cent*. However, the *number* of people who are illiterate has also grown. The increase in literacy has not kept up with the population growth. Consequently the number of illiterates has increased by nearly 70 million since 1960 to an estimated 900 million in 1985.[25]

People in the industrialised North have enjoyed the security offered by modern medicine for so long that we assume it must now be available for all. Over a billion people lack access to elementary health services, and 1.6 billion people do not even have safe water to drink.[26] The cost of such services is relatively small. The World Health Organization has reported that if we would only increase our annual investments in preventive care by 45 pence per person in the Third World, we could save 5 million people every year. That would take less than £2 billion. Surely the people of the wealthier nations can help find £2 billion to save the lives of 5 million people. US citizens alone spend £3 billion a year on special diets to lower their calorie intake.[27]

The results of such efforts can be dramatic. During the 1980s, a few, inexpensive actions have saved the lives of millions of children. In 1980, less than 10 per cent of children in the developing world were immunised. Measles, tetanus, whooping cough, and other common illnesses were killing 5 million children a year and disabling several million more. Today, the immunisation rate has risen to over 50 per cent. Vaccines now save the lives of at least 1.5 million children annually. And the vaccines only cost an average of 90 pence per child.[28]

Oral rehydration therapy (ORT), also an inexpensive health procedure, prevents children from dehydrating from diarrhoea. In 1980, dehydration from diarrhoea claimed almost 10,000 children a day. The use of ORT saves 750,000 to 1 million children's lives a year. Of an estimated 4 million deaths a year from diarrhoeal disease, approximately 60 per cent, or over 2 million, are caused by dehydration and could, therefore, be treated by ORT. Bags of oral rehydration salts cost about 6 pence each. They can be used by parents themselves.[29]

Infants, Brain Damage and Protein

Lacking both food and medicine, poor nations have high infant mortality rates. As shown in Table 1, the rate of infant mortality is much higher in less developed countries than it is in the developed world.

Permanent brain damage caused by protein deficiency is one of the most devastating aspects of world poverty. Eighty per cent of total brain development takes place between the moment of conception and age two. Adequate protein intake – precisely what over 150 million children under five do not have – is necessary for proper brain

Table 1 Infant Mortality Per 1,000 Live Births (1988)

Sweden	—7
West Germany	—8
Australia	—9
UK	—9
US	—10
Chile	—19
USSR	—25
Guatemala	—58
Egypt	—83
India	—98
Rwanda	—121
Malawi	—149
Mozambique	—172

Source: James P. Grant, The State of the World's Children 1990 *(New York: Oxford University Press, 1990), pp. 76–7.*

development.[30] A study in the early 1980s in Mexico found that a group of severely malnourished children under five had an IQ thirteen points lower than a scientifically selected, adequately fed control group.[31] Medical science now agrees that severe malnutrition produces irreversible brain damage.

When a poor family runs out of food, the children suffer most. For the immediate future, an inactive child is not as serious a problem as an inactive wage earner. But malnutrition produces millions of retarded children.

Little Marli, a happy six-year-old girl from Rio de Janeiro is just one of these. Little Marli looked normal in every way. Healthy. Happy. There was just one thing wrong with her. She couldn't learn. At first the teachers thought perhaps her difficulty was psychological, the result of neglect in a family of eleven children. Her younger sister had the same problem. But after careful observation and testing, it was evident that Marli, a child of Brazil's poor and wretched favelas [slums], was unable to learn because as an infant her malnourished body could not produce a healthy brain.[32]

No one knows how many poor children have suffered irreversible brain damage because of insufficient protein during childhood. But there were 151 million malnourished children under the age of five in 1988 and at the current rate there will be 180 million in 2000.[33]

Hunger, illiteracy, disease, brain damage, death. That's what grinding poverty means. The 1.3 billion impoverished people of the world experience its daily anguish.

Population

The population explosion is another fundamental problem. Not until 1830 did the world have 1 billion people. But then it took only a hundred years (1930) to add another billion. Within a mere thirty years another billion human beings appeared. The fourth billion arrived in only fifteen years (1975). By 1990, we had more than 5 billion people. The Population Reference Bureau's 1989 Population Data

Table 2 Years Required to Add One Billion People

	Years required	*Years reached*
First billion	10,000 plus	1830
Second billion	100	1930
Third billion	30	1960
Fourth billion	15	1975
Fifth billion	12	1987
Sixth billion	9	1996

Source: Lester Brown, The Twenty-Ninth Day (*New York: Norton, 1978*), *p. 74 (slightly updated).*

Sheet projects that the world population in 2000 will be 6.3 billion (see Table 2).[34]

Table 3 shows how quickly the population expands at different growth rates. A population of 100 million people growing at 1.5 per cent per year expands to 145 million in 25 years, and 443 million in 100 years. And a population of 100 million growing at 3 per cent (Nigeria, Pakistan and the Philippines are close to that) expands to 438 million in 50 years and 1,922 million in 100 years.

The population explosion prompts some people to despair completely. The Environmental Fund ran an advertisement in 1976 in many newspapers, including the *New York Times* and the *Wall Street Journal*. Drafted by William Paddock and Garrett Hardin, among others, the statement declared, 'The world as we know it will likely be ruined before the year 2000 . . . The momentum toward tragedy is at this moment so great that there is probably no way of halting it.'[35]

Such views, of course, are clearly too pessimistic. Population trends in the last twenty years offer some hope. Whereas the overall population growth rate in the world was about 2 per cent in 1960, the Population Reference Bureau's 1989 World Population Data Sheet indicates that it has dropped to 1.8 per cent. We can be grateful for the improvement. But the present rate of population growth is still dangerously high. At this rate, the population will

Table 3   Population Increase Over 25, 50, and 100 years

Population growth rate per cent per year	Ratio of projected population to current population		
	25 years	50 years	100 years
0.5	1.13	1.28	1.65
1.0	1.28	1.65	2.70
1.5	1.45	2.11	4.43
2.0	1.64	2.69	7.24
2.5	1.85	3.44	11.81
3.0	2.09	4.38	19.22
3.5	2.36	5.58	31.19

Table 4 Population Growth Rate Per Year for Selected
Countries (mid 1989)

	Growth rate	Population mid 1989 (in millions)
West Germany	−0.1%	61.5
UK	0.2%	57.3
Japan	0.5%	123.2
United States	0.7%	248.8
Australia	0.8%	16.8
Canada	0.8%	26.3
USSR	1.0%	289
China	1.4%	1,103.9
World	1.8%	5,234
Brazil	2.0%	147.4
Ethiopia	2.1%	49.8
India	2.2%	835
Mexico	2.4%	86.7
Mozambique	2.6%	15.2
Philippines	2.8%	64.9
Pakistan	2.9%	110.4
Nigeria	2.9%	115.3

Source: Population Reference Bureau, *1989 World Population Data Sheets.*

double in thirty-nine years to over 10 billion people.[36] We are already ravaging the environment to feed today's 5 billion.

In considering the issue of population growth, it is important to remember that the number of children per family in Western Europe and North America was much higher in the latter half of the last century than the two or three children per family common now. Infant mortality rates were of course higher. Despite this, however, family size and population growth in the industrialising nations at that time were quite close to size and growth rates in many developing countries since World War II. Affluence and decline in population growth seem to go together, in the long term anyway. See Table 4 for a comparison of the population growth rates for selected countries.

Limits to Growth?

Along with the food crisis and the population explosion, a third set of complex, interrelated issues makes our dilemma even more desperate. How long can the earth sustain the present rate of industrialisation? What will be the effect of the resulting pollution?

World-famous economist Robert Heilbroner undoubtedly has a point: 'Ultimately, there is an absolute limit to the ability of the earth to support or tolerate the process of industrial activity, and there is reason to believe that we are now moving toward that limit very rapidly.'[37]

From 1950 to 1990, the world lost one-fifth of all topsoil and one-fifth of all tropical forests.[38] Scientists warn that carbon dioxide and other 'greenhouse gases' are slowly warming the world to a point where catastrophic changes in climate are quite possible in the next century. We will explore this problem more in chapter 6.

The Future and Our Response

The population explosion, environmental pollution and the possible necessity of slowing industrialisation (at least in the affluent nations) compound the difficulties involved in trying to share the world's resources more justly. Not surprisingly, predictions of doomsday are legion. What are our future prospects?

No one can predict with any certainty what will happen in the next decades. Widespread famine in poorer nations might tempt their leaders to unleash wars of redistribution in a demand for a fairer share of the earth's resources. Such a prospect is not sheer fantasy. Professor Heilbroner has predicted nuclear terrorism and wars of redistribution. He has suggested that the world is like 'an immense train, in which a few passengers, mainly in the advanced capitalist world, ride in first-class coaches, in conditions of comfort unimaginable to the enormously greater numbers crammed into the cattle cars that make up the bulk of the train's carriages'.[39] As millions die and imminent starvation threatens even more, Heilbroner fears that desperate Third World leaders might threaten to use their nuclear weapons. In 1989, several developing countries possessed nuclear weapons and eight more were emerging nuclear powers.[40] By the end of the 'eighties, thirteen developing countries possessed chemical weapons. The number with ballistic missiles could double to fifteen in the 'nineties.[41]

The result of such a confrontation could only be ghastly bloodshed on a massive scale. We would undoubtedly use our vast military might to defend our unfair share of the world's goods. Realism demands that we honestly face the fact than unless the affluent quarter of the world makes fundamental changes, North-South tension will increase. Wars of redistribution are even possible.

A former president of World Vision helps us to understand why: 'The [developing nations] have suffered long with "aid" that isn't, with discriminatory trade, with the rape of their resources.'[42] US Senator Mark Hatfield concurs. He has warned, 'The greatest threat to this nation [the United States] and the stability of the entire world is hunger. It's more explosive than all the atomic weaponry possessed by the big powers. Desperate people do desperate things, and remember that nuclear fission is now in the hands of even the developing nations.'[43]

In 1980, a US Presidential Commission on World Hunger (composed of Democrats and Republicans, conservatives and liberals) repeated this warning:

> The most potentially explosive force in the world today is the frustrated desire of poor people to attain a decent standard of living. . . . The Commission believes that promoting economic development in general, and overcoming hunger in particular, are tasks far more critical to US national security than most policy makers acknowledge or even believe. Since the advent of nuclear weapons, most Americans have been conditioned to equate national security with the strength of strategic military forces. The Commission considers this prevailing belief to be a simplistic illusion.[44]

Global co-operation to reduce hunger and injustice is the only path to enduring peace.

Professor Georg Borgstrom, a world-renowned specialist in food science and nutrition, fears that 'the rich world is on a direct collision course with the poor of the world . . . We cannot survive behind our Maginot Line of missiles and bombs.'[45]

What will Christians do in such a time? Will we dare to insist that the God revealed in Scripture is always at work seeking to 'set at liberty those who are oppressed' (Luke 4:18)? Will Christians have the courage to seek justice for the poor, even if that means disapproval by affluent neighbours? Where will you and I stand? With the starving or the overfed? With poor Lazarus or the rich man? Most of the rich countries are white and at least nominally Christian. What an ironic tragedy that a white, affluent, 'Christian' minority in the world continues to hoard its wealth while hundreds of millions of people hover on the edge of starvation!

One popular fundamentalist newsletter (with a circulation of over sixty thousand) has called on Christians to stockpile new dried foods. In a most ingenious combination of apocalyptic piety and slick salesmanship, the newsletter quoted several 'Bible scholars' to prove that some Christians will live through the tribulation. And the conclusion? Since we cannot be absolutely certain where we will be during the tribulation, we ought to purchase a seven-year supply of reserve foods for £1,000 or so![46]

In an Age of Hunger most Christians, regardless of theological label, are severely tempted to succumb to the heresy of following current cultural and societal values rather than biblical truth.[47] Society offers demonically convincing justifications for enjoying our affluence and forgetting about over a billion desperately poor neighbours.

But if the Christ of Scripture is our Lord, then we will believe his paradoxical word that true happiness comes from giving. We will refuse to be squeezed into the mould of our affluent, sinful culture. In an Age of Hunger,

Christians of necessity must be radical nonconformists. But nonconformity is painful. Only if we are thoroughly grounded in the scriptural view of possessions, wealth, and poverty will we be capable of living an obedient lifestyle.

Study Questions

1. What were your strongest feelings as you read this chapter?
2. What facts were most surprising to you? Most disturbing?
3. How has famine been redefined?
4. What concretely does poverty mean in day-to-day life?
5. How do you think most Christians you know would respond if they truly understood the problem of world hunger?

THE AFFLUENT MINORITY

I used to think when I was a child, that Christ might have been exaggerating when he warned about the dangers of wealth. Today I know better. I know how very hard it is to be rich and still keep the milk of human kindness. Money has a dangerous way of putting scales on one's eyes, a dangerous way of freezing people's hands, eyes, lips, and hearts[1] (Dom Helder Camara).

The North-South division is one of the most dangerous divisions in the world today. With one or two exceptions, the rich countries are in the Northern Hemisphere, and the poor countries are in the South. North America, Europe, and Japan are an affluent northern aristocracy. Our standard of living is at least as luxurious in comparison with that of over a billion poor neighbours As was the life-style of the medieval aristocracy in comparison with their serfs.

And the chasm widens every year. Table 5 starkly outlines the growing inequality. 'The gap in per capita income between countries is now over twice as large as it was 30 years ago; the gap in public health expenditures is four times as large.'[2]

A Widening Chasm

The Gross National Product (GNP) provides one standard of comparison. A country's GNP is the sum of all goods and services produced in a year.[3] If you divide a country's GNP by the number of persons in the country, you arrive at a per capita GNP which can be compared with that of other nations.[4] As Table 6 shows, the per capita GNP in the United States was $18,530 in 1987. In India it was a mere $330.

Virtually all authorities agree that the chasm will widen still more by the year 2000. The *Global 2000 Report to the President* (1980) reported that 'for every $1 increase in GNP per capita in the LDCs, a $20 increase is projected for the industrialised countries'.[5] Between 1965 and 1985, the least developed countries (LDCs), the thirty-one poorest countries in Africa, had an average per capita income growth rate of minus 0.3 per cent. During the same period, all the developed countries experienced an average annual growth rate per capita of 1.7 per cent. So the growth-rate gap between the poorest and richest countries increased at a rate of 2 per cent per year.

Table 5   Growing Inequality, 1950–90

Adjusted Income per Person, Four Economic Classes of Nations, 1950-88

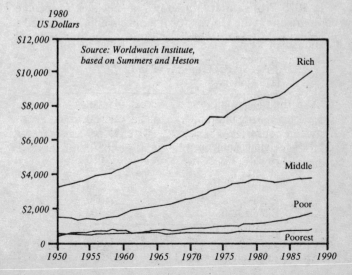

Fortunately, the overall picture for all non-oil-producing developing nations was better. They had an average per capita GNP growth rate of approximately 2.8 per cent per year. So the percentage growth in developing countries was higher (by 1.1 per cent) than in developed nations for 1965–85.

Yet, the absolute income gap still widened! An increase of 2.8 per cent in a poor country's per capita income of $300 only adds $8.40 more. But an increase of 1.7 per cent to a rich country's per capita income of $15,000 adds $255 more! Thus, as development economist Professor Todaro points out, 'the absolute and per capita income gap between all rich and poor nations continued to widen appreciably' for 1965–85.[6]

Recognising that per capita GNP comparisons are open to several criticisms (see note 3), some development specialists have tried to improve on the GNP comparisons. A frequently quoted conclusion is that 'differences in income per head between the poor and rich countries were around 1:2 at the beginning of the nineteenth century; they are . . . today . . . around 1:20'.[7]

In 1975 Professor Irving Kravis, a specialist in income comparisons at the University of Pennsylvania, published a massive, painstaking comparison of total output and real

Table 6   Per Capita GNP in 1987
(US Dollars)

Switzerland	21,330
United States	18,530
Japan	15,760
United Kingdom	10,420
Brazil	2,020
Nigeria	370
Kenya	330
India	330
Bangladesh	160

Source: World Bank, World Development Report 1989 *(New York: Oxford University Press, 1989), pp. 164–5.*

purchasing power in different countries. He concluded that
the real income per person in the United States was
fourteen times that of India and seventeen times that of
Kenya.[8]

These calculations compare average figures for each
country. *State of the World 1990*, however, points out that if
we had the data to compare the average incomes of the
richest one-fifth of the world, regardless of where they live,
with the poorest one-fifth, we would discover that the rich
have thirty to forty times as much.[9]

A comparison of energy usage simply underscores our
affluence. Because of a lengthening list of luxuries – numerous electrical gadgets and toys, large air-conditioned cars,
skyscrapers, and so on – North Americans consume more
than twice as much energy per person as their counterparts
in industrialised countries like France and Switzerland.
And they use 140 times as much as the average person in
Zaire.[10]

There are many ways of showing our incredible affluence
in the North relative to that of the developing nations, but
undoubtedly the most striking measure of the gap between
the rich and poor is our consumption of the most basic
commodity of all – food. As Table 7 indicates, US citizens
consume six times as much grain per person as do people in
LDCs.

The major reason for the glaring difference between the
consumption of grain in the United States and that of the
LDCs is that Americans eat much grain indirectly – via
grain-fed livestock and fowl. Why is this important? Because it takes many pounds of grain to produce just one
pound of beef.

In July 1983, I talked with George Allen, an agricultural
economist in the Economic Research Service of the US
Department of Agriculture (USDA).[11] Allen reported that
a steer in a feedlot gains one pound of edible meat for every
thirteen pounds of grain equivalents consumed. (In a
typical feedlot, a steer would consume about eight and a
half pounds of grain and four and a half pounds of silage,
hay, and protein for every pound of weight gained.) But the

Table 7 Average Annual Per Capita Grain Consumption, 1985–6 (in pounds; includes grain fed to animals)

	Population (millions)	Total Use (million metric tons)	Per Capita Use (kg)	Per Capita Use (lb)
World	4,924,342	1,340,550	272.2	600.2
USA	239,744	208,705	870.5	1919.2
USSR	278,704	213,120	764.7	1685.8
European Community	322,188	142,703	442.9	976.5
Japan	121,067	37,765	311.9	687.7
China	1,041,563	312,639	300.2	661.7
Less developed countries	2,921,076	425,618	145.7	321.2

Source: USDA, Foreign Agricultural Service – production, supply and disappearance computer database *(Michael Trueblood, March 1990).*

animal also spends time on the range eating grass. It does not, however, spend as much time on the range as in the past. In November 1974, the *New York Times* reported that in the 1940s only one-third of all beef was grain-fed. By 1970, 82 per cent of all cattle slaughtered came from feedlots where they had been fed grain. It was expected that 78 per cent of cattle slaughtered in 1990 would be grain-fed.[12] USDA economist Allen said that when the total life of the animal is considered, each pound of edible beef represents seven pounds of grain. That means that, in addition to all the grass, hay and other food involved, seven pounds of grain are required to produce a typical pound of beef purchased in the supermarket. Fortunately, the conversion rates for chicken and pork are lower. Although the exact calculations differ slightly, the overall ratios are striking. Table 8 shows that the conversion rates are 3:1 for chicken and 6:1 for pork.[13] Beef is the Rolls-Royce of meat products.[14] Should we move to a Mini?

Because of this high level of meat consumption, the rich minority of the world devours an unequal share of the world's available food. Table 9 shows that in the years 1987–9, 816 million people in the developed nations consumed almost as much grain (440 million tons) as the 2.812 billion people (551 million tons) in less developed nations. We eat much of our grain (63.2 per cent) indirectly via meat. People in the poor countries eat almost all of their grain (81.8 per cent) directly. The United Nations reported in 1974 that livestock in the rich countries ate as much grain as did all the people of India and China.[15]

Table 9 shows that the less developed nations feed only 18.2 per cent of their grain to livestock. In the developed nations we feed 63.2 per cent of our grain to cattle, which is why we consume so much more grain than poor nations.

The final irony is that our high meat and fat consumption is harmful to our health. As is now well known, a diet high in saturated fats contributes to heart disease. Beef, especially choice and prime cuts, and pork, as well as eggs, cream and butter all contain large amounts of saturated fats. Diets high in meat and fat and low in roughage are also harmful for the bowel. Dr Mark Hegsted of the Harvard School of Public Health has pointed out that 'meat consumption in this country is preposterously high, relative to need, and cannot be justified on a nutritional basis'.[16] Fortunately, trends in meat consumption have moved in the right direction recently. From 1940 to 1972, the annual per-person consumption of beef in the UK jumped from 39 pounds to 52 pounds but since then it has dropped steadily to 43 pounds in 1987. In the United States the figure

Table 8 Pounds of Grain and Soy Fed to Get One Pound of Meat, Poultry, or Eggs

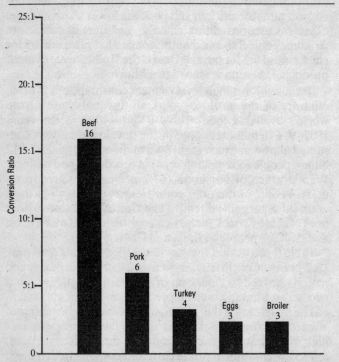

Source: Hollender, Jeffrey. How to Make the World A Better Place *(New York: William Morrow, 1990), p. 124.*

jumped from 55 to 116 pounds from 1940 to 1972, but by 1982 it was down to 79 pounds, and by 1987 it was 73.4 pounds.[17]

The percentage of disposable personal income spent on food in different countries provides another stark comparison. In the United States it is a mere 9.7 per cent. In the United Kingdom, it is 12.8 per cent. In the Philippines it is *51.6 per cent.*

Agony and anguish are concealed in the simple statistics of Table 10. For persons spending 10 per cent of disposable income on food, a 50 per cent increase in food costs is a minor irritation. But for the one already spending 50 per cent of income on food, a 50 per cent increase means hunger and malnutrition.

Table 11, on available calories, tells the same story. Whereas people in many poor nations have less than the daily minimal requirements, people in North America and Western Europe have more calories than they need. While lack of food destroys millions in poor lands, too much food devastates millions in affluent countries. According to a 1980 survey by the National Center for Health Statistics, 32 per cent of American men and 36 per cent of American women between the ages of twenty and seventy-four are overweight.[18] Although the figure for the UK is lower than this, obesity is a problem here too.

The facts are clear. North Americans, Europeans, and Japanese devour an incredibly unequal share of the world's available food. Whether measured in terms of GNP or energy and food consumption, we are many, many times more affluent than the poor majority of our sisters and brothers. And the chasm widens every year.

Poverty at £20,000 a Year?

It was late 1974. Millions were literally dying from starvation. But that was not the concern of Judd Arnett, a syndicated columnist with Knight Newspapers. In a column read (and probably believed) by millions of North Americans, Arnett lamented the fact that people earning $15,000

Table 9 Average Annual Grain Consumption by Main Uses, 1987–9 (in million metric tons)

	Population (millions)	Total Consumption	Used Directly as Food	Used Indirectly as Feed to Animals	Per Cent Fed to Animals
World	5,143	1,669	1,029	640	38.4
Centrally planned economies	1,514	678	416	262	38.7
Less developed countries	2,812	551	451	100	18.2
Developed countries	816	440	162	278	63.2

Source: USDA, Foreign Agricultural Service – production, supply and disappearance computer database (*Michael Trueblood, March 1990*).

a year were on the edge of poverty (remember that $15,000 in 1974 was equal to $37,728 or £23,000 in 1989).[19]

> One of the great mysteries of life to me is how a family in the $15,000 [= $37,728 or £23,000] bracket, before taxes, or even $18,000 [= $45,274 or £27,606], can meet all its obligations and still educate its children.[20]

It was September 1985. Millions were still dying of starvation, but the British public were shocked to read that a member of the Government was resigning from his post as Minister because he could not afford to live in London on £33,000 a year. This is, of course, an extreme example, but at the same time other professionals had embarked on a lengthy and damaging strike because they found it impossible to manage on £10,000.

A few years later *Newsweek* did a story on 'The Middle Class Poor', calmly reporting that US citizens earning $30,693 (£18,715), $36,832 (£22,458) or even $51,155 (£31,192) a year (in 1989 dollars) felt they were at the edge of poverty.[21]

To the vast majority of the world's people, such state-

Table 10 Expenditures for Food – 1987
(as per cent of disposable personal income)

United States	9.7
Canada	10.2
United Kingdom	12.8
Australia	13.9
Germany	14.0
France	14.4
Colombia	27.9
Korea	29.3
Thailand	34.7
Sri Lanka	41.3
Philippines	51.6

Source: World Agricultural Trends and Indicators 1970–88 (Economic Research Service, USDA, Statistical Bulletin No. 781, July 1989).

ments would be unintelligible – or dishonest. To be sure, we do need £20,000, £25,000 or even more each year if we insist on two cars, an expensively furnished, sprawling suburban home, a £50,000 life insurance policy, new clothes every time fashions change, the most recent 'labour-saving devices' for home and garden, an annual three-week holiday to travel, and so on. Many people in North America and Europe have come to expect precisely that. But that is hardly life at the edge of poverty.

By any objective criterion, the 5 per cent of the world's people who live in the United States and the rest of us who live in the industrialised Northern Hemisphere are an incredibly rich aristocracy living in the midst of impoverished masses. Surely one of the most astounding things, therefore, about this affluent minority is that we honestly think we barely have enough to survive in modest comfort.

Constant, seductive advertising helps to create this destructive delusion. Advertisers regularly con us into

Table 11   Calorie Supply Per Capita as Percentage of Requirements, 1984–6

United States	138
USSR	133
France	130
Canada	129
Japan	122
Brazil	111
China	111
Guatemala	105
Pakistan	97
Afghanistan	94
Zambia	92
Haiti	84
Bangladesh	83
Ghana	76
Ethiopia	71
Chad	69

Source: James P. Grant, The State of the World's Children 1990 *(New York: Oxford University Press, 1989), pp. 78–9.*

believing that we genuinely need one luxury after another. We are convinced that we must keep up with or even go one better than our neighbours. So we buy another dress, sports jacket or sports car and thereby drive up the standard of living. The ever-more affluent standard of living is the god of the twentieth-century Northern Hemisphere and the adman is its prophet.

The purpose of advertising is no longer primarily to inform. It is to create desire. 'CREATE MORE DESIRE' shrieked an inch-high headline for an unusually honest ad in the *New York Times*. It continued: 'Now, as always, profit and growth stem directly from the ability of salesmanship to create more desire.'[22] Luxurious houses in *Country Life* or *Homes and Gardens* make our perfectly adequate houses shrink by comparison into dilapidated, tiny cottages in need of immediate renovation. The advertisements for the new season's fashions make our almost new dresses and suits from previous years look shabby and positively old-fashioned.

We are bombarded by costly, manipulative advertising at every turn. The average Briton watches television containing 5–10,000 commercials every year.[23] Americans spend more money on advertising than on all public institutions of higher education. In America, too, in 1987, $109.6 billion went into advertising 'to convince us that Jesus was wrong about the abundance of possessions'.[24]

Luxuries are renamed 'necessities' by advertising. Our postman once delivered an elegant brochure complete with glossy photographs of exceedingly expensive homes. The brochure announced the seductive lie that *Architectural Digest* would help one quench 'man's passionate *need* for beauty and *luxury*' (my emphasis). Evidently we 'need' luxury!

Sometimes advertising overkill is hilarious. An evangelical book discount house once created this promotional gem: 'Your mouth is going to water, and your soul is going to glow, when you feast your eyes on the bargains we have providentially provided for your benefit this month.' (I promptly ordered books worth twenty-four dollars.)

Promises, Promises

Perhaps the most devastating, demonic part of advertising is that it attempts to persuade us that material possessions will bring joy and fulfilment. 'That happiness is to be attained through limitless material acquisition is denied by every religion and philosophy known to man, but is preached incessantly by every television set.'[25] Advertisers promise that their products will satisfy our deepest needs and inner longings for love, acceptance, security and sexual fulfilment. The right deodorant, they promise, will bring acceptance and friendship. The newest toothpaste or shampoo will make one irresistible. A comment by New York jewellery designer Barry Kieselstein shows how people search for meaning and friendship in things: 'A nice piece of jewelry you can relate to is like having a friend who's always there.'[26]

Examples are everywhere. A bank in Washington, DC, advertised for new savings accounts with the question, 'Who's gonna love you when you're old and grey?' For a decade, our savings bank used a particularly enticing ad: 'Put a little love away. Everybody needs a penny for a rainy day. Put a little love away.' Those words are unbiblical, heretical, demonic. They teach the Big Lie of our secular, materialistic society. But the words and music were so seductive that they danced through my head hundreds of times.

If no one paid any attention to these lies, they would be harmless. But that is impossible. Advertising has a powerful effect on all of us. It shapes the values of our children.

In a sense, we pay too little attention to advertisements. Most of us think we ignore them. But in fact they seep into our unconscious minds. We experience them instead of analysing them. We should examine their blatant lies and then laugh hilariously at their preposterous promises. John V. Taylor has suggested that Christian families ought to adopt the slogan 'Who are you kidding?' and shout it in unison every time a commercial appears on the screen.[27] An alternative is simply to turn down the sound whenever a commercial break comes on.

Perhaps the 'TV Victim's Lament' (sung to the tune of 'Blowin' in the Wind') could be the theme song of our lighthearted (yet deadly serious) crusade against advertising.

> How many times must a guy spray with [Sure]
> Before he doesn't offend?
> And how many times must he gargle each day
> Before he can talk to a friend?
> How many tubes of shampoo must he buy
> Before his dandruff will end?
> The sponsors, my friend, will sell you all they can.
> The sponsors will sell you all they can.
>
> How many times must a man use Gillette
> Before shaving won't make him bleed?
> And how many cartons of Kent must he smoke
> Before the girls all pay him heed?
> How many products must one person buy
> Before he has all that he'll need?
> The sponsors, my friend, will sell you all they can.
> The sponsors will sell you all they can.
>
> How many times must a girl clean her sink
> Before Ajax scours that stain?
> And how many times must she rub in [Deep Heat]
> Before she can rub out the pain?
> How many ads on TV must we watch
> Before we are driven insane?
> The sponsors, my friend, will broadcast all they can.
> The sponsors will broadcast all they can.[28]

Theologian Patrick Kerans has argued that our society's commitment to a growth economy and an ever-increasing standard of living promoted by constant advertising is really a sell-out to the Enlightenment. During the eighteenth century, Western society decided that the scientific method would shape our relationship to reality. Since only quantitative criteria of truth and value were acceptable, more intangible values such as community, trust, friendship and the beauty of creation became less important. Unlike friendship, the gorgeous splendour of unspoiled nature, and justice, GNP can be measured. The result is our competitive growth economy where winning and economic success (and they are usually the same) are all-important.[29]

The result, if Kerans is correct, can only be social disintegration. If our basic social structures are built on the heretical supposition of the Enlightenment that the scientific method is the only way to truth and value, and if Christianity is true, then our society must eventually collapse.

Advertising itself contains a fundamental inner contradiction.[30] We all long for those qualities of life that satisfy our deepest needs; we long for significance and joy. Marketing recognises our needs and hooks into them. Now Christians know that affluence does not guarantee love, beauty, acceptance and joy. But advertising promises them to those who strive for more gadgets and bigger bank accounts. Our inherent bent for idolatry gives advertising the power to be convincing; so people persist in the fruitless effort to quench the thirst for meaning and fulfilment with an ever-rising river of possessions.

The result within the person is agonising distress and undefined dissatisfaction. The broader, external result is structural injustice. Our affluence fails to satisfy our restless hearts. And it also keeps us from sharing badly needed food and development assistance with over 1 billion hungry neighbours. Will we affluent Christians have the courage and faithfulness to learn how to be unconformed to this world's seductive, Satanic advertising?

How Generous Are We?

The United States is one of the richest nations in the world. But the data in Table 12 reveal that the US government ranks second from the bottom (in percentage of GNP given) among major Western donors of foreign aid. The

United Kingdom ranks only slightly higher – fifth from the bottom.

Popular opinion does not reflect this reality. One survey discovered that more than two-thirds (69 per cent) of Americans thought that the United States is more generous in foreign aid than other developed nations.[31] Perhaps the illusion of generosity is a necessary protective device. In order to justify Western affluence, we foster an image of a generous nation dispensing foreign aid on a grand scale.

Table 12   Estimated Official Development Assistance from Industrialised Countries as Percentage of GNP (1988)

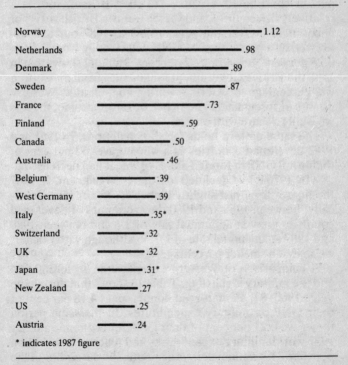

Norway	1.12
Netherlands	.98
Denmark	.89
Sweden	.87
France	.73
Finland	.59
Canada	.50
Australia	.46
Belgium	.39
West Germany	.39
Italy	.35*
Switzerland	.32
UK	.32
Japan	.31*
New Zealand	.27
US	.25
Austria	.24

* indicates 1987 figure

Source: World Bank, The World Development Report 1989 *(New York: Oxford University Press, 1989), p. 200.*

The United States did display national generosity at the end of World War 2. At the height of the Marshall Plan (begun in 1947 to rebuild war-torn Europe) the US actually gave annually 2.79 per cent of its total GNP.[32] But in 1960 the figure for foreign aid had dropped to .53 per cent of GNP; and by 1988 it had plummeted to a mere .25 per cent (see Table 12). From 1960 to 1987, per-capita income in the United States had risen from $6,036 to $11,012 (calculated in terms of constant prices and wages based on the year 1982).[33] But foreign aid to help the poor did not follow the same trend. In 1960 the average person in the United States contributed $21.7 a year to foreign aid. In 1981 the average person contributed a paltry $13.10.[34] Britain, too, is a relatively rich country, and yet the trend in British aid is not encouraging. Over the period 1965 to 1987 our aid, expressed as a percentage of GNP, fell steadily from 0.48 to 0.28 per cent. It is now 0.32 per cent. Table 12 shows that in 1988 the British Government ranked fifth from the bottom (in percentage of GNP given) among major Western donors of foreign aid. The richer we have become, the less we want to share with others.

The same pattern holds for all rich nations. In 1961 and 1962 developed countries as a whole gave .52 per cent of their total GNP in foreign aid. By 1965, it had decreased to .48; by 1970 it had declined to a mere .34 per cent. In 1987 the figure stood just slightly higher at .35 per cent. Ironically, between 1965 and 1980 the economies of developed countries grew at an annual rate of 3.6 and between 1980 and 1987 at an annual rate of 2.7.[35] Although vastly richer, we shared a smaller percentage.

A comparison of Western expenditures on foreign aid and the military is startling. Table 13 shows that during the years 1960–87, all major aid donors spent 4.78 per cent of their GNP on military expenditures. In the same period they gave 0.21 per cent of their GNP for economic aid. By 1987 world military expenditures had reached $944 billion per year – 1.9 million dollars a minute. As the author of the widely respected annual *World Military and Social Expenditures* pointed out, 'In total, the developed countries have

Table 13   Comparative Expenditures of Major Aid Donors

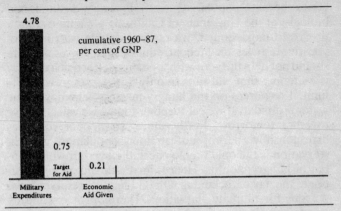

4.78

cumulative 1960–87,
per cent of GNP

0.75

Target
for Aid

0.21

Military
Expenditures

Economic
Aid Given

*Source: Sivard, Ruth Leger. World Military and Social Expenditures 1989.
(Washington, DC: World Priorities, 1989), p. 19.*

spent over twenty times more on arms since 1960 than on development assistance to the poorer countries.'[36] Is that the way we want to use our abundance?

Fortunately, we live in a day when it may be politically possible to reduce military expenditures dramatically. The breathtaking changes in Eastern Europe and the Soviet Union made possible by President Gorbachev's reforms have led almost all politicians to discuss substantial reductions in military spending. Of course, not everyone agrees — especially the military-industrial complex. But the possibility of major cuts in military spending and the reallocation of those dollars to empower the poor is more realistic today than at any time in decades.

Rationalising Our Affluence

It would be impossible for those of the rich minority to live with themselves if they did not invent plausible justifications. These rationalisations take many forms. Analysing a few of the most common may help us spot each year's new models.

In the 'seventies, concepts like 'triage'[37] and 'lifeboat ethics' became popular. Garrett Hardin, a distinguished biologist at the University of California at Santa Barbara, provoked impassioned, widespread debate with his provocative articles on lifeboat ethics.[38] He argues that we should not help the poor with food or aid. Each rich country is a lifeboat that will survive only if it refuses to waste its limited resources on the hungry masses swimming in the water around it. If we eat together today, we will all starve together tomorrow. Furthermore, since poor countries 'irresponsibly' permit unrestrained population growth, starvation is the only way to check the ever-growing number of hungry mouths. Hence, increased aid merely postpones the day of reckoning. Our aid simply preserves more persons for ultimate starvation. Therefore it is ethically correct to help them to learn the hard way – by letting them starve now.

There are, however, fatal flaws in Hardin's argument.

Hardin ignores data which show that poor countries can (and have) cut population growth fairly rapidly if, instead of investing in advanced technology and industrial development, they concentrate on improving the lot of the poor masses. If the poor masses have a secure food supply, access to some (relatively inexpensive) health services and modest educational opportunities, population growth tends to decline quickly. Lester Brown summarises these findings:

There is striking evidence that in an increasing number of poor countries . . . birth rates have dropped sharply despite relatively low per capita income . . . Examination of societies as different as China, Barbados, Sri Lanka, Uruguay, Taiwan, the Indian Punjab, Cuba and South Korea suggests a common factor. In all these countries, a large portion of the population has gained access to modern social and economic services – such as education, employment, and credit systems . . . There is increasing evidence that the very strategies which cause the greatest improvement in the welfare of the entire population also have the greatest effect on reducing population growth.[39]

The right kind of aid – focused especially on empowering the poorest through labour-intensive development using intermediate technology – will help check population growth.[40] Hardin's thesis suggests doing nothing at a time when the right kind of action could probably avoid disaster.

Another omission in Hardin's thesis is even more astonishing. He totally ignores the fact that the ever-increasing affluence among the rich minority is one of the fundamental causes of the present crisis. It is simply false to suggest that there is not enough food to feed everyone. There is enough – if it is more evenly distributed. In a world where the rich minority feed more grain to their livestock than is eaten by one quarter of all the world's people, it is absurd and immoral to talk of the necessity of letting selected hungry nations starve. The boat in which the rich sail is not an austerely equipped lifeboat. It is a lavishly stocked luxury liner.

Hardin's proposal, of course, is also unrealistic. Hungry nations left to starve would not disappear in submissive silence. India is one of the nations frequently nominated for this dubious honour. A nation with nuclear weapons would certainly not tolerate such a decision.[41]

A second rationalisation has a pious ring to it. Some evangelical Christians argue that they must adopt an affluent lifestyle in order to evangelise wealthy persons. Rationalisation is dreadfully easy. Garden Grove Community Church in California has a lavish, multimillion-dollar plant complete with a series of water fountains that begin spraying when the minister touches a button in the pulpit. The pastor, Robert Schuller, defends his luxurious facilities:

We are trying to make a big, beautiful impression upon the affluent non-religious American who is riding by on this busy freeway. It's obvious that we are not trying to impress the Christians! . . . Nor are we trying to impress the social workers in the County Welfare Department. They would tell us that we ought to be content to remain in the Orange Drive-In Theater and give the money to feed the poor. But suppose we had given this money to feed the poor? What would we have today? We would still have hungry, poor people and God would not have this tremendous base of operations which He is using to inspire people to become more successful, more affluent, more generous, more genuinely unselfish in their giving of themselves.[42]

Where does valid justification end and rationalisation begin? We must avoid simplistic legalism. Christians certainly ought to live in the suburbs as well as the inner city. But those who defend an affluent lifestyle on the basis of a call to witness to the rich must ask themselves hard questions: How much of my affluent lifestyle is directly related to my witnessing to rich neighbours? How much of it could I abandon for the sake of Christ's poor and still be able to witness effectively? Indeed, how much of it must I abandon in order faithfully to proclaim the biblical Christ who taught that failure to feed the poor entails eternal damnation (Matt. 25:45–6)?

The response of top US leaders to proposals by developing nations shows how rationalisation can degenerate into double talk. In 1974 there was a historic meeting at the United Nations. The developing nations adopted a document calling for a new international economic order. They insisted on higher prices for their raw materials and other changes in trade patterns and international monetary arrangements that they believed would facilitate their development. US Secretary of State Henry Kissinger and other US leaders charged the large coalition of poor countries with 'using' the United Nations. Some highly placed US officials suggested that this 'tyranny of the majority' warranted US withdrawal from the UN. Is not the democratic principle of majority rule our principle? Is it not dishonest double talk to speak of tyranny when the majority use their numbers to demand justice? It would surely be ironic if we were to belittle democratic principles in order to defend our affluence.

In the coming decades, rationalisations for our affluence will be legion. They will be popular and persuasive. 'Truly, I say to you, it will be hard for a rich man to enter the kingdom of heaven' (Matt. 19:23). But all things are possible with God – if we will hear and obey his Word. We can move towards a more hopeful future for our world and more genuine joy and fulfilment in our personal lives if we affluent Christians will dare to allow the Bible to shape our relationship to a billion sons and daughters of poor Lazarus. The next four chapters discuss how to do that by developing a biblical perspective on poverty and possessions.

Study Questions

1. Is the gap between rich and poor different from what you had thought? How?

2. What are some of the best measures of that gap?

3. How does advertising contribute to our problem? Do you have theological questions about (some) advertising?

4. How does solving poverty help reduce over-population?

5. What rationalisations of affluence are most convincing? For yourself? Your friends?

6. What do you think about the first line of the Preface: 'This book is about joy and self-fulfilment'?

Part 2

A Biblical Perspective on the Poor and Possessions

Martin Luther once said that 'if you preach the gospel in all aspects with the exception of the issues which deal specifically with your time you are not preaching the gospel at all'.[1]

Luther's comment relates directly to the findings of a recent scholarly study. Social scientists examined the factors that shape American attitudes on matters related to the development of the poor nations. They discovered that religion plays no significant role at all! Those with deep religious beliefs are no more concerned about assistance and development for the poor than are persons with little or no religious commitment.[2]

Christians in the West have failed to declare God's perspective on the plight of our billion hungry neighbours – surely one of the most pressing issues of our time.

But I refuse to believe that this failure must inevitably continue. I believe there are millions of Christians in affluent lands who care more about Jesus than anything else in the world. There are millions of Christians who will take any risk, make any sacrifice, forsake any treasure, if they see clearly that God's Word demands it. That is why Part 2, 'A Biblical Perspective on the Poor and Possessions', is the most important section of our study.

Part 2 is full of Scripture. But even so it is only a small selection of the vast volume of biblical material. *Cry Justice* contains almost two hundred pages of biblical texts that relate directly to the theme of this section.[3]

3

GOD AND THE POOR

He who is kind to the poor lends to the Lord. (Prov. 19:17)
I know that the Lord maintains the cause of the afflicted, and
executes justice for the needy (Ps. 140:12).

What is God's attitude towards the poor and oppressed?

Is God biased in favour of the poor? Some theologians
have said yes.[1] The question, however, is ambiguous. Does
it mean that God desires the salvation of poor people more
than the salvation of the rich? Does it mean that God and
his people treat the poor so conspicuously differently from
the way the rich and powerful normally treat them that we
can only say that God seems to have a special concern for
the poor and oppressed? Is God on the side of the poor in a
way that he is not on the side of the rich? Just who are 'the
poor' in the Bible?

The Hebrew words for the poor are '*ānî*, '*ānāw*, '*ebyôn*,
dal and *rāš*. '*Ānî* (and '*ānāw*, which originally had approximately the same meaning) denotes one who is 'wrongfully
impoverished or dispossessed'.[2] '*Ebyôn* refers to a beggar
imploring charity. *Dal* connotes a thin, weakly person, that
is, an impoverished, deprived peasant.[3] Unlike the others,
rāš is an essentially neutral term. In their persistent polemic
against the oppression of the poor, the prophets used the
terms '*ebyôn*, '*ānî*, and *dal*. Thus the primary connotation
of 'the poor' in the Scriptures is economic. Usually, too,
calamity or some form of oppression is the assumed cause
of the poverty.

The Scriptures also teach that some folk are poor because they are lazy and slothful (for example, Prov. 6:6–11;

19:15; 20:13; 21:25; 24:30–4). And the Bible knows of
voluntary poverty for the sake of the kingdom. The most
common biblical connotation of 'the poor', however, is of
those who are economically impoverished because of
calamity or exploitation.[4] In this chapter, we use this last
meaning of 'the poor'.

We can only answer the questions about God's bias
towards the poor after we have searched for biblical
answers to five related questions: (1) What concern for the
poor did God disclose at those pivotal points (especially
the Exodus, the destruction of Israel and Judah, and the
Incarnation) where he acted in history to reveal himself?
(2) In what sense does God identify with the poor? (3) How
significant is the fact that God frequently chooses to work
through the poor and oppressed? (4) What does the Bible
mean by the recurring teaching that God destroys the rich
and exalts the poor? (5) Does God command his people to
have a special concern for the poor?

Pivotal Points of Revelation History

The Bible clearly and repeatedly teaches a fundamental
point that we have often overlooked. At the crucial mo-
ments when God displayed his mighty acts in history to
reveal his nature and will, God also intervened to liberate
the poor and oppressed.

1 The Exodus   God displayed his power at the Exodus
in order to free oppressed slaves. When he called Moses at
the burning bush, God's intent was to end suffering and
injustice: 'I have seen the affliction of my people who are
in Egypt, and have heard their cry because of their task-
masters; I know their sufferings, and I have come down to
deliver them out of the hand of the Egyptians' (Exod.
3:7–8). This text does not reflect an isolated perspective on
the great event of the Exodus. Each year at the harvest
festival the Israelites repeated a liturgical confession cel-
ebrating the way God had acted to free a poor, oppressed
people.

A wandering Aramean was my father; and he went down into Egypt and sojourned there. . . . And the Egyptians treated us harshly, and afflicted us, and laid upon us hard bondage. Then we cried to the Lord the God of our fathers, and the Lord heard our voice, and saw our affliction, our toil, and our oppression; and the Lord brought us out of Egypt with a mighty hand (Deut. 26:5–8).

The God of the Bible cares when people enslave and oppress others. At the Exodus he acted to end economic oppression and bring freedom to slaves.

Now of course the liberation of oppressed slaves was not God's only purpose in the Exodus. God also acted because of his covenant with Abraham, Isaac and Jacob. In addition, he wanted to create a special people to whom he could reveal himself.[5] Both of these concerns were clearly central to God's activity at the Exodus. The liberation of a poor, oppressed people, however, was also right at the heart of God's design. The following passage discloses God's multifaceted purpose in the Exodus:

Moreover I have heard the groaning of the people of Israel whom the Egyptians hold in bondage and I have remembered my covenant [with Abraham, Isaac and Jacob]. . . . I will bring you out from under the burdens of the Egyptians, and I will deliver you from their bondage, and I will redeem you with an outstretched arm and with great acts of judgment, and I will take you for my people, and I will be your God; and you shall know that I am the Lord your God, who has brought you out from under the burdens of the Egyptians (Exod. 6:5–7).

Yahweh wanted his people to know him as the One who freed them from slavery and oppression.

The preamble to the Ten Commandments, probably the most important portion of the entire law for Israel, begins with this same revolutionary truth. Before he gives the two tables of the law, Yahweh identifies himself: 'I am the Lord your God, who brought you out of the land of Egypt, out of the house of bondage' (Deut. 5:6; Exod. 20:2). Yahweh is the one who frees from bondage. The God of the Bible wants to be known as the liberator of the oppressed.

The Exodus was certainly the decisive event in the creation of the chosen people. We distort the biblical interpretation of this momentous occasion unless we see that at this pivotal point the Lord of the universe was at work correcting oppression and liberating the poor.

2 Destruction and Captivity   When they settled in the Promised Land, the Israelites soon discovered that Yahweh's passion for justice was a two-edged sword. When they were oppressed, it led to their freedom. But when they became the oppressors, it led to their destruction.

When God called Israel out of Egypt and made his covenant with them, he gave them his law so that they could live together in peace and justice. But Israel failed to obey the law of the covenant. As a result, God destroyed Israel and sent his chosen people into captivity.

Why?

The explosive message of the prophets is that God destroyed Israel because of mistreatment of the poor. Idolatry, of course, was an equally prominent reason. Too often, however, we remember only Israel's 'spiritual' problem of idolatry and overlook the clear, startling biblical teaching that economic exploitation also sent the chosen people into captivity.

The middle of the eighth century BC was a time of political success and economic prosperity unknown since the days of Solomon.[6] But it was precisely at this moment that God sent his prophet Amos to announce the unwelcome news that the northern kingdom of Israel would be destroyed. Penetrating beneath the façade of current prosperity and fantastic economic growth, Amos saw oppression of the poor. He saw the rich 'trample the head of the poor into the dust of the earth' (2:7). He saw that the affluent lifestyle of the rich was built on oppression of the poor (6:1–7). He denounced the rich women ('cows' was his word!) 'who oppress the poor, who crush the needy, who say to their husbands, "Bring, that we may drink!"' (4:1). Even in the courts the poor had no hope because the rich bribed the judges (5:10–15).

Archaeologists have confirmed Amos's picture of shocking extremes of wealth and poverty.[7] In the early days of settlement in Canaan, the land was distributed equally among the families and tribes. All Israelites enjoyed a similar standard of living. In fact, as late as the tenth century BC, archaeologists have found that houses were all approximately the same size. But by Amos's day, two centuries later, everything is different. Archaeologists have uncovered bigger, better-built houses in one area and poorer houses huddled together in another section.[8] No wonder Amos warned the rich, 'You have built houses of hewn stone, but you shall not dwell in them' (5:11)!

God's word through Amos was that the northern kingdom would be destroyed and the people taken into exile (7:11, 17).

> Woe to those who lie upon beds of ivory,
>   and stretch themselves upon their couches, and eat
>   lambs from the flock,
>   and calves from the midst of the stall. . . .
> Therefore they shall now be the first of those to go into
>   exile,
>   and the revelry of those who stretch themselves shall
>   pass away (6:4, 7).

Only a few years after Amos spoke it happened just as God had said. The Assyrians conquered the northern kingdom and took thousands into captivity. Because of their mistreatment of the poor, God destroyed the northern kingdom – for ever.

As in the case of the Exodus, we must not ignore another important factor. The prophet Hosea, a contemporary of Amos, disclosed that the nation's idolatry was another cause of impending destruction. Because they had forsaken Yahweh for idols, the nation would be destroyed (Hos.

8:1–6; 9:1–3).[9] According to the prophets, then, the northern kingdom fell because of both idolatry and economic exploitation of the poor.

God sent other prophets to announce the same fate for the southern kingdom of Judah. Isaiah warned that destruction from afar would befall Judah because of its mistreatment of the poor:

> Woe to those who decree iniquitous decrees. . . .
> to turn aside the needy from justice
> and to rob the poor of my people of their right. . . .
> What will you do on the day of punishment,
> in the storm which will come from afar? (Isa. 10:1–3)

Micah denounced those in Judah who 'covet fields, and seize them; and houses, and take them away; they oppress a man and his house, a man and his inheritance' (2:2). As a result, he warned, Jerusalem would one day become 'a heap of ruins' (3:12).

Fortunately, Judah was more open to the prophetic word, and the nation was spared for a time. But oppression of the poor continued. A hundred years after the time of Isaiah, the prophet Jeremiah again condemned the wealthy who had amassed riches by oppressing the poor:

> Wicked men are found among my people;
> they lurk like fowlers lying in wait.
> They set a trap;
> they catch men.
> Like a basket full of birds,
> their houses are full of treachery;
> therefore, they have become great and rich, they have
>   grown fat and sleek.
> They know no bounds in deeds of wickedness;
> they judge not with justice
> the cause of the fatherless, to make it prosper,
> and they do not defend the rights of the needy.
> Shall I not punish them for these things?

says the Lord,
and shall I not avenge myself
on a nation such as this? (Jer. 5:26–9)

Even at that late date Jeremiah could promise hope if the
people would forsake *both* injustice *and* idolatry. 'If you
truly execute justice one with another, if you do not oppress
the alien, the fatherless or the widow . . . and if you do not
go after other gods to your own hurt, then I will let you
dwell in this place, in the land that I gave of old to your
fathers for ever' (Jer. 7:5–7).

But they continued to oppress the poor and helpless (Jer.
34:3–17). As a result Jeremiah persisted in saying God
would use the Babylonians to destroy Judah. In 587 BC
Jerusalem fell and the Babylonian captivity began.

The destruction of Israel and Judah, however, was not
mere punishment. God wanted to use the Assyrians and
Babylonians to purge his people of oppression and injustice. In a remarkable passage Isaiah showed how God
would attack his foes and enemies (that is, his chosen
people!) in order to purify them and restore justice.

How the faithful city [Jerusalem]
has become a harlot,
she that was full of justice!
Righteousness lodged in her,
but now murderers.
Your silver has become dross,
your wine mixed with water. . . .
Every one loves a bribe
and runs after gifts.
They do not defend the fatherless,
and the widow's cause does not come to them.
Therefore the Lord says,
the Lord of hosts,
the Mighty One of Israel:
'Ah, I will vent my wrath on my enemies,
and avenge myself on my foes.
I will turn my hand against you

> and will smelt away your dross as with lye
> and remove all your alloy.
> And I will restore your judges as at the first,
> and your counsellors as at the beginning.
> Afterwards you shall be called the city of righteousness,
> the faithful city.' (Isa. 1:21–6)

The catastrophe of national destruction and captivity reveals the God of the Exodus still at work correcting the oppression of the poor.

3 The Incarnation Christians believe that God revealed himself most completely in Jesus of Nazareth. How did the Incarnate One define his mission?

Jesus's words in the synagogue at Nazareth, spoken near the beginning of his public ministry, throb with hope for the poor. He read from the prophet Isaiah:

> The Spirit of the Lord is upon me,
> because he has anointed me to preach good news to the
>   poor.
> He has sent me to proclaim release to the captives
> and recovering of sight to the blind,
> to set at liberty those who are oppressed,
> to proclaim the acceptable year of the Lord (Luke
>   4:18–19).

After reading these words, Jesus informed his audience that this Scripture was now fulfilled in himself. The mission of the Incarnate One was to free the oppressed and heal the blind. (It was also to preach the gospel. And this is equally important, although the focus of this book precludes further discussion of it.)[10] The poor are the only group specifically singled out as recipients of Jesus's gospel. Certainly the gospel he proclaimed was for all, but he was particularly concerned that the poor realise that his good news was for them.

Some try to avoid the clear meaning of Jesus's statement by spiritualising his words. Certainly, as other texts show, he came to open our blinded hearts, to die for our sins and to free us from the oppression of guilt. But that is not what he means here. The words about releasing captives and liberating the oppressed are from Isaiah. In their original Old Testament setting they unquestionably referred to physical oppression and captivity. In Luke 7:18–23, which contains a list similar to that in Luke 4:18–19, it is clear that Jesus is referring to material, physical problems.[11]

Jesus's actual ministry corresponded precisely to the words of Luke 4. He spent most of his time not among the rich and powerful in Jerusalem, but among the poor in the cultural and economic backwater of Galilee. He healed the sick and blind. He fed the hungry. And he warned his followers in the strongest possible words that those who do not feed the hungry, clothe the naked, and visit the prisoners will experience eternal damnation (Matt. 25:31–46).

At the supreme moment of history when God took on human flesh, the God of Israel was still liberating the poor and oppressed and summoning his people to do the same. That is the central reason for Christian concern for the poor.

It is not just at the Exodus, captivity, and Incarnation, however, that we learn of God's concern for the poor, the weak, and the oppressed. The Bible is full of passages which speak of this. Two illustrations from the Psalms are typical of a host of other texts.

Psalm 10 begins with despair. God seems to have hidden himself far away while the wicked prosper by oppressing the poor (vv. 2, 9). But the psalmist concludes with hope:

The hapless commits himself to thee;
thou hast been the helper of the fatherless. . . .
O Lord, thou wilt hear the desire of the meek . . .
thou wilt incline thy ear
to do justice to the fatherless and the oppressed (vv. 14,
    17–18).

Psalm 146 is a ringing declaration that to care for the poor is central to the very nature of God. The psalmist exults in the God of Jacob because he is both the creator of the universe and the defender of the oppressed.

Praise the Lord!
Praise the Lord, O my soul! . . .
Happy is he whose help is the God of Jacob,
whose hope is in the Lord his God,
who made heaven and earth,
the sea, and all that is in them;
who keeps faith for ever;
who executes justice for the oppressed;
who gives food to the hungry.
The Lord sets the prisoners free;
the Lord opens the eyes of the blind.
The Lord lifts up those who are bowed down;
the Lord loves the righteous.
The Lord watches over the sojourners,
he upholds the widow and the fatherless;
but the way of the wicked he brings to ruin (vv. 1, 5–9).

According to Scripture it is just as much a part of God's
essence to defend the weak, the stranger and the oppressed
as to create the universe. Because of who he is, Yahweh
lifts up the mistreated.[12] The foundation of Christian
concern for the hungry and oppressed is that God cares
especially for them.

God Identifies with the Poor

God not only acts in history to liberate the poor, but in a
mysterious way that we can only half fathom the Sovereign
of the universe identifies with the weak and destitute. Two
proverbs state this beautiful truth. Proverbs 14:31 puts it
negatively: 'He who oppresses a poor man insults his
Maker.' Even more moving is the positive formulation: 'He
who is kind to the poor lends to the Lord' (19:17). What a
statement! Helping a poor person is like helping the
Creator of all things with a loan.

Only in the Incarnation can we begin to perceive what
God's identification with the weak, oppressed and poor
really means. 'Though he was rich,' Paul says of our Lord
Jesus, 'yet for your sake he became poor' (2 Cor. 8:9).

He was born in a small, insignificant province of the Roman Empire. His first visitors, the shepherds, were persons viewed by Jewish society as thieves. His parents were too poor to bring the normal offering for purification. Instead of a lamb, they brought two pigeons to the Temple (Luke 2:24; compare Lev. 12:6–8). Jesus was a refugee and then an immigrant in Galilee (Matt. 2:13–15, 19–23). Since Jewish rabbis received no fees for their teaching, Jesus had no regular income during his public ministry. (Scholars belonged to the poorer classes in Judaism.)[13] Nor did he have a home of his own. Jesus warned an eager follower who promised to follow him everywhere, 'Foxes have holes, and birds of the air have nests; but the Son of man has nowhere to lay his head' (Matt. 8:20). He sent out his disciples in extreme poverty (Luke 9:3; 10:4).

His identification with the poor and unfortunate was, Jesus said, a sign that he was the Messiah. When John the Baptist sent messengers to ask him if he were the long-expected Messiah, Jesus simply pointed to his deeds: he was healing the sick and preaching to the poor (Matt. 11:2–6). Jesus also preached to the rich. But apparently it was his particular concern to preach to the poor that validated his claim to messiahship. His preoccupation with the poor and disadvantaged contrasted sharply with the style of his contemporaries. Was that perhaps why he added a final word to take back to John: 'Blessed is he who takes no offence at me' (Matt. 11:6)?

Only as we feel the presence of the incarnate God in the form of a poor Galilean can we begin to understand his words: 'I was hungry and you gave me food, I was thirsty and you gave me drink. . . . I was naked and you clothed me. . . . Truly, I say to you, as you did it to one of the least of these my brethren, you did it to me' (Matt. 25:35–6, 40). What does it mean to feed and clothe the Creator of all things? We cannot know. We can only look on the poor and oppressed with new eyes and resolve to heal their hurts and help end their oppression.

If Jesus's saying in Matthew 25:40 is awesome, its parallel is terrifying: 'Truly, I say to you, as you did it not to one of the least of these, you did it not to me' (v. 45). What does that mean in a world where millions die each year while rich Christians live in affluence? What does it mean to see the Lord of the universe lying by the roadside starving and walk by on the other side? We cannot know. We can only pledge, in fear and trembling, not to kill him again.

God's Special Instruments

When God selected a chosen people, he picked poor slaves in Egypt. When God called the early church, most of the members were poor folk. When God became flesh, he came as a poor Galilean. Are these facts isolated phenomena or part of a significant pattern? This is our third question in discerning God's special concern for the poor.

God might have selected a rich, powerful nation as his chosen people. Instead he chose oppressed slaves. God picked an impoverished, enslaved people to be his special instrument of revelation and salvation for all people. (See also Gideon in Judges 6:15–16; 7:2.)

In the early church most members were poor. In a recent book sketching the social history of early Christianity, Martin Hengel points out that the early gentile Christian communities 'were predominantly poor'.[14] St Paul marvelled at the kind of people God called into the church: 'Not many of you were wise according to worldly standards, not many were powerful, not many were of noble birth; but God chose what is foolish in the world to shame the wise, God chose what is weak in the world to shame the strong, God chose what is low and despised in the world, even things that are not, to bring to nothing things that are, so that no human being might boast in the presence of God' (1 Cor. 1:26–9).

Likewise James:

> My brethren, show no partiality as you hold the faith of our Lord Jesus Christ, the Lord of glory. For if a man with gold rings and in fine clothing comes into your assembly, and a poor man in shabby clothing also comes

in, and you pay attention to the one who wears the fine
clothing and say, 'Have a seat here, please,' while you
say to the poor man, 'Stand there,' or, 'Sit at my feet,'
have you not made distinctions among yourselves, and
become judges with evil thoughts? Listen, my beloved
brethren. Has not God chosen those who are poor in the
world to be rich in faith and heirs of the kingdom which
he has promised to those who love him? But you have
dishonoured the poor man. Is it not the rich who oppress
you, is it not they who drag you into court? Is it not they
who blaspheme the honourable name which was invoked
over you? (Jas. 2:1–7)

The rhetorical question in verse 5 indicates that the
Jerusalem church too was far from rich. But the entire
passage illustrates the way the church so often forsakes
God's way and opts instead for the way of the world. At
both the Exodus and the emergence of the early church,
God chose poor folk as his special instruments.

Of course one must not overstate the case. Abraham
seems to have been well off. Moses lived at Pharaoh's court
for forty years. Paul and Luke were neither poor nor
uneducated. God does not work exclusively through impoverished, oppressed people. There is a sharp contrast,
none the less, between God's procedure and ours. When
we want to effect change, we almost always contact people
with influence, prestige, and power. When God wanted to
save the world, he selected slaves, prostitutes and sundry
other disadvantaged folk.

Again the Incarnation is the most important example.
Nowhere is the contrast between God's ways and ours
clearer than here. God might have entered history as a
powerful Roman emperor or at least as an influential
Sadducee with a prominent place in the Sanhedrin. Instead he came and lived as a poor carpenter in Nazareth, a
humble hamlet too insignificant to be mentioned either in
the Old Testament or the writings of Josephus, the first-
century Jewish historian.[15] Yet this is how God chose to
effect our salvation.

When Jesus chose his disciples, those who were to carry on his mission, all except Matthew were fishermen and other common folk. Those who think that only the rich and powerful change history continue to take offence at Jesus's preoccupation with the poor and weak.

Again we must oppose the view that God never uses rich, powerful people as his chosen instruments. He has and does. But we always choose such people. God, on the other hand, frequently selects the poor to carry out his most important tasks. He sees potential that we do not. And when the task is done, the poor and weak are less likely to boast that they deserve the credit. God's selection of the lowly to be his special messengers of salvation to the world is striking evidence of his special concern for them. And his incarnation as a poor Galilean suggests that the frequent use of the poor as his special instruments is not insignificant historical trivia. It points to something significant about the very nature of God.

Is God a Marxist?

Jesus's story of the rich man and Lazarus echoes and illustrates a fourth teaching prominent throughout Scripture: The rich may prosper for a time, but eventually God will destroy them; the poor, on the other hand, God will exalt. Mary's Magnificat puts it simply and bluntly:

> My soul magnifies the Lord. . . .
> He has put down the mighty from their thrones,
> and exalted those of low degree;
> he has filled the hungry with good things,
> and the rich he has sent empty away (Luke 1:46, 52–3).

Centuries earlier Hannah's song had proclaimed the same truth:

> There is none holy like the Lord,
> there is none besides thee. . . .
> Talk no more so very proudly,

let not arrogance come from your mouth. . . .
The bows of the mighty are broken,
but the feeble gird on strength.
Those who were full have hired themselves out for
    bread,
but those who were hungry have ceased to hunger. . . .
The Lord makes poor and makes rich. . . .
He raises up the poor from the dust;
he lifts the needy from the ash heap (1 Sam. 2:2–8).

Jesus pronounced a blessing on the poor and a curse on the rich:

Blessed are you poor, for yours is the kingdom of God.
Blessed are you that hunger now, for you shall be
    satisfied. . . .
Woe to you that are rich, for you have received your
    consolation.
Woe to you that are full now, for you shall hunger
    (Luke 6:20–5).[16]

'Come now, you rich, weep and howl for the miseries that are coming upon you' (Jas. 5:1) is a constant theme of biblical revelation.

Why does Scripture declare that God regularly reverses the good fortunes of the rich? Is God engaged in class warfare? Our texts never say that God loves the poor more than the rich. But they do constantly assert that God lifts up the poor and disadvantaged. They persistently insist that God casts down the wealthy and powerful precisely because they became wealthy by oppressing the poor or because they failed to feed the hungry.

Why did James warn the rich to weep and howl because of impending misery? Because they had cheated their workers: 'You have laid up treasure for the last days. Behold, the wages of the labourers who mowed your fields, which you kept back by fraud, cry out; and the cries of the harvesters have reached the ears of the Lord of hosts. You have lived on the earth in luxury and in pleasure; you have fattened your hearts in a day of slaughter' (Jas. 5:3–5). God does not have class enemies. But he hates and punishes injustice and neglect of the poor. And the rich, if we accept the repeated warnings of Scripture, are frequently guilty of both.[17]

Long before the days of James, the psalmist knew that the rich were often rich because of oppression. He took comfort in the faith that God would punish such evildoers.

> In arrogance the wicked hotly pursue the poor. . . .
> His ways prosper at all times. . . .
> He thinks in his heart, 'I shall not be moved;
> throughout all generations I shall not meet
>   adversity. . . .'
> He lurks in secret like a lion in his covert;
> he lurks that he may seize the poor,
> he seizes the poor when he draws him into his net. . . .
> Arise, O Lord; O God, lift up thy hand;
> forget not the afflicted. . . .
> Break thou the arm of the wicked and evildoer. . . .
> O Lord, thou wilt hear the desire of the meek;
> thou wilt strengthen their heart,
> thou wilt incline thy ear
> to do justice to the fatherless and the oppressed
>   (Ps. 10).

God announced the same message through the prophet Jeremiah:

> Wicked men are found among my people;
> they lurk like fowlers lying in wait.
> They set a trap;
> they catch men.
> Like a basket full of birds
> their houses are full of treachery;
> *therefore they have become great and rich,*
> *they have grown fat and sleek.*
> They know no bounds in deeds of wickedness;
> they judge not with justice
> the cause of the fatherless, to make it prosper,

and they do not defend the rights of the needy.
Shall I not punish them for these things?
says the Lord (Jer. 5:26–9).

Nor was the faith of Jeremiah and the psalmist mere wishful thinking. Through the prophets God announced devastation and destruction for both rich individuals and rich nations who oppressed the poor. And it happened as they predicted. Jeremiah pronounced one of the most biting, satirical diatribes in all of Scripture against the unjust King Jehoiakim of Judah:

'Woe to him who builds his house by unrighteousness,
and his upper rooms by injustice;
who makes his neighbour serve him for nothing,
and does not give him his wages;
who says, "I will build myself a great house
with spacious upper rooms,"'
and cuts out windows for it,
panelling it with cedar,
and painting it with vermilion.
Do you think you are a king
because you compete in cedar?
Did not your father eat and drink
and do justice and righteousness?
Then it was well with him.
He judged the cause of the poor and needy;
then it was well.
Is not this to know me?
says the Lord.
But you have eyes and heart
only for your dishonest gain,
for shedding innocent blood,
and for practising oppression and violence.'
Therefore thus says the Lord concerning
    Jehoiakim: . . .
'With the burial of an ass he shall be buried,
dragged and cast forth beyond the gates of Jerusalem'
    (Jer. 22:13–19).

Jehoiakim, historians think, was assassinated.[18]

God destroys whole nations as well as rich individuals because of oppression of the poor. We have already examined a few of the pertinent texts.[19] One more is important. Through Isaiah God declared that the rulers of Judah were rich because they had cheated the poor. Surfeited with affluence, the wealthy women had indulged in self-centred wantonness, oblivious to the suffering of the oppressed. The result, God said, would be destruction.

> The Lord enters into judgment
> with the elders and princes of his people:
> 'It is you who have devoured the vineyard,
> *the spoil of the poor is in your houses*.
> What do you mean by crushing my people,
> by grinding the face of the poor?'
> says the Lord God of hosts.
> The Lord said:
> Because the daughters of Zion are haughty
> and walk with outstretched necks,
> glancing wantonly with their eyes,
> mincing along as they go,
> tinkling with their feet;
> the Lord will smite with a scab
> the heads of the daughters of Zion. . . .
> In that day the Lord will take away the finery
> of the anklets, the headbands, and the crescents. . . .
> Instead of perfume there will be rottenness;
> and instead of a girdle, a rope;
> and instead of well-set hair, baldness;
> and instead of a rich robe, a girding of sackcloth;
> instead of beauty, shame.
> Your men shall fall by the sword
> and your mighty men in battle (Isa. 3:14–25).

Because the rich oppress the poor and weak, the Lord of history is at work pulling down their houses and kingdoms. Sometimes Scripture does not charge the rich with direct oppression of the poor. It simply accuses them of failure to share with the needy. But the result is the same.

In the story of the rich man and Lazarus, Jesus does not say that the rich man exploited Lazarus (Luke 16). He merely shows that he had no concern for the sick beggar lying outside his gate. 'Clothed in purple and fine linen [the rich man] feasted sumptuously every day' (Luke 16:19). Lazarus, on the other hand, 'desired to be fed with what fell from the rich man's table' (Luke 16:21). Did the rich man deny hungry Lazarus even the scraps? Perhaps not. But obviously he had no real concern for him.

Such sinful neglect of the needy infuriates the God of the poor. When Lazarus died, God comforted him in Abraham's bosom. When the rich man died, torment confronted him.[20] The meaning of the name *Lazarus*, 'one whom God has helped', underlines the basic point.[21] God aids the poor, but the rich he sends empty away.

Clark Pinnock is surely correct when he notes that 'a story like that of Dives and Lazarus ought to explode in our hands when we read it sitting at our well-covered tables while the third world stands outside'.[22] Not only the Law and the Prophets declare the terrifying word that God destroys the rich when they fail to assist the poor; our Lord himself declares it.

The biblical explanation of Sodom's destruction provides another illustration of this terrible truth. If asked why Sodom was destroyed, virtually all Christians would point to the city's gross sexual perversity. But that is a one-sided recollection of what Scripture actually teaches. Ezekiel shows that one important reason God destroyed Sodom was that it stubbornly refused to share with the poor!

Behold, this was the guilt of your sister Sodom: she and her daughters had pride, *surfeit of food, and prosperous ease, but did not aid the poor and needy*. They were haughty, and did abominable things before me; therefore I removed them, when I saw it (Ezek. 16:49–50; see also Isa. 1:10–17).

The text does not say that they oppressed the poor, although they probably did. It simply accuses them of failing to assist the needy.

Affluent Christians remember Sodom's sexual misconduct and forget its sinful unconcern for the poor. Is it because the former is less upsetting? Have we allowed our economic self-interest to distort our interpretation of Scripture? Undoubtedly we have. But precisely to the extent that our affirmation of scriptural authority is sincere, we will permit painful texts to correct our thinking. As we do, we will acknowledge in fear and trembling that the God of the Bible wreaks horrendous havoc on the rich. But it is not because he does not love rich persons. It is because the rich regularly oppress the poor or neglect the needy.

God's Concern and Ours

Since God cares so much for the poor, it is hardly surprising that he wants his people to do the same. God's command to believers to have a special regard for the poor, weak and disadvantaged is the fifth theme of biblical literature we shall follow.

Equal justice for the poor in court is a constant concern of Scripture. The law commanded it (Exod. 23:6). The psalmist invoked divine assistance for the king so that he could provide it (Ps. 72:1–4). And the prophets announced destruction because the rulers stubbornly subverted it (Amos 5:10–15).

Widows, orphans and strangers also receive particularly frequent attention. 'You shall not wrong a stranger or oppress him, for you were strangers in the land of Egypt. You shall not afflict any widow or orphan. If you do afflict them, and they cry out to me, I will surely hear their cry; and my wrath will burn, and I will kill you with the sword, and your wives shall become widows and your children fatherless' (Exod. 22:21–4).

'The fatherless, widows, and foreigners,' John F. Alexander observes, 'each has about forty verses that command justice for them. God wants to make it very clear that in a special sense he is the protector of these weak ones. Strangers are to be treated nearly the same as Jews, and woe to people who take advantage of orphans or widows.'[23]

Rare indeed are the Christians who pay any attention to Jesus's command to show bias towards the poor in their dinner invitations. 'When you give a dinner or a banquet, do not invite your friends or your brothers or your kinsmen or rich neighbours. . . . But when you give a feast, invite the poor, the maimed, the lame, the blind, and you will be blessed, because they cannot repay you' (Luke 14:12–14; see also Heb. 13:1–3).

Obviously Jesus was employing hyperbole, a typical technique of Hebrew literature to emphasise his point. He did not mean to forbid parties with friends and relatives. But he certainly did mean that we ought to entertain the poor and disadvantaged (who cannot reciprocate) at least as often – and perhaps a lot more often than we entertain friends, relatives and 'successful' folk. Have you ever known a Christian who took Jesus that seriously?

The Bible specifically commands believers to imitate God's special concern for the poor and oppressed. In the Old Testament, Yahweh frequently reminded the Israelites of their former oppression in Egypt when he commanded them to care for the poor. God's unmerited concern for the Hebrew slaves in Egyptian bondage is the model to imitate (Exod. 22:21–4; Deut. 15:13–15).

Jesus taught his followers to imitate God's mercy in their lending as well. 'If you do good to those who do good to you, what credit is that to you? . . . And if you lend to those from whom you hope to receive, what credit is that to you? . . . Lend, expecting nothing in return; and your reward will be great, and you will be sons of the Most High; for he is kind to the ungrateful and the selfish. Be merciful, even as your Father is merciful' (Luke 6:33–6). Why lend without expecting return? Because that is the way our Father acts. Jesus's followers are to reverse normal human patterns precisely because they are sons and daughters of God and want to reflect his nature.

When Paul took up the collection for the poor in Jerusalem, he pointedly reminded the Corinthians that the Lord Jesus became poor so that they might become rich (2 Cor. 8:9). When the author of 1 John called on Christians to share with the needy, he first mentioned the example of Christ: 'By this we know love, that he laid down his life for us; and we ought to lay down our lives for the brethren' (1 John 3:16). Then, in the very next verse, he urged Christians to give generously to the needy. It is the amazing self-sacrifice of Christ which Christians are to imitate as they relate to the poor and oppressed.

We have seen that God's Word commands believers to care for the poor. In fact the Bible underlines the command by teaching that when God's people care for the poor, they imitate God himself. But that is not all. God's Word teaches that those who neglect the poor and oppressed are really not God's people at all – no matter how frequent their religious rituals or how orthodox their creeds and confessions.

God thundered again and again through the prophets that worship in the context of mistreatment of the poor and disadvantaged is an outrage. Isaiah denounced Israel (he called it Sodom and Gomorrah!) because it tried to worship Yahweh and oppress the weak at the same time:

Hear the word of the Lord,
you rulers of Sodom!
Give ear to the teaching of our God,
you people of Gomorrah!
'What to me is the multitude of your sacrifices? . . .
Bring no more vain offerings;
incense is an abomination to me.
New moon and sabbath and the calling of assemblies –
I cannot endure iniquity and solemn assembly.
Your new moons and your appointed feasts
my soul hates; . . .
even though you make many prayers,
I will not listen;
your hands are full of blood' (Isa. 1:10–15).

What does God want? 'Cease to do evil, learn to do good; seek justice, correct oppression; defend the fatherless, plead for the widow' (Isa. 1:16–17).

Equally powerful are Isaiah's words against mixing fasting and injustice:

'Why have we fasted, and thou seest it not?
Why have we humbled ourselves,
and thou takest no knowledge of it?'
Behold, in the day of your fast you seek your own
     pleasure, and oppress all your workers. . . .
Is not this the fast that I choose:
to loose the bonds of wickedness,
to undo the thongs of the yoke,
to let the oppressed go free,
and to break every yoke?
Is it not to share your bread with the hungry,
and bring the homeless poor into your house?
(Isa. 58:3–7)

God's words through the prophet Amos are also harsh:

I hate, I despise your feasts,
and I take no delight in your solemn assemblies.
Even though you offer me your burnt offerings and
     cereal offerings,
I will not accept them. . . .
But let justice roll down like waters,
and righteousness like an ever-flowing stream
(Amos 5:21–4).[24]

Earlier in Amos 5 the prophet had condemned the rich and powerful for oppressing the poor. They even bribed judges to prevent redress in the courts. God wants justice, not mere religious rituals, from such people.[25] Their worship is a mockery and abomination to the God of the poor.

God has not changed. Jesus repeated the same theme. He warned the people about the scribes 'who devour

widows' houses and for a pretence make long prayers'
(Mark 12:40). Their pious-looking garments and frequent
visits to the synagogue were a sham. Jesus was a Hebrew
prophet in the tradition of Amos and Isaiah. Like them he
announced God's outrage against those who try to mix
pious practices and mistreatment of the poor.

The prophetic word against religious hypocrites raises a
difficult question. Are the people of God truly God's
people if they oppress the poor? Is the church really the
church if it does not work to free the oppressed?

We have seen how God declared that the people of Israel
were really Sodom and Gomorrah rather than the people of
God (Isa. 1:10). God simply could not tolerate their exploitation of the poor and disadvantaged any longer. Hosea
solemnly announced that, because of their sins, Israel was
no longer God's people and he was no longer their God
(Hos. 1:8–9). In fact God destroyed them. Jesus was even
more blunt and sharp. To those who do not feed the
hungry, clothe the naked, and visit the prisoners, he will
speak a terrifying word at the final judgment: 'Depart from
me, you cursed, into the eternal fire prepared for the devil
and his angels' (Matt. 25:41). The meaning is clear and
unambiguous. Jesus intends that his disciples imitate his
own special concern for the poor and needy. Those who
disobey will experience eternal damnation.

But perhaps we have misinterpreted Matthew 25. Some
people think that 'the least of these' (v. 45) and 'the least of
these my brethren' (v. 40) refer only to Christians. This
exegesis is not certain. But even if the primary reference of
these words is to poor believers, other aspects of Jesus's
teaching not only permit but require us to extend the
meaning of Matthew 25 to both believers and unbelievers
who are poor and oppressed. The story of the good
Samaritan teaches that anybody in need is our neighbour
(Luke 10:29–37). Matthew 5:43–5 is even more explicit:
'You have heard that it was said, "You shall love your
neighbour and hate your enemy." But I say to you, Love
your enemies and pray for those who persecute you, so that
you may be sons of your Father who is in heaven; for he

makes his sun rise on the evil and on the good, and sends rain on the just and on the unjust.'

The ideal in the Qumran community (known to us through the Dead Sea Scrolls) was indeed to 'love all the sons of light' and 'hate all the sons of darkness' (1 QS 1:9–10, the Essenes' Community Rule). Even in the Old Testament, Israelites were commanded to love the neighbour who was the son of their own people and ordered not to seek the prosperity of Ammonites and Moabites (Lev. 19:17–18; Deut. 23:3–6). But Jesus explicitly forbids his followers to limit their loving concern to the neighbour who is a member of their own ethnic or religious group. He explicitly commands his followers to imitate God who does good for all people everywhere.

As George Ladd has said, 'Jesus redefines the meaning of love for neighbor; it means love for any man in need.'[26] In the light of the parable of the good Samaritan and the clear teaching of Matthew 5:43–8, one is compelled to say that part of the full teaching of Matthew 25 is that those who fail to aid the poor and oppressed (whether they are believers or not) are simply not the people of God.

In 1 John 3:17–18 we find the same message: 'If any one has the world's goods and sees his brother in need, yet closes his heart against him, how does God's love abide in him? Little children, let us not love in word or speech but in deed and in truth.' (See also James 2:14–17.) Again the words are plain. What do they mean for Western Christians who demand increasing affluence each year while Christians in the Third World suffer from malnutrition, deformed bodies and brains – even starvation? The text clearly says that if we fail to aid the needy, we do not have God's love – no matter what we may say. It is deeds that count, not pious phrases and saintly speeches. Regardless of what we do or say at 11.00 a.m. Sunday morning, affluent people who neglect the poor are not the people of God.

But still the question persists. Are professing believers no longer Christians because of continuing sin? Obviously not. The Christian knows that sinful selfishness continues to plague even the most saintly. Salvation is by grace alone, not works-righteousness. We are members of the people of God not because of our own righteousness but solely because of Christ's death for us.

That response is true – but inadequate by itself. Matthew 25 and 1 John 3 surely mean more than that the people of God are disobedient (but still justified all the same) when they neglect the poor. These verses pointedly assert that some people so disobey God that they are not his people at all in spite of their pious profession. Neglect of the poor is one of the oft-repeated biblical signs of such disobedience. Certainly none of us would claim that we fulfil Matthew 25 perfectly. And we cling to the hope of forgiveness. But there comes a point (and, thank God, he alone knows where!) when neglect of the poor is not forgiven. It is punished. Eternally.

Is it not possible that many Western 'Christians' have reached that point? North Americans earn fourteen times as much as the people in India, but give only a small amount to the church. Most churches spend much of that pittance on themselves. Can we claim we are obeying the biblical command to have a special concern for the poor? Can we honestly say we are imitating God's concern for the poor and oppressed? Can we seriously hope to experience eternal love rather than eternal separation from the God of the poor?

The biblical teaching that Yahweh has a special concern for the poor and oppressed is unambiguous. But does that mean, as some assert today, that God is biased in favour of the poor? Not really. Scripture explicitly forbids being partial. 'You shall do no injustice in judgment; you shall not be partial to the poor or defer to the great, but in righteousness shall you judge your neighbour' (Lev. 19:15; also Deut. 1:17). Exodus 23:3 contains precisely the same injunction: 'Nor shall you be partial to a poor man in his suit.' God instructs his people to be impartial because he himself is not biased.

The most crucial point for us, however, is not God's impartiality, but rather the result of his freedom from bias. The text declares Yahweh's impartiality and then immediately portrays God's tender care for the weak and disadvantaged. 'For the Lord your God is God of gods and Lord of lords, the great, the mighty, and the terrible God, who is not partial and takes no bribe. He executes justice for the fatherless and the widow, and loves the sojourner, giving him food and clothing (Deut. 10:17–18).

God is not partial. He has the same loving concern for each person he has created.[27] Precisely for that reason he cares as much for the weak and disadvantaged as he does for the strong and fortunate. By contrast with the way you and I, as well as the comfortable and powerful of every age and society, always act towards the poor, God seems to have an overwhelming bias in favour of the poor. But it is biased only in contrast with our sinful unconcern. It is only when we take our perverse preference for the successful and wealthy as natural and normative that God's concern appears biased.

On the Side of the Poor

When I say that God is on the side of the poor, there are several important things I do not mean. First, God is not biased. Second, material poverty is not a biblical ideal. Third, the poor and oppressed, just because they are poor and oppressed, are not thereby members of the church. (The poor sinfully disobey God just as do middle-class sinners, and they, too, need to repent and be saved by God's justifying grace.) Fourth, God does not care more about the salvation of the poor than the salvation of the rich. Fifth, we dare not start with some ideologically interpreted context of oppression (for example, Marxist analysis) and then reinterpret Scripture from that ideological bias. Sixth, God does not overlook the sin of those who are poor because of sloth or alcoholism. God punishes such sinners.[28]

God, however, is not neutral. His freedom from bias does not mean that he maintains neutrality in the struggle for justice. He is indeed on the side of the poor! The Bible clearly and repeatedly teaches that God is at work in history casting down the rich and exalting the poor because frequently the rich are wealthy precisely because they have oppressed the poor or have neglected to aid the needy. God also sides with the poor because of their special vulnerability. As we shall see in the next chapter, God also sides with the poor because he disapproves of great extremes of wealth and poverty. The God of the Bible is on the side of the poor just because he is *not* biased, for he is a God of impartial justice.

The rich neglect or oppose justice because justice demands that they end their oppression and share with the poor. Therefore God actively opposes the rich. But that does not in any way mean that he loves the rich less than the poor. God longs for the salvation of the rich as much as for the salvation of the poor. He desires fulfilment, joy, and happiness for all his creatures. But that does not contradict the fact that he is on the side of the poor. Genuine biblical repentance and conversion lead people to turn away from all sin – including economic oppression.[29] Salvation for the rich will include liberation from their injustice. Thus God's desire for the salvation and fulfilment of the rich is in complete harmony with the scriptural teaching that God is on the side of the poor.

God's concern for the poor is astonishing and boundless. At the pivotal points of revelation history, Yahweh was at work liberating the oppressed. We can only begin to fathom the depth of his identification with the poor disclosed in the Incarnation. Frequently the poor are his specially chosen instruments of revelation and salvation. His passion for justice compels him to obliterate rich societies and individuals that oppress the poor and neglect the needy. Consequently, God's people – if they are indeed his people – follow in the footsteps of the God of the poor.

In light of this clear biblical teaching, how biblical is our theology? I think we must confess that Christians in North America and Europe are largely on the side of the rich oppressors rather than the oppressed poor. Imagine what would happen if all our church institutions – our youth organisations, our publications, our colleges and sem-

inaries, our congregations and denominational headquarters – would all dare to undertake a comprehensive
two-year examination of their total programme and activity
to answer this question: Is there the same balance and
emphasis on justice for the poor and oppressed in our
programmes as there is in Scripture? I am willing to predict
that, if we did that with an unconditional readiness to
change whatever did not correspond with the scriptural
revelation of God's special concern for the poor and
oppressed, we would unleash a new movement of biblical
social concern that would change the course of modern
history.

But our problem is not primarily one of ethics. It is not
that we have failed to live what our teachers have taught.
Our theology itself has been unbiblical. By largely ignoring
the central biblical teaching that God is on the side of the
poor, our theology has been profoundly unorthodox. The
Bible has just as much to say about this doctrine as it does
about Jesus's resurrection. And yet we insist on the resurrection as a criterion of orthodoxy and largely ignore the
equally prominent biblical teaching that God is on the side
of the poor and the oppressed.

Now please do not misunderstand me at this point. I am
not saying that the resurrection is unimportant. The bodily
resurrection of Jesus of Nazareth is absolutely central to
Christian faith and anyone who denies it or says it is
unimportant has fallen into heresy.[30] But if centrality in
Scripture is any criterion of doctrinal importance, then the
biblical teaching that God is on the side of the poor ought to
be an extremely important doctrine for Christians.

I am afraid those who have thought themselves most
orthodox, however, have fallen into theological liberalism.
Of course, we usually think of theological liberalism in
terms of classical nineteenth-century liberals who denied
the deity, the atonement, and the bodily resurrection of
Jesus our Lord. And that is correct. People who abandon
those central biblical doctrines have fallen into terrible
heresy. But notice what the essence of theological liberalism is – it is allowing our thinking and living to be shaped by

the surrounding society's views and values rather than by biblical revelation. Liberal theologians thought that belief in the deity of Jesus Christ and his bodily resurrection was incompatible with a modern scientific world view. So they followed surrounding scientific society rather than Scripture.

Orthodox Christians rightly called attention to this heresy – and then tragically made exactly the same move in another area. We have allowed the values of our affluent materialistic society to shape our thinking and acting towards the poor. It is much easier in theologically conservative circles today to insist on an orthodox Christology than to insist on the biblical teaching that God is on the side of the poor. We have allowed our theology to be shaped by the economic preferences of our materialistic contemporaries rather than by Scripture. And that is to fall into theological liberalism. We have not been nearly as orthodox as we have claimed.

Past failure, however, is no reason for despair. I think we mean it when we sing, 'I'd rather have Jesus than houses or lands.' I think we mean it when we write and affirm doctrinal statements that boldly declare that we will not only believe but also live whatever Scripture teaches. But if we do mean it, then we must teach and live, in a world full of injustice and starvation, the important biblical doctrine that God and his faithful people are on the side of the poor and oppressed. Unless we drastically reshape both our theology and our entire institutional church life so that the fact that God is on the side of the poor and oppressed becomes as central to our theology and institutional programmes as it is in Scripture, we will demonstrate to the world that our verbal commitment to *sola scriptura* is a dishonest ideological support for an unjust, materialistic status quo.

I hope and believe that in the next decade millions of Christians will allow the biblical teaching that God is on the side of the poor and oppressed to reshape fundamentally our culturally conditioned theology and our unbiblically one-sided programmes and institutions. If that happens, we

will forge a new, truly biblical theology of liberation that
will change the course of modern history.

Study Questions

1. What are the five major foundations for the thesis that
God is on the side of the poor? Which of these do you find
most convincing? Least convincing? Why?

2. Does the author conclude that God is biased?

3. Has there been as much emphasis on God's concern
for the poor in Christian preaching and teaching you have
heard as there is in the Bible? If not, how do you explain the
difference?

4. Are we heretical if we ignore God's concern for the
poor?

5. What does Matthew 25:31–46 really mean?

4

ECONOMIC RELATIONSHIPS AMONG THE PEOPLE OF GOD

I do not mean that others should be eased and you burdened, but that as a matter of equality your abundance at the present time should supply their want, so that their abundance may supply your want, that there may be equality. As it is written, 'He who gathered much had nothing over, and he who gathered little had no lack' (2 Cor. 8:13–15).

God requires radically transformed economic relationships among his people. Sin has alienated us from God and from each other. The result has been personal selfishness, structural injustice and economic oppression. Among the people of God, however, the power of sin is broken. The new community of the redeemed begins to display an entirely new set of personal, social and economic relationships. The present quality of life among the people of God is to be a sign of that coming perfection and justice which will be revealed when the kingdoms of this world finally and completely become the kingdom of our Lord at his second coming.

In this chapter we will look at some central biblical models of transformed economic relationships. We discover in the Scriptures that God created mechanisms and structures to prevent great economic inequality among his people. As economic relationships are redeemed in the body of Christ, the church's common life of mutual availability is to point convincingly to the coming kingdom. And – as if that were not enough – the loving oneness among

Christians is to become so visible and concrete that it convinces the world that Jesus came from the Father (John 17:20–3).

The Jubilee Principle

Leviticus 25 is one of the most radical texts in all of Scripture. At least it seems that way for people born in countries committed to either laisser-faire economics or communism. Every fifty years, God said, all land was to return to the original owners – without compensation! Physical handicaps, death of a breadwinner or lack of natural ability may lead some people to become poorer than others. But God does not want such disadvantages to lead to greater and greater divergence of wealth and poverty. God therefore gave his people a law which would equalise land ownership every fifty years (Lev. 25:10–24).

In an agricultural society, land is capital. Land was the basic means of producing wealth in Israel. At the beginning, of course, the land had been divided more or less equally among the tribes and families (Num. 26:52–6).[1] Apparently God wanted that basic economic equality to continue. Hence his command to return all land to the original owners every fifty years. Private property was not abolished. But the means of producing wealth were to be equalised regularly.

What is the theological basis for this startling command? Yahweh's ownership of everything is the presupposition. The land cannot be sold permanently because Yahweh owns it: 'The land shall not be sold in perpetuity, *for the land is mine*; for you are strangers and sojourners with me' (Lev. 25:23). God owns the land. For a time he permits his people to sojourn on his good earth, cultivate it, eat its produce and enjoy its beauty. But we are only stewards. Stewardship is one of the central theological categories of any biblical understanding of our relationship to the land and economic resources generally.[2]

Before and after the year of jubilee, land could be bought or sold. But the buyer actually purchased a specific number of harvests, not the land itself (Lev. 25:16). And woe betide the person who tried to make a killing by demanding what the market would bear rather than a just price for the intervening harvests from the date of purchase to the next jubilee! 'If the years are many you shall increase the price, and if the years are few you shall diminish the price, for it is the number of the crops that he is selling to you. You shall not wrong one another, but you shall fear your God; for I am the Lord your God' (Lev. 25:16–17). Yahweh is Lord – even of economics. There is no hint here of some sacred law of supply and demand totally independent of biblical ethics and the Lordship of Yahweh. The people of God submit to him, and he demands economic justice among his people.

That this passage prescribes justice rather than haphazard handouts by wealthy philanthropists is extremely significant. The year of jubilee envisaged an institutionalised structure that affected all Israelites automatically. It was to be the poor person's *right* to receive back his inheritance at the time of jubilee. Returning the land was not a charitable courtesy that the wealthy might extend if they pleased.[3]

The jubilee principle also provided for self-help and self-development. With his land returned, the poor person could again earn his own living. The biblical concept of jubilee underlines the importance of institutionalised mechanisms and structures that promote justice.

It is striking that this jubilee passage challenges both capitalism and communism in an equally fundamental way. Only God is an absolute owner. Furthermore, the right of each person to have the means to earn his own way takes priority over a purchaser's 'property rights' or a totally free market economy. At the same time, this text clearly affirms not only the right but the importance of private property managed by families who understand that they are stewards responsible to God. God wants each family to have the resources to produce their own livelihood – in order to strengthen the family, in order to give people the freedom to be co-creators of history, and in order to prevent the centralisation of power and totalitarianism that almost always accompanies centralised ownership of land or capital by either the state or small élites.

One final aspect of Leviticus 25 is striking. It is surely more than coincidental that the trumpet blast announcing the jubilee sounded forth on the Day of Atonement (Lev. 25:9). Reconciliation with God is the precondition for reconciliation with brothers and sisters.[4] Conversely, genuine reconciliation with God leads inevitably to a transformation of all other relationships. Reconciled with God by the sacrifice on the Day of Atonement, the more prosperous Israelites were to liberate the poor by freeing Hebrew slaves as well as returning all land to the original owners.[5]

Unfortunately, we do not know whether the people of Israel ever practised the year of jubilee. The absence of references to jubilee in the historical books suggests that it may never have been implemented.[6] Regardless of its antiquity or implementation, Leviticus 25 remains a part of God's authoritative Word. Because he disapproves of extremes of wealth among his people, God ordains equalising mechanisms like the year of jubilee.

The Sabbatical Year

The law also provides for liberation of soil, slaves and debtors every seven years. Again the concern is justice for the poor and disadvantaged.

Every seven years the land is to lie fallow (Exod. 23: 10–11; Lev. 25:2–7).[7] The purpose, apparently, is both ecological and humanitarian. Not planting any crops every seventh year certainly helps preserve the fertility of the soil. God, however, is particularly concerned with the poor: 'For six years you shall sow your land and gather in its yield; but the seventh year you shall let it rest and lie fallow, *that the poor of your people may eat*' (Exod. 23:10–11). In the seventh year the poor are free to gather for themselves whatever grows spontaneously in the fields and vineyards.

Hebrew slaves also receive their freedom in the sabbatical year (Deut. 15:12–18). Poverty sometimes forced

Israelites to sell themselves as slaves to more prosperous neighbours (Lev. 25:39–40).[8] But this inequality, God decrees, is not to be permanent. At the end of six years the Hebrew slaves are to be set free. And masters are to share the proceeds of their joint labours with the departing brothers: 'And when you let him go free from you, you shall not let him go empty-handed; you shall furnish him liberally out of your flock, out of your threshing floor, and out of your wine press; as the Lord your God has blessed you, you shall give to him' (Deut. 15:13–14; see also Exod. 21:2–6). The freed slave would thereby have the means to earn his own way.[9]

The sabbatical provision on loans is even more revolutionary (Deut. 15:1–6). Every seven years all debts are to be cancelled! Yahweh even adds a footnote for those with a sharp eye for loopholes: It is sinful to refuse a loan to a poor man just because it is the sixth year and the money will be lost in twelve months.

Take heed lest there be a base thought in your heart, and you say,

> 'The seventh year, the year of release is near,' and your eye be hostile to your poor brother, and you give him nothing, and he cry to the Lord against you, and it be sin in you. You shall give to him freely, and your heart shall not be grudging when you give to him; because for this the Lord your God will bless you (Deut. 15:9–10).[10]

As in the case of the year of jubilee, it is crucial to note that Scripture prescribes justice rather than mere charity. The sabbatical release of debts was an institutionalised mechanism for preventing an evergrowing gap between rich and poor.

Deuteronomy 15 is both an idealistic statement of God's perfect demand and also a realistic reference to Israel's probable performance concerning debts. Verse 4 promises that there will be no poor in Israel – if they obey all the commands God provides! But God knew they would not attain that standard. Hence the recognition in verse 11 that

poor people will always exist in Israel. But the conclusion is
not that one can therefore ignore the needy because hordes
of paupers will always far exceed one's resources. It is
precisely the opposite. 'For the poor will never cease out of
the land; *therefore* I command you, you shall open wide
your hand to your brother, to the needy and to the poor, in
the land.'

Jesus knew and Deuteronomy implies that sinful persons
and societies will always produce poor people (Matt.
26:11). Rather than justifying negligence, however, God
intends this insight to lead to renewed concern for the
needy and to the creation of structural mechanisms for
promoting justice.

The sabbatical year, unfortunately, was practised only
sporadically. Some texts suggest that failure to obey this
law was one reason for the Babylonian exile (2 Chron.
36:20–1; Lev. 26:34–6).[11] Israel's disobedience, however,
does not weaken God's demand. Institutionalised structures to reduce poverty and great economic inequality are
God's will for his people.

Laws on Tithing and Gleaning

Other legal provisions extend the concern of the year of
jubilee and the sabbatical year. The law calls for one-tenth
of all farm produce, whether animal, grain or wine, to be
set aside as a tithe. 'At the end of every three years you shall
bring forth all the tithe of your produce in the same year;
. . . and the Levite . . . and the sojourner, the fatherless,
and the widow, who are within your towns, shall come and
eat and be filled; that the Lord your God may bless you'
(Deut. 14:28–9; see also Lev. 27:30–2; Deut. 26:12–15;
Num. 18:21–32).[12]

The poor widow Ruth was able to survive because of
this law of gleaning. When she and Naomi returned to
Bethlehem penniless, the grandmother of King David went
into the fields at harvest time and gathered the stalks of
grain dropped by the gleaners (Ruth 2). She could do that
because God's law decreed that farmers should leave some

of the harvest, including the corners of grain fields, for the poor. Grapes that had been dropped accidentally were to be left. 'You shall leave them for the poor and for the sojourner: I am the Lord your God' (Lev. 19:10).

The memory of their own poverty and oppression in Egypt was to prompt them to leave generous gleanings for the poor sojourner, the widow and the fatherless. 'You shall remember that you were a slave in the land of Egypt; therefore I command you to do this' (Deut. 24:22). The law of gleaning was an established method for preventing debilitating poverty among the people of God and sojourners in the land.

Models to Follow and Avoid

How do we apply biblical revelation on the year of jubilee, the sabbatical year, tithes and gleaning today? Should we attempt to implement these mechanisms? Are these laws, even the basic principles, applicable to the church at all?

God gave Israel the law so that his people would know how to live together in peace and justice. The church is now the new people of God (Gal. 3:6–9; 6:16; 1 Pet. 2:9–10). Certainly, as Paul and other New Testament writers indicate, parts of the Mosaic law (the ceremonial law, for instance) no longer apply to the church. But there is no indication that the moral law has ceased to be normative for Christians (Matt. 5:17–20; Rom. 8:4).[13] The Old Testament's revelation about the kind of economic relationships that promote love and harmony among God's people should still guide the church today. (Whether these laws have any relevance for society as a whole will be discussed in chapter 9.)

How then do we apply the actual laws we have discussed? Should we attempt to revive the specific mechanisms proposed in Leviticus 25 and Deuteronomy 15?

Certainly not. The specific provisions of the year of jubilee are not binding today. Modern technological society is vastly different from rural Palestine. If farmers left grain standing in the corners of their fields, it would not help the hungry in the inner city or those in rural India. We need methods appropriate to our own civilisation. It is the basic principles, not the specific details, which are important and normative for Christians today.

The history of the prohibition against charging interest is instructive at this point. The annual rate of interest in the ancient Near East was incredibly high – often as much as 25 per cent or more.[14] It is not hard, therefore, to see why the law includes prohibitions against charging interest to fellow Israelites (Exod. 22:25; Deut. 23:19–20; Lev. 25:35–8).[15] The *International Critical Commentary* suggests that this legislation reflects a time when most loans were charitable loans rather than commercial ones. Commercial loans to establish or extend a business were not common. Most were charitable loans needed by a poor person or by someone facing a temporary emergency.[16] It is quite clear that the well-being of the poor is a central concern of the texts on interest. 'If you lend money to any of my people with you who is poor, you shall not be to him as a creditor, and you shall not exact interest from him' (Exod. 22:25). The legislation on interest is one part of an extensive set of laws designed to protect the poor and prevent great extremes of wealth and poverty among the people of God.

Failing to understand this, the Christian church attempted to apply the texts on interest in a legalistic way. Several church councils wrestled with the question. Eventually, all interest on loans was prohibited in 1179 (Third Lateran Council). But the results were tragic. Medieval monarchs invited Jews, who were not bound by the church's teaching, into their realms to be money lenders. Anti-Semitism was one demonic result. Increasingly, theologians developed casuistic schemes for circumventing the prohibition.[17] Tragically, the misguided preoccupation with the letter of the law and the resulting adoption of an unworkable, legalistic application helped discredit or at least obscure the important biblical teaching that the God of the poor is Lord of economics – Lord even of interest rates. Legalistic utilisation of the texts on interest thus helped create the modern mentality which views loans, banking, indeed the whole field of economics, as completely independent and autonomous. From the standpoint of revealed faith, of course, such a view is heretical. It stems from modern secularism, not from the Bible.[18]

This history warns us against a wooden application. But it dare not lead to timid silence. These texts unquestionably teach that the borrower's need, rather than careful calculation of potential profit, must be decisive for the Christian lender. (Low-interest or no-interest loans for development provided by Christian organisations to Christians in the Third World are an example of meaningful, contemporary application of God's Word on interest.)

In applying the biblical teaching on the year of jubilee, the sabbatical year, gleaning and tithing, then, we must discover the underlying principles. Then we can search for contemporary strategies to give flesh to these basic principles. The texts we have examined clearly show that God wills justice, not mere charity. Therefore Christians should design and institute new structures that can effectively eliminate indigence among believers, and drastically reduce the scandalous extremes of wealth and poverty between rich and poor members of the one body of the risen Jesus.

Jesus's New Community

Let us see how the first-century Christians reaffirmed the Old Testament teaching. Jesus walked the roads of Galilee announcing the startling news that the kingdom of peace and righteousness was at hand. Economic relationships in the new community of his followers were a powerful sign confirming this awesome announcement.

The Hebrew prophets had predicted more than that Israel would be destroyed because of her idolatry and oppression of the poor. They had also proclaimed a message of hope – the hope of a future messianic kingdom. The days are coming, they promised, when God will raise up a righteous branch from the Davidic line. Peace, righteousness and justice will then abound in a new, redeemed society. When the shoot from the stump of Jesse comes, Isaiah predicted, the poor and meek will finally receive their due: 'With righteousness he shall judge the poor, and decide with equity for the meek of the earth' (Isa. 11:4; see also Isa. 9:6–7; 61:1; Jer. 23:5; Hos. 2:18–20).

The essence of the good news which Jesus proclaimed was that the expected messianic kingdom had come.[19] Certainly the kingdom Jesus announced disappointed popular Jewish expectations. He did not recruit an army to drive out the Romans. He did not attempt to establish a free Jewish state. But neither did he remain alone as an isolated, individualistic prophet. He called and trained disciples. He established a visible community of disciples joined together by their submission to him as Lord. His new community began to live the values of the promised kingdom which was already breaking into the present. As a result, all relationships, even economic ones, were transformed in the community of Jesus's followers.

They shared a common purse (John 12:6).[20] Judas administered the common fund, buying provisions or giving to the poor at Jesus's direction (John 13:29). Nor did this new community of sharing end with Jesus and the Twelve. It included a number of women whom Jesus had healed. The women travelled with Jesus and the disciples, sharing their financial resources with them (Luke 8:1–3; see also Mark 15:40–1).[21]

From this perspective, some of Jesus's words gain new meaning and power. Consider his advice to the rich young man.

When Jesus asked the rich young man to sell his goods and give to the poor, he did not say 'Become destitute and friendless.' Rather, he said, 'Come, follow me' (Matt. 19:21). In other words, he invited him to join a community of sharing and love, where his security would not be based on individual property holdings, but on openness to the Spirit and on the loving care of new-found brothers and sisters.[22]

Jesus invited the rich young man to share the joyful common life of his new kingdom.

Jesus's words in Mark 10:29–30 have long puzzled me: 'Truly, I say to you, there is no one who has left house or brothers or sisters or mother or father or children or lands, for my sake and for the gospel, who will not receive a hundredfold *now in this time, houses and brothers and sisters and mothers and children and lands*, with persecutions, and in the age to come eternal life.' Matthew 6 contains a similar saying. We are all very – indeed embarrassingly – familiar with the way Jesus urged his followers to enjoy a carefree life unburdened by anxiety over food, clothing, and possessions (Matt. 6:25–33). But he ended his advice with a promise too good to be true: 'But seek first his kingdom and his righteousness, and all these things [that is, food, clothing and so on] shall be yours as well.' These promises used to seem at least a trifle naïve. But his words came alive with meaning when I read them in the context of the new community of Jesus's followers. Jesus began a new social order, a new kingdom of faithful followers who were to be almost completely available to each other.

The common purse of Jesus's disciples symbolised that almost unlimited liability for each other. In that new community there would be genuine economic security. Each would indeed have many more loving brothers and sisters than before. The economic resources available in difficult times would in fact be compounded a hundredfold and more. The resources of the entire community of obedient disciples would be available to anyone in need. To be sure, that kind of unselfish, sharing lifestyle would challenge surrounding society so pointedly that there would be persecutions. But even in the most desperate days, the promise would not be empty. Even if persecution led to death, children of martyred parents would receive new mothers and fathers in the community of believers.

In the community of the redeemed, all relationships are being transformed. Jesus and his first followers vividly demonstrate that the old covenant's pattern of economic relationships among the people of God is continued and deepened.

The Jerusalem Model

However embarrassing it may be to some, the massive economic sharing of the earliest Christian church is indisputable. 'Now the company of those who believed were of one heart and soul, and no one said that any of the things which he possessed was his own, but they had everything in common' (Acts 4:32). Everywhere in the early chapters of Acts, the evidence is abundant and unambiguous (Acts 2:43–7; 4:32–7; 5:1–11; 6:1–7). The early church continued the pattern of economic sharing practised by Jesus.

Economic sharing in the Jerusalem church started in the earliest period. Immediately after reporting the three thousand conversions at Pentecost, Acts notes that 'all who believed were together and had all things in common' (2:44). Whenever anyone was in need, they shared. Giving surplus income to needy brothers and sisters was not enough. They regularly dipped into capital reserves, selling property to aid the needy. Barnabas sold a field he owned (4:36–7). Ananias and Sapphira sold property, although they lied about the price. God's promise to Israel that faithful obedience would eliminate poverty among his people came true (Deut. 15:4)! 'There was not a needy person among them, for as many as were possessors of lands or houses sold them; . . . and distribution was made to each as any had need' (Acts 4:34–5).

Two millenniums later the texts still throb with the first community's joy and excitement. They ate meals together 'with glad and generous hearts' (Acts 2:46). They experienced an exciting unity as all sensed they 'were of one heart and soul' (4:32). They were not isolated individuals, struggling alone to follow Jesus. A new community, in which all areas of life (including economics) were being transformed, became a joyful reality.

The evangelistic impact of their demonstration of oneness is striking. The texts repeatedly relate the transformed economic relationships in the Jerusalem church to the phenomenal evangelistic outreach. 'And day by day, attending the temple together and breaking bread in their homes, they partook of food with glad and generous hearts, praising God *and having favour with all the people.* And the Lord added to their number day by day' (Acts 2:46–7). The joy and love exhibited in their common life were contagious. I mentioned that the author records in Acts 4 that they had all things in common instead of clinging to their private possessions. In the very next verse he adds, 'And with great power the apostles gave their testimony to the resurrection of the Lord Jesus' (v. 33). Jesus's prayer that the loving unity of his followers would be so striking that it would convince the world that he had come from the Father has been answered – at least once! It happened in the Jerusalem church. The unusual quality of their life together gave power to the apostolic preaching.

The account in Acts 6 is particularly instructive. Apparently there was a significant minority of Hellenists in the Jerusalem church. (Hellenists were Greek-speaking Jews, perhaps even Greeks that had converted to Judaism.) Somehow, the Jewish-speaking majority had overlooked the needs of the Hellenist widows until they complained about the injustice. The church's response is startling. The seven men chosen to look after this matter were all from the minority group! Every one of their names is Greek.[23] The church turned over their entire programme and funds for needy widows to the minority group that had been discriminated against. What was the result of this new act of financial fellowship? 'And the word of God increased; and the number of disciples multiplied greatly in Jerusalem' (Acts 6:7).

Redeemed economic relationships in the early church resulted in an increase of the Word of God. What a sobering thought! Is it perhaps the same today? Would similar economic changes produce a dramatic increase of believers today? Probably so. Are those who talk about the importance of evangelism prepared to pay *that* price?

But what is the price to be paid? What was the precise nature of the Jerusalem church's costly *koinōnia*? The earliest church did not insist on absolute economic equality. Nor did they abolish private property. Peter reminded Ananias that he had been under no obligation either to sell his property or to donate the proceeds to the church (Acts 5:4). Sharing was voluntary, not compulsory.[24] But love for brothers and sisters was so overwhelming that many freely abandoned legitimate claims to private possessions. 'No one said that any of the things which he possessed was his own' (4:32). That does not mean that everyone donated everything. Later in Acts we see that John Mark's mother, Mary, still owned her own house (12:12). Others also undoubtedly retained some private property.

The tense of the Greek words confirms this interpretation. In both Acts 2:45 and 4:34, the verbs are in the imperfect tense. In Greek the imperfect tense denotes continued, repeated action over an extended period of time. Thus the meaning is, 'they often sold possessions', or, 'they were in the habit of regularly bringing the proceeds of what was being sold'.[25] The text does not suggest that the community decided to abolish all private property or that everyone instantly sold everything. Rather it suggests that over a period of time, whenever there was need, believers regularly sold lands and houses to aid the needy.

What then was the essence of the transformed economic relationships in the Jerusalem church? The best way to describe their practice is to speak of almost unlimited liability and near total availability. Their sharing was not superficial or occasional. Regularly and repeatedly, 'they sold their possessions and goods and distributed them to all, as any had need' (2:45). If the need was greater than current cash reserves, they sold property. They simply gave until the needs were met. The needs of the sister and brother, not legal property rights or future financial security, were decisive. They made their financial resources unconditionally available to each other. Oneness in Christ for the earliest Christian community meant almost unlimited economic liability for, and sweeping economic availability to, the other members of Christ's body.

Unfortunately most Christians ignore the example of the Jerusalem church. Perhaps it is because of the economic self-interest of affluent Christians. At any rate, we have developed a convenient rationale for relegating the pattern of the Jerusalem church to the archivists' attic of irrelevant historical trivia. Why did Paul have to take a collection for the Jerusalem church a few decades later? A recent book offers the familiar response:

> The trouble in Jerusalem was that they turned their capital into income, and had no cushion for hard times, and the Gentile Christians had to come to their rescue. It is possible not to live for bread alone, not to be overcome by materialist values, and at the same time to act responsibly; and this is why the Church may be grateful for the protest of the commune movement, but still consider that it has no answer.[26]

But were the Jerusalem Christians really irresponsible, naïve communal-types whom we should respect but certainly not imitate? It is absolutely essential to insist that the Jerusalem principle of almost unlimited economic liability and sweeping financial availability does not necessarily require communal living. It did not in Jerusalem. The Christian commune is only one of many faithful models. We dare not let the communal hobgoblin distort our discussion of the Jerusalem model.

But why did the Jerusalem church run into financial difficulty? It is quite unlikely that their economic sharing was to blame. Rather, it was due to a unique set of historical circumstances. Jerusalem attracted an unusually large number of poor. Since Jews considered alms given in Jerusalem particularly meritorious, the many pilgrims to the city were especially generous. As a result vast crowds of impoverished beggars flocked to the city. In addition, a disproportionately large number of older people gravitated to the Holy City to die or wait for the Messiah (see Luke 2:25, 36). There was also an unusually large number of rabbis living in Jerusalem because it was the centre of Jewish faith. Rabbis depended on charity, however, since they were not paid for teaching. Their students likewise were often poor. Hence the large number of religious scholars in Jerusalem swelled the ranks of the destitute.[27]

Nor was that all. Natural disasters struck at mid-century. The Roman historians Suetonius and Tacitus report recurring food shortages and famines during the reign of the Emperor Claudius (AD 41–54). Josephus dates such shortages in Palestine around AD 44 to 48.[28] Famine in Palestine was so severe at one point that the Antioch church quickly sent assistance (Acts 11:27–30).

Special reasons within the first church itself also caused unusual poverty. Jesus's particular concern for the poor and oppressed probably attracted a disproportionately large number of impoverished persons into the early church. Persecution, too, must have wreaked havoc with the normal income of Christians. Acts records considerable open persecution (8:1–3; 9:29; 12:1–5; 23:12–15). Undoubtedly Christians also experienced subtle forms of discrimination in many areas including employment.[29] Finally, the Twelve must have given up their means of livelihood when they moved from their native Galilee to Jerusalem. Hence their support increased the demand on the resources of the Jerusalem church.

These are some of the many reasons why the first community of Christians faced financial difficulty at mid-century. But misguided generosity was hardly a significant factor. In fact, it was probably precisely the unusually large number of poor in their midst that made dramatic sharing such an obvious necessity. That the rich among them gave with overflowing generosity to meet a desperate need in the body of Christ indicates not naïve idealism but unconditional discipleship.

The costly sharing of the first church stands as a constant challenge to Christians of all ages. They dared to give concrete, visible expression to the oneness of believers. In the new messianic community of Jesus's first followers after Pentecost, God was redeeming all relationships. The result

was far-reaching economic liability for and financial availability to the other brothers and sisters in Christ.

Whatever the beauty and appeal of such an example,
however, was it not a vision which quickly faded? Most
people believe it was. But the actual practice of the early
church proves the contrary.

Economic *Koinōnia*

Paul broadened the vision of economic sharing among the
people of God in a dramatic way. He devoted a great deal
of time to raising money for Jewish Christians among
gentile congregations. In the process he developed intra-
church assistance (within one local church) into interchurch
sharing among all the scattered congregations of believers.

From the time of the Exodus, God had taught his chosen
people to exhibit transformed economic relations among
themselves. With Peter and Paul, however, biblical religion
moved beyond one ethnic group and became a universal,
multi-ethnic faith. Paul's collection demonstrated that the
oneness of that new body of believers entails economic
sharing across ethnic and geographic lines.

Paul's concern for economic sharing in the body of Christ
began early. Famine struck Palestine in AD 46. In response,
the believers at Antioch gave '*every one according to his
ability*, to send relief to the brethren who lived in Judaea'
(Acts 11:29). Paul helped Barnabas bring this economic
assistance from Antioch to Jerusalem.[30] That trip was just
the beginning of Paul's extensive concern for economic
sharing. For several years he devoted much time and
energy to his great collection. He discusses his concern in
several letters. Already in Galatians he expresses eagerness
to assist the poor Jerusalem Christians (Gal. 2:10). He
mentions it in the letter to Rome (Rom. 15:22–8). Briefly
noted in 1 Corinthians 16:1–4, the collection became a
major preoccupation in 2 Corinthians 7–9. He also
arranged for the collection in the churches of Macedonia,
Galatia, Corinth, Ephesus and probably elsewhere.[31]

Paul knew he faced certain danger and possible death.

But he still insisted on personally accompanying the offering. It was while delivering this financial assistance that Paul was arrested for the last time. His letter to the Romans shows that he was not blind to the danger (Rom. 15:31). Repeatedly friends and prophets warned Paul as he and the representatives of the contributing churches journeyed towards Jerusalem (Acts 21:4, 10–14). But Paul had a deep conviction that this financial symbol of Christian unity mattered far more even than his own life. 'What are you doing, weeping and breaking my heart?' he chided friends imploring him not to accompany the others to Jerusalem. 'For I am ready not only to be imprisoned but even to die at Jerusalem for the name of the Lord Jesus' (Acts 21:13). And he continued the journey. His passionate commitment to economic sharing with brothers and sisters led to his final arrest and martyrdom (see Acts 24:17).

Why was Paul so concerned with the financial problems of the Jerusalem church? Because of his understanding of fellowship. *Koinōnia* is an extremely important concept in Paul's theology. And it is central in his discussion of the collection.

Koinōnia means fellowship with someone or participation in something. Believers enjoy fellowship with the Lord Jesus (1 Cor. 1:9).[32] Experiencing the *koinōnia* of Jesus means having his righteousness imputed to us. It also entails sharing in the self-sacrificing, cross-bearing life he lived (Phil. 3:8–10). Nowhere is the Christian's fellowship with Christ experienced more powerfully than in the Eucharist. Sharing in the Lord's Supper draws the believer into a participation (*koinōnia*) in the mystery of the cross: 'The cup of blessing which we bless, is it not a participation [*koinōnia*] in the blood of Christ? The bread which we break, is it not a participation [*koinōnia*] in the body of Christ?' (1 Cor. 10:16).

Paul's immediate inference is that *koinōnia* with Christ inevitably involves *koinōnia* with all the members of the body of Christ. 'Because there is one bread, we who are many are one body, for we all partake of the one bread' (1 Cor. 10:17; see also 1 John 1:3–4). As seen in Ephesians

2, Christ's death for Jew and gentile, male and female, has broken down all ethnic, sexual and cultural dividing walls. In Christ there is one new person, one new body of believers. When the brothers and sisters share the one bread and the common cup in the Lord's Supper, they symbolise and actualise their participation in the one body of Christ.

That is why the class divisions at Corinth so horrified Paul. Apparently wealthy Christians feasted at the Eucharistic celebration while poor believers went hungry. Paul angrily denied that they were eating the Lord's Supper at all (1 Cor. 11:20–2). In fact, they were profaning the Lord's body and blood because they did not discern his body (1 Cor. 11:27–9).

But what did Paul mean when he charged that they did not discern the Lord's body? To discern the Lord's body is to understand and live the truth that fellowship with Christ is inseparable from membership in his body where our oneness in Christ far transcends differences of race or class. Discernment of that one body of believers leads to sweeping availability to and responsibility for the other sisters and brothers. Discernment of that one body prompts us to weep with those who weep and rejoice with those who rejoice. Discernment of that one body is totally incompatible with feasting while other members of the body go hungry. Those who live a practical denial of their unity and fellowship in Christ, Paul insists, drink judgment on themselves when they go to the Lord's table. In fact, they do not really partake of the Lord's Supper at all.

Once we understand the implication of Paul's teaching on discerning the body in the Lord's Supper, we dare not rest content until the scandal of starving Christians is removed. As long as any Christian anywhere in the world is hungry, the Eucharistic celebration of all Christians everywhere in the world is imperfect.

For Paul, the intimate fellowship in the body of Christ has concrete economic implications, for he uses precisely this same word, *koinōnia*, to designate financial sharing among believers. Early in his ministry, the Jerusalem leaders endorsed his mission to the gentiles after a dramatic debate. When they extended the 'right hand of fellowship' (*koinōnia*), they stipulated just one tangible expression of that fellowship. Paul promised financial assistance for his fellow Christians in Jerusalem (Gal. 2:9–10).[33]

Paul frequently employs the word *koinōnia* as a virtual synonym for 'collection'. He speaks of the 'liberality of the fellowship' (*koinōnia*) that the Corinthians' generous offering would demonstrate (2 Cor. 9:13, my translation; see also 8:4).[34] He employed the same language to report the Macedonian Christians' offering for Jerusalem. It seemed good to the Macedonians 'to make fellowship [*koinōnia*] with the poor among the saints at Jerusalem (Rom. 15:25, my translation). Indeed, this financial sharing was just one part of a total fellowship. The gentile Christians had come to share in (he uses the verb form of *koinōnia*) the spiritual blessings of the Jews. Therefore it was fitting for the gentiles to share their material resources. Economic sharing was an obvious and crucial part of Christian fellowship for St Paul.[35]

Paul's first guideline for sharing in the body of believers was general: Give all you can. Each person should give 'as he may prosper' (1 Cor. 16:2). But that does not mean a small donation that costs nothing. Paul praised the Macedonians who 'gave according to their means . . . and beyond their means' (2 Cor. 8:3). The Macedonians were extremely poor. Apparently they faced particularly severe financial difficulties just when Paul asked for a generous offering (2 Cor. 8:2). But still they gave beyond their means. No hint here of a mechanical 10 per cent for pauper and millionaire. Giving as much as you can is the Pauline pattern.

Second, giving was voluntary (2 Cor. 8:3). Paul specifically noted that he was not issuing a command to the Corinthians (2 Cor. 8:8). Legalism is not the answer.

Paul's third guideline is the most startling. The norm, he suggests, is something like economic equality among the people of God. 'I do not mean that others should be eased and you burdened, but that as a matter of equality your abundance at the present time should supply their want, so that their abundance may supply your want, that there may be equality.' To support his principle, Paul quotes from the biblical story of the manna. 'As it is written, "He who gathered much had nothing over, and he who gathered little had no lack"' (2 Cor. 8:13–15).

According to the Exodus account, when God started sending daily manna to the Israelites in the wilderness, Moses commanded the people to gather only as much as they needed for one day (Exod. 16:13–21). One omer (about four pints) per person would be enough, Moses said. Some greedy souls, however, apparently tried to gather more than they could use. But when they measured what they had gathered, they discovered that they all had just one omer per person. 'He that gathered much had nothing over, and he that gathered little had no lack' (16:18).

Paul quotes from the biblical account of the manna to support his guideline for economic sharing. Just as God had insisted on equal portions of manna for all his people in the wilderness, so now the Corinthians should give 'that there may be equality' in the body of Christ.

This may be startling and disturbing to rich Christians in the Northern Hemisphere. But the biblical text clearly shows that Paul enunciates the principle of economic equality among the people of God to guide the Corinthians in their giving. '*It is a question of equality*. At the moment your surplus meets their need, but one day your need may be met from their surplus. *The aim is equality*' (NEB).[36]

It is exciting to see how the biblical teaching on transformed economic relationships among God's people created in the early church a concern for the poor which was unique in late antiquity. Writing about AD 125, the Christian philosopher Aristides painted the following picture of economic sharing in the church.

They walk in all humility and kindness, and falsehood is not found among them, and they love one another. They despise not the widow, and grieve not the orphan. He that hath, distributeth liberally to him that hath not. If they see a stranger, they bring him under their roof, and rejoice over him, as it were their own brother: for they call themselves brethren, not after the flesh, but after the spirit and in God; but when one of their poor passes away from the world, and any of them see him, then he provides for his burial according to his ability; and if they hear that any of their number is imprisoned or oppressed for the name of their Messiah, all of them provide for his needs, and if it is possible that he may be delivered, they deliver him. And if there is among them a man that is poor and needy, and they have not an abundance of necessaries, they fast two or three days that they may supply the needy with their necessary food.[37]

By AD 250 the church at Rome supported fifteen hundred needy persons. According to the German scholar Martin Hengel, this kind of economic sharing was unique in the late Roman Empire.[38]

That this transformed lifestyle made a powerful impression on outsiders is clear from a grudging comment by a pagan emperor. During his short reign (AD 361–3), Julian the Apostate tried to stamp out Christianity. But he was forced to admit to a fellow pagan 'that the godless Galileans [Christians] feed not only their poor but ours also'. With chagrin he acknowledged that the pagan cult which he had tried to revive had failed miserably in the task of aiding the poor.[39]

The practice of second-century Christians, however interesting it may be, is, of course, not normative today. In fact, many would eagerly insist that neither is the practice of Paul at Corinth or the first Christians in Jerusalem. What relevance then does their economic sharing have for the contemporary church?

Certainly the church today need not slavishly imitate every detail of the life of the early church depicted in Acts. It is scriptural teaching, not the action of the Jerusalem church, that is normative. But that does not mean that we can simply dismiss the economic sharing described in Acts and the Pauline letters.

Over and over again God specifically commanded his people to live together in community in such a way that they would avoid extremes of wealth and poverty. That is the point of the legislation concerning the jubilee and the sabbatical year. That is the point of the legislation on tithing, gleaning and loans. Jesus, our only perfect model, shared a common purse with the new community of his disciples. Again and again, Jesus instructed his followers to share with those in need. The first-century Christians were simply implementing what both the Old Testament and Jesus commanded.

The powerful evangelistic impact of the economic sharing at Jerusalem indicates that God approved and blessed the practice of the Jerusalem church. When in some places Scripture commands transformed economic relationships among God's people and in other places describes God's blessing on his people as they implement these commands, then we can be sure that we have discovered a normative pattern for the church today.

What is striking, in fact, is the fundamental continuity of biblical teaching and practice at this point. The Bible repeatedly and pointedly reveals that God wills transformed economic relationships among his people. Paul's collection was simply an application of the basic principle of the jubilee. The particular method, of course, was different because the people of God at his time were a multi-ethnic body living in different lands. But the principle was the same. Since the Greeks at Corinth were now part of the people of God, they were to share with the poor Jewish Christians at Jerusalem – that there might be equality.

Conclusion

We have looked carefully at the kind of economic relationships God desires among his people. What does this biblical revelation mean for affluent Christians in the Northern Hemisphere? Only one conclusion seems possible to me.

Present economic relationships in the worldwide body of

Christ are unbiblical and sinful, a hindrance to evangelism and a desecration of the body and blood of Jesus Christ. The value of the food North Americans throw in the rubbish bin each year equals about one-fifth of the total annual income of all the Christians in Africa.[40] It is a sinful abomination for one part of the world's Christians living in the Northern Hemisphere to grow richer year by year while our brothers and sisters in the Third World ache and suffer for lack of minimal health care, minimal education, and even – in some cases – just enough food to escape starvation.

We are like the rich Corinthian Christians who feasted without sharing their food with the poor members of the church (1 Cor. 11:20–9). Like them we fail today to discern the reality of the one worldwide body of Christ. The tragic consequence is that we profane the body and blood of the Lord Jesus we worship. Christians in the United States spent $5.7 billion on new church construction alone in the six years from 1967 to 1972.[41] Would we go on building lavishly furnished expensive church plants if members of our own congregations were starving? Do we not flatly contradict Paul if we live as if African or Latin American members of the body of Christ are less a part of us than the members of our home congregation?[42]

The present division between the haves and have nots in the body of Christ is a major hindrance to world evangelism. Hungry people in the Third World find it difficult to accept a Christ preached by people who always symbolise (and often defend the affluence of) the richest society on earth.

Lost opportunities and past and present sin, however, must not blind us to present potential. We live in a world dangerously divided between rich and poor. If a mere fraction of North American and European Christians would begin to apply biblical principles on economic sharing among the worldwide people of God, the world would be utterly astounded. There is probably no other step that would have such a powerful evangelistic impact today. Is it not likely that millions and millions of unbelievers would confess Christ? Jesus's prayer might be answered. The mutual love and unity within Christ's body might convince the world that Jesus indeed came from the Father (John 17:20–3).

The church is the most universal body in the world today. It has the opportunity to live a new model of sharing at a crucial moment in world history. Because of its concern for the poor, the church in the past pioneered in developing schools and hospitals. Later, secular governments institutionalised the new models. In the late twentieth century, a dangerously divided world awaits a new model of economic sharing.

The Bible clearly teaches that God wills fundamentally transformed economic relationships among his people. Do we have the faith and obedience to start living the biblical vision?

Study Questions

1. Do most Christians you know think that their faith in Christ has anything to do with their economic relationships with others in the worldwide body of Christ? How does the Bible challenge their assumptions?

2. What are the basic implications of the jubilee and the sabbatical release of debts for today?

3. What would be the best words to describe the economic sharing occurring in the earliest church at Jerusalem?

4. What are the implications of Paul's intercontinental offering for the global church today?

5. How do you evaluate the statement: 'God is opposed to great extremes of wealth and poverty'?

A BIBLICAL ATTITUDE TOWARDS PROPERTY AND WEALTH

In the house of the righteous there is much treasure (Prov. 15:6).
Blessed are you poor, for yours is the kingdom of God (Luke 6:20).

The title of this chapter, 'A Biblical Attitude Towards Property and Wealth', promptly suggests an important question: Does the Bible sanction or condemn private property? Unfortunately, for many this is the only important question raised by the title. The biblical viewpoint is strikingly different. The Bible teaches many things about property and wealth.

Private Property

The Ten Commandments sanction private property implicitly and explicitly.[1] God forbids stealing, indeed even coveting, the house, land or animals of one's neighbours (Exod. 20:15, 17; Deut. 5:19, 21; see also Deut. 27:17; Prov. 22:28). Apparently Jesus likewise assumed the legitimacy of private property. His disciple Simon Peter owned a house that Jesus frequented (Mark 1:29). Jesus commanded his followers to give to the poor and loan money even when there was no reasonable hope of repayment (Matt. 6:2–4; 5:42; Luke 6:34–5). Such advice would have made little sense if Jesus had not also assumed that the possession of property and money was legitimate so that one could make loans. As we saw in the previous chapter, not even the dramatic economic sharing in the first Jerusalem church led to a rejection of private ownership. Throughout biblical revelation the legitimacy of private property is constantly affirmed.[2]

But the right of private property is not absolute. From the perspective of biblical revelation, property owners are not free to seek their own profit without regard for the needs of their neighbours. Such an outlook derives from the secular laisser-faire economics of the deist Adam Smith, not from Scripture.

Smith published a book in 1776 which has profoundly shaped Western society in the last two centuries.[3] (Since the Keynesian revolution, of course, Smith's ideas have shaped Western societies less than previously, but his fundamental outlook, albeit in somewhat revised form, still provides the basic ideological framework for many of us.) Smith argued that an invisible hand would guarantee the good of all if each person would pursue his or her own economic self-interest in the context of a competitive society. Supply and demand for goods and services must be the sole determinant of prices and wages. If the law of supply and demand reigns and if all seek their own advantage within a competitive, non-monopolistic economy, the good of society will be served. Owners of land and capital therefore have not only the right but also the obligation to seek as much profit as possible.

Such an outlook may be extremely attractive to successful Westerners. Indeed laisser-faire economics has been espoused by some as *the* Christian economics.[4] In reality, however, it is a product of the Enlightenment.[5] It reflects a modern, secularised outlook rather than a biblical perspective.

It is interesting to note the striking parallel between the laisser-faire and the pagan Roman attitude towards private property. Carl F. H. Henry, former editor of *Christianity Today*, rightly contrasts the biblical and Roman understandings: 'The Roman or Justinian view derives ownership from natural right; it defines ownership as the individual's unconditional and exclusive power over property. It implies an owner's right to use property as he pleases . . . irrespective of the will of others.' And Henry admits that this pagan view, 'still remains the silent presupposition of much of the free world's common practice today'.[6]

According to biblical faith, Yahweh is Lord of all things. He is the sovereign Lord of history. Economics is not a neutral, secular sphere independent of his Lordship. Economic activity, like every other area of life, should be subject to his will and revelation.

How does the biblical view that Yahweh is Lord of all of life require a modification of the common belief that the right of private property is absolute and inviolable? The Bible insists that God alone has an absolute right to property. Furthermore, it teaches that this Absolute Owner places significant limitations on how his people acquire and use his property.

The psalmist summarised the biblical view of Yahweh's absolute ownership: 'The earth is the Lord's and the fullness thereof, the world and those who dwell therein' (Ps. 24:1). 'Whatever is under the whole heaven is mine,' God informed Job (Job 41:11; see also Ps. 50:12; Deut. 26:10; Exod. 19:5). In chapter 4 we examined the year of jubilee. It is precisely because absolute ownership of the land rested with Yahweh rather than the Israelite farmers that he could command the redistribution of land every fiftieth year: 'The land shall not be sold in perpetuity, for the land is mine; for you are strangers and sojourners with me' (Lev. 25:23; see also Deut. 10:14). Because he is the creator and sustainer of all things, God alone has absolute property rights.

As absolute owner, God places limitations on the acquisition and use of property. According to the Old Testament, 'the right to property was in principle subordinated to the obligation to care for the weaker members of society'.[7] That is the clear implication of the legislation on the jubilee, the sabbatical year, gleaning and interest. Property owners did not have the right to harvest everything in their fields. They were to leave some for the poor. When an Israelite farmer purchased land, he really only

bought the use of the land until the year of jubilee (Lev.
25:15–17). Indeed, even the right to use the land for the
intervening years was not absolute. If a relative of the seller
appeared, the purchaser had to sell the land back promptly.
Or if the seller recovered financial solvency, he had the
right to buy back his land immediately (Lev. 25:25–8). The
purchaser's right of ownership was subordinate to the
original owner's right to earn a living.

God was concerned to avoid extremes of wealth and
poverty among his people. He wanted each family to
possess the means to earn its own way. These human rights,
even of the less advantaged who regularly fell behind the
more aggressive, more prosperous people, were more
significant than the property rights of the person able to pay
the market price for land. Thus the rights of the poor and
disadvantaged to possess the means to earn a just living
have precedence over the rights of the more prosperous to
make a profit.[8]

At the same time, biblical principles by no means support
a communist economic system. Biblical principles point in
the direction of decentralised private ownership which
allows families to control their economic destinies. As
stewards of the land and other economic resources that
belong ultimately to God, they have the responsibility and
privilege of earning their own way and sharing generously
with others as they have need. This kind of decentralised
economic system empowers all people to be co-workers
with God. It also protects everyone against centralised
economic power (as when the state owns the means of
production or when small groups of élite control huge
multinational corporations), which threatens freedom and
promotes totalitarianism.

The Old Testament attitude towards property stems
from the high view of persons held in Israel. Old Testament
scholars have pointed out that Israel, unlike other ancient
civilisations such as Babylon, Assyria, and Egypt, considered all citizens equal before the law. In other societies
the social status of the offender (royal official, poor man,
priest) determined how his offence was judged and

punished. In Israel all citizens were equal before the law. Because of this high view of people, property seemed less significant by comparison.

> This equality before the law is accompanied by a new respect for human life. Whereas in neighbouring states offences connected with property such as theft, robbery, etc., were frequently punished with the death penalty, this was no longer the case in the law of the Old Testament. The life of even the most degraded person is worth more than the richest possession.[9]

The case of slaves illustrates this point. In all other ancient civilisations slaves were viewed as mere property. The owner was completely free to treat the slave according to his whim. But in Israel the slave was a person, not a piece of property. Specific laws guaranteed him certain rights (Exod. 21:20, 26–8; Deut. 23:15–16). 'The fact that, in accordance with God's order, the life of every individual, even of the poorest, is of greater value than all material things – this fact represents an insurmountable stumbling-block to all economic developments which make profits for the few out of human misery.'[10]

A Carefree Attitude Towards Possessions

Jesus calls his followers to a joyful life of carefree unconcern for possessions:

> I bid you put away anxious thoughts about food to keep you alive and clothes to cover your body. Life is more than food, the body more than clothes. Think of the ravens: they neither sow nor reap; they have no storehouse or barn; yet God feeds them. You are worth far more than the birds! Is there a man among you who by anxious thought can add a foot to his height? If, then, you cannot do even a very little thing, why are you anxious about the rest?
> Think of the lilies: they neither spin nor weave; yet I

tell you, even Solomon in all his splendour was not attired like one of these. But if that is how God clothes the grass, which is growing in the field today, and tomorrow is thrown on the stove, how much more will he clothe you! How little faith you have! And so you are not to set your mind on food and drink; you are not to worry. For all these are things for the heathen to run after; but you have a Father who knows that you need them. No, set your mind upon his kingdom, and all the rest will come to you as well. (Luke 12:22–31 NEB; see also 2 Cor. 9:8–11)

Jesus's words are anathema to Marxists and capitalists alike: to Marxists because they worship Mammon by claiming that economic forces are the ultimate causal factors in history; to capitalists because they worship Mammon by idolising economic efficiency and success as the highest goods.[11] Indeed, at another level, Jesus's words are anathema to the ordinary, comfortable 'Christian'. In fact, I must confess that I cannot read them without an underlying sense of uneasiness. The beauty and appeal of the passage always overwhelm me. But it also reminds me that I have not, in spite of continuing struggle and effort, attained the kind of carefree attitude Jesus depicts.

What is the secret of such carefree living? First, many people cling to their possessions instead of sharing them because they are worried about the future. But is not such an attitude finally unbelief? If we really believe that God is who Jesus said he is, then we can begin to live without anxiety for the future. Jesus taught us that God is our loving Father. His word *abba* is a tender, intimate word like *papa* (Mark 14:36). If we really believe that the almighty creator and sustainer of the cosmos is our loving papa, then we can begin to cast aside anxiety about earthly possessions.

Second, such carefree living presupposes an unconditional commitment to Jesus as Lord. We must genuinely want to seek first the kingdom of heaven. Jesus was blunt. We cannot serve God and possessions. 'No one can serve two masters; for either he will hate the one and love the other, or he will be devoted to the one and despise the other. You cannot serve God and mammon' (Matt. 6:24). Mammon is not some mysterious pagan God. The word *mammon* is simply the Aramaic word for wealth or property.[12] Like the rich young ruler and Zacchaeus, we must decide between Jesus and riches. Like the merchant in Jesus's parable, we must decide between the kingdom of heaven and our affluent life: 'The kingdom of heaven is like a merchant in search of fine pearls, who, on finding one pearl of great value, went and sold all that he had and bought it' (Matt. 13:45–6; see also v. 44). Either Jesus and his kingdom matter so much that we are ready to sacrifice everything else, including our possessions, or we are not serious about Jesus.

If Jesus is truly Lord and if we trust in a loving heavenly Father, then we can take courage to live without anxiety about possessions. That kind of carefree unconcern for possessions, however, is not merely an inner spiritual attitude. It involves concrete action. Immediately following the moving statement about the carefree life of the ravens and lilies, Jesus says, 'Sell your possessions, and give alms; provide yourselves with purses that do not grow old, with a treasure in the heavens that does not fail. . . . For where your treasure is, there will your heart be also' (Luke 12:33–4).

If there are poor people who need assistance, Jesus's carefree disciple will help – even if that means selling possessions. People are vastly more important than property. 'Laying up treasure in heaven' means exactly the same thing. 'In Jewish literature, the good deeds of a religious person are often described as treasures stored up in heaven.'[13] One stores up treasure in heaven by doing righteousness on earth. And aiding the poor is one of the most basic acts of righteousness. Jesus does not mean, of course, that we earn salvation by assisting the needy. But he does mean to urge his followers – out of gratitude for God's forgiving grace – to be so unconcerned with property that they eagerly sell it to aid the poor and oppressed. Such activity is an integral part of living a life of joyful unconcern for possessions.

But a difficult question remains. Did Jesus mean that we should sell all our possessions? How literally should we understand what he said in Luke 6:30: 'Give to every one who begs from you; and of him who takes away your goods do not ask them again'? Jesus sometimes engaged in typical Jewish hyperbole to make a point. He hardly meant in Luke 14:26 that one must actively hate father and mother in order to be his disciple. But we have become so familiar with Jesus's words, so accustomed to compromising their call to radical discipleship and unconditional commitment, that we weaken his real intent. What 99 per cent of all of us need to hear 99 per cent of the time is this: 'Give to everyone who begs from you', and 'sell your possessions'. It is certainly true that Jesus's followers continued to own some private property. But Jesus clearly taught that the kind of substantial sharing he desired would involve selling possessions. His first followers at Jerusalem took him seriously. If Christians today in affluent countries want to experience Jesus's carefree outlook on property and possessions, they will need to do the same.

Other parts of the New Testament continue the same theme. Bishops must not be lovers of money (1 Tim. 3:3; Tit. 1:7). Deacons likewise dare not be 'greedy for gain' (1 Tim. 3:8). In many churches today, 'success' in business is one of the chief criteria for selection to the church board. Is that not a blatant reversal of biblical teaching on the importance of possessions? Even those who are rich should be careful not to set their hope in 'uncertain riches'. Instead, they should trust in God and share generously (1 Tim. 6:17–18). 'Keep your life free from love of money, and be content with what you have; for he has said, "I will never fail you nor forsake you"' (Heb. 13:5). Our future is secure not because of our possessions but because it rests in the hands of a loving, omnipotent Father. If we truly trust in him and are unconditionally submitted to his Lordship, we can confidently imitate Jesus's carefree unconcern for property and possessions.

The Rich Fool

Most Christians in the Northern Hemisphere simply do not believe Jesus's teaching about the deadly danger of possessions. We all know that Jesus warned that possessions are highly dangerous – so dangerous, in fact, that it is extremely difficult for a rich person to be a Christian at all. 'It is easier for a camel to go through the eye of a needle than for a rich man to enter the kingdom of God' (Luke 18:25). But we do not believe Jesus. Christians in the United States live in the richest society in the history of the world, surrounded by a billion needy neighbours. In Britain too we are relatively well off. Yet we demand that our governments foster an ever-expanding economy in order that our incomes might increase each year. We insist on more and more. If Jesus was so un-American that he considered riches dangerous, then we must ignore or reinterpret his message.

But he said it all the same. Matthew, Mark and Luke all record the terrible warning: 'How hard it is for those who have riches to enter the kingdom of God!' (Luke 18:24; Matt. 19:23; Mark 10:23). The context of this saying shows why possessions are dangerous. Jesus spoke these words to his disciples immediately after the rich young man had decided to cling to his wealth rather than follow Jesus (Luke 18:18–23). Riches are dangerous because their seductive power frequently persuades us to reject Jesus and his kingdom.

The sixth chapter of 1 Timothy underlines and reinforces Jesus's teaching. Christians should be content with the necessities of food and clothing (1 Tim. 6:8). Why? 'Those who desire to be rich fall into temptation, into a snare, into many senseless and hurtful desires that plunge men into ruin and destruction. For the love of money is the root of all evils; it is through this craving that some have wandered away from the faith and pierced their hearts with many pangs' (1 Tim. 6:9–10). A desire for riches prompts people to do anything for the sake of economic success. The result, Scripture warns, is anguish now and damnation later.

That economic success tempts people to forget God was

already a biblical theme in the Old Testament. Before they entered the Promised Land, God warned the people of Israel about the danger of riches.

> Take heed lest you forget the Lord your God . . . lest, when you have eaten and are full, and have built goodly houses and live in them, and when your herds and flocks multiply, and your silver and gold is multiplied, and all that you have is multiplied, then your heart be lifted up, and you forget the Lord your God. . . . Beware lest you say in your heart, 'My power and the might of my hand have gotten me this wealth' (Deut. 8:11–14, 17).

An abundance of possessions can easily lead us to forget that God is the source of all good. We trust in ourselves and our wealth rather than in the Almighty.

Not only do possessions tempt us to forsake God. War and neglect of the poor often result from the pursuit of wealth. 'What causes wars, and what causes fightings among you? . . . You desire and do not have; so you kill. And you covet and cannot obtain; so you fight and wage war' (Jas. 4:1–2). A cursory reading of world history confirms this point.

Instead of fostering more compassion towards the poor, riches often harden the hearts of the wealthy. Scripture is full of instances in which rich persons are unconcerned about the poor at their doorstep (Isa. 5:8–10; Amos 6:4–7; Luke 16:19–31; James 5:1–5). Dom Helder Camara, a Brazilian archbishop who has devoted his life to seeking justice for the poor, makes the point forcefully:

> I used to think, when I was a child, that Christ might have been exaggerating when he warned about the dangers of wealth. Today I know better. I know how very hard it is to be rich and still keep the milk of human kindness. Money has a dangerous way of putting scales on one's eyes, a dangerous way of freezing people's hands, eyes, lips and hearts.[14]

Possessions are positively dangerous because they often encourage unconcern for the poor, because they lead to strife and war, and because they seduce people into forsaking God.

The usage of the word *covetousness* (it occurs nineteen times in the New Testament) reflects the biblical under-standing of the dangers of riches. The Greek word *pleonexia* (translated 'covetousness') means 'striving for material possessions'.[15]

Jesus's parable of the rich fool vividly portrays the nature of covetousness. When a man came running to Jesus for help in obtaining his share of a family inheritance, Jesus refused to consider the case. Perceiving the real problem, Jesus instead warned of the danger of covetousness. 'Take heed, and beware of all covetousness [*pleonexia*]; for a man's life does not consist in the abundance of his possessions' (Luke 12:15). Knowing that the man was obsessed with material things, Jesus told him a story about a rich fool.

> The land of a rich man brought forth plentifully; and he thought to himself, 'What shall I do, for I have nowhere to store my crops?' And he said, 'I will do this: I will pull down my barns, and build larger ones; and there I will store all my grain and my goods. And I will say to my soul, Soul, you have ample goods laid up for many years; take your ease, eat, drink, be merry.' But God said to him, 'Fool! This night your soul is required of you; and the things you have prepared, whose will they be?' So is he who lays up treasure for himself, and is not rich towards God (Luke 12:16–21).

The rich fool is the epitome of the covetous person. He has a greedy compulsion to acquire more and more possessions, even though he does not need them. And his phenomenal success at piling up more and more property and wealth leads to the blasphemous conclusion that material possessions can satisfy all his needs. From the divine perspective, however, this attitude is sheer madness. He is a raving fool.

One cannot read the parable of the rich fool without thinking of our own society. We madly multiply more sophisticated gadgets, larger and taller buildings, and faster means of transportation – not because such things truly enrich our lives but because we are driven by an obsession for more and more. Covetousness, a striving for more and more material possessions, has become a cardinal vice of Western civilisation.

The New Testament has a great deal to say about covetousness. It is divine punishment for sin. In its essence, it is idolatry. Scripture teaches that greedy persons must be expelled from the church. Certainly no covetous person will inherit the kingdom.

In Romans 1 Paul indicates that God sometimes punishes sin by letting sinners experience the ever more destructive consequences of their continuing rebellion against him. 'And since they did not see fit to acknowledge God, God gave them up to a base mind and to improper conduct. They were filled with all manner of wickedness, evil, *covetousness* . . . murder, strife, deceit' (Rom. 1:28–9). Covetousness is one of the sins with which God punishes our rebellion. The parable of the rich fool suggests how the punishment works out. Since we are made for communion with the Creator, we cannot obtain genuine fulfilment when we seek it in material possessions. Hence we seek ever more frantically and desperately for more houses and bigger barns. Eventually we worship our possessions. As Paul indicates, covetousness is finally sheer idolatry (Eph. 5:5; Col. 3:5).

Paul actually commanded the Corinthians to exercise church discipline against the covetous (1 Cor. 5:11). Christians today are not at all surprised that he urged the Corinthians to excommunicate a church member living with his father's wife (1 Cor. 5:1–5). But we quietly overlook the fact that Paul went right on to urge Christians not to associate or even eat meals with persons who claim to be Christians but who are guilty of greed. Are we not guilty of covetousness when we demand an ever higher standard of living while millions of children starve to death each year? Is it not time for the church to begin applying church discipline to those guilty of this sin?[16] Would it not be more biblical to apply church discipline to people whose greedy acquisitiveness has led to 'financial success' than to elect them to the board of elders?

Such action may be the last means we have of communicating the biblical warning that greedy persons will not inherit the kingdom. 'Do you not know that the unrighteous will not inherit the kingdom of God? Do not be deceived; neither the immoral, nor idolators, nor adulterers, nor homosexuals, nor thieves *nor the greedy* [the covetous], nor drunkards, nor revilers, nor robbers will inherit the kingdom of God' (1 Cor 6:9–10). Covetousness is just as sinful as idolatry and adultery.

The same vigorous, unambiguous word appears in Ephesians: 'Be sure of this, that no fornicator or impure man, or one who is covetous (that is, an idolater), has any inheritance in the kingdom of Christ' (Eph. 5:5). These biblical passages should drive us all to our knees. I am afraid that I have been repeatedly and sinfully covetous. The same is true of the vast majority of Western Christians.

Possessions are dangerous. They lead to a multitude of sins, including idolatry. Western Christians today desperately need to turn away from their covetous civilisation's grasping materialism.

The Ring and the Beloved

Possessions are dangerous. But they are not innately evil.[17] Biblical revelation begins with creation. And created things, God said, are good (Gen. 1).

Biblical faith knows nothing of the ascetic notion that forsaking food, possessions or sex is inherently virtuous. To be sure, these created goods are, as St Augustine said, only rings from our Beloved. They are not the Beloved himself. Sometimes particular circumstances – such as an urgent mission or the needs of the poor – may require their renunciation. But these things are part of God's good creation. Like the ring given by the Beloved, they are signs of his love. If we treasure them as good tokens of his affection instead of mistaking them for the Beloved, they are marvellous gifts which enrich our lives.

God's provision for Israel's use of the tithe symbolises the scriptural perspective (Deut. 14:22–7). Every third year, as we saw earlier, the tithe was given to the poor. In the other years, however, the people were to go to the place of worship and have a fantastic feast. They were to have a great big, joyful celebration! 'Before the Lord your God, in the place which he will choose, to make his name dwell there, you shall eat the tithe of your grain, of your wine, and of your oil, and the firstlings of your herd and flock' (Deut. 14:23). Those who lived far from the place of worship could sell the tithe of their produce and take the money with them. Listen to God's directions for the party: 'Spend the money for whatever you desire, oxen, or sheep, or wine or strong drink, whatever your appetite craves; and you shall eat there before the Lord your God and rejoice' (Deut. 14:26). God wants his people to celebrate the glorious goodness of his creation.

Jesus's example fits in perfectly with the Old Testament view. Certainly he said a great deal about the danger of possessions. But he was not an ascetic. He was happy to join in marriage celebrations and even contribute the beverage (John 2:1–11). He dined with the prosperous. Apparently he was sufficiently fond of feasts and celebrations that his enemies could spread the false rumour that he was a glutton and a drunkard (Matt. 11:19). Christian asceticism has a long history, but Jesus's life undermines its basic assumptions.

A short passage in 1 Timothy succinctly summarises the biblical view. In the latter days people will forbid marriage and advocate abstinence from foods. But this is misguided, 'for everything created by God is good, and nothing is to be rejected if it is received with thanksgiving' (1 Tim. 4:4).

The biblical teaching on the goodness of creation does not contradict the other biblical themes we have explored.

It is also true that possessions are dangerous and that God's people must practise self-denial to aid the poor and feed the hungry. But it is important to focus the biblical mandate to liberate the poor without distorting other aspects of Scripture. It is not because food, clothes and property are inherently evil that Christians today must lower their standard of living. It is because others are starving. Creation is good. But the one who gave us this gorgeous token of his affection has asked us to share it with our sisters and brothers.

Righteousness and Riches

Does obedience guarantee prosperity? Is it true that 'in the house of the righteous there is much treasure' (Prov. 15:6)? Is the reverse also true? Are riches a sure sign of righteousness?

The Bible certainly does not romanticise poverty. It is a curse (2 Sam. 3:29; Ps. 109:8–11). Sometimes it is the result of sin, but not always. A fundamental point of the book of Job is that poverty and suffering are not always due to disobedience. In fact, they can be redemptive (Isa. 53). Even so, poverty and suffering are not inherently good. They are tragic distortions of God's good creation.

Prosperity, on the other hand, is good and desirable. God repeatedly promised his people Israel that obedience would bring abundant prosperity in a land flowing with milk and honey (Deut. 6:1–3). 'All these blessings shall come upon you . . . if you obey the voice of the Lord your God. . . . And the Lord will make you abound in prosperity, in the fruit of your body, and in the fruit of your cattle, and in the fruit of your ground' (Deut. 28:2, 11; see also Deut. 7:12–15). That God frequently rewards obedience with material abundance is a clear teaching of Scripture.

But the threat of a curse always accompanied the promise of blessing (Deut. 6:14–15; 8:11–20; 28:15–68). As we discovered in the last two chapters, one of God's most frequent commands to his people was to feed the hungry and to bring justice to the poor and oppressed. For repeatedly ignoring this command, Israel experienced God's curse. Israel's prosperity in the days of Amos and Isaiah was not the result of divine blessing. It was the result of sinful oppression of the poor. God consequently destroyed the nation.

More biblical texts warn of God's punishment of the rich and powerful because of their neglect or oppression of the poor than tell us that material abundance results from obedience.[18] The two statements, however, are not mutually contradictory. Both are true. It is the biblical balance that we need.

The Bible does teach that God rewards obedience with prosperity. But it denies the converse. It is a heresy, particularly common in the West, to think that wealth and prosperity are always a sure sign of righteousness. They may be the result of sin and oppression, as in the case of Israel (see chapter 3). The crucial test is whether the prosperous are obeying God's command to bring justice to the oppressed.[19] If they are not, they are living in damnable disobedience to God. On biblical grounds, therefore, one can be sure that prosperity in the context of injustice results from oppression rather than obedience and that it is not a sign of righteousness.

The connection between righteousness, prosperity and concern for the poor is explicitly taught in Scripture. The picture of the good wife in Proverbs 31 provides one beautiful illustration. This is of a diligent businesswoman who buys fields and engages in trade (vv. 14, 16, 18). She is a righteous woman who fears the Lord (v. 30). Her obedience and diligence clearly bring prosperity. But material possessions do not harden her heart against the poor: 'She opens her hand to the poor, and reaches out her hands to the needy' (v. 20). Psalm 112 is equally explicit:

Blessed is the man who fears the Lord,
who greatly delights in his commandments! . . .
Wealth and riches are in his house; . . .
The Lord is gracious, merciful, and righteous.

> It is well with the man who deals generously and lends,
>   who conducts his affairs with justice. . . .
> He has distributed freely, he has given to the poor
>   (Ps. 112:1, 3–5, 9).

The righteous person distributes his riches freely to the poor. He works to establish justice for the oppressed. That kind of life is a sign that one's prosperity results from obedience rather than oppression.

God wills prosperity with justice. As John V. Taylor has pointed out so beautifully, the biblical norm for material possessions is 'sufficiency'.[20] Proverbs 30:8–9 is a perfect summary:

> Give me neither poverty nor riches;
>   feed me with the food that is needful for me,
> lest I be full, and deny thee,
>   and say, 'Who is the Lord?'
> or lest I be poor, and steal,
>   and profane the name of my God.

Western Christians, however, must be careful not to distort the biblical teaching that God sometimes rewards obedience with material abundance. Wealthy persons who make up Christmas hampers and give to relief have not satisfied God's demand. God wills justice for the poor. And justice, as we have seen, means things like the jubilee and the sabbatical remission of debts. It means economic structures that check the emergence of extremes of wealth and poverty. It means massive economic sharing among the people of God. Prosperity without that kind of biblical concern for justice unambiguously signifies disobedience.

We have seen that the Old Testament teaches that material possessions sometimes result from divine blessing. But is this view compatible with Jesus's saying: 'Blessed are you poor, for yours is the kingdom of God' (Luke 6:20)? Does Jesus consider poverty itself a virtue? Furthermore, how can one reconcile the Lucan version of this beatitude with Matthew's version: 'Blessed are the poor *in spirit*' (Matt. 5:3)?

The development of the idea of the 'pious poor' in the centuries just prior to Christ helps answer these questions. Already in the Psalms the poor were often identified as the special objects of God's favour and protection precisely because they were oppressed by the wicked rich (see, for example, Ps. 9:18; 10:1–2).[21] When Greece and then Rome conquered Palestine, Hellenistic culture and values were foisted on the Jews. Those who remained faithful to Yahweh often suffered financially. Thus the term *poor* came to be used to describe faithful Jews. 'It was virtually equivalent to pious, God-fearing, and godly, and reflects a situation where the rich were mainly those who had sold out to the incoming culture and had allowed their religious devotion to become corrupted by the new ways. If the poor were the pious, the faithful and largely oppressed, the rich were the powerful, ungodly, worldly, even apostate.'[22]

In such a setting the righteous are often poor, hungry and sad, not just 'in spirit' but in physical life. Matthew has not 'spiritualised' Jesus's words. He has simply captured another aspect of Jesus's original meaning. Jesus was talking about those faithful persons who so hungered for righteousness that they sacrificed even their material prosperity when that became necessary. Jesus did not mean that poverty and hunger are desirable in themselves. But in a sinful world where, frequently, success and prosperity are possible only if one transgresses God's law, poverty and hunger are indeed a blessing. The kingdom is for precisely such people.

Jesus's comment in Mark 10:29–30 adds further clarification. He promised that those who forsake all for the kingdom will receive a hundredfold even in this life. He even included houses and lands, part of the good creation intended for our enjoyment. In the same sentence, however, he also promised persecution. Sometimes – perhaps most of the time – the wicked, powerful and rich will persecute those who dare to follow Jesus's teaching without compromise. Hunger and poverty often result. In such a time the poor and hungry disciples are indeed blessed.

I fear that we may be at the threshold of such an age. The

time may soon come when those who dare to preach and live what the Bible teaches about the poor and possessions will experience terrible persecution. Indeed that day has already arrived in some lands. Many Christians in Latin America have experienced torture, some even death, because they identified with the poor. If the wars of redistribution envisaged by Heilbroner become a reality, if affluent lands go to war to protect their unfair share of the world's food and resources, then persecution in affluent countries will inevitably occur.[23]

In such an age faithful Christians will continue to assert that property rights are not absolute. They will courageously insist that the right of individuals and nations to use land and resources as they please is subordinate to the right of all people to have the resources to earn a just living. They will understand more profoundly than today Jesus's carefree unconcern for possessions. As they see fellow church members choose security and affluence rather than faithfulness and persecution, they will realise how dangerous indeed are possessions and wealth. Certainly they will not despise the good gifts of creation. But, when forced to choose between possessions and the kingdom, they will gladly forsake the ring for the Beloved.

Study Questions

1. How does the biblical perspective on private property challenge modern ideas?

2. What are the dangers of possessions? Is this part of biblical truth especially difficult for modern folk to grasp? Why?

3. What is the actual biblical connection between righteousness and riches? How is this truth perverted today?

4. How would you change your life if you were truly to implement Jesus's teaching about carefree living?

5. How does St Augustine's image of the ring and the Beloved summarise the proper attitude towards possessions?

6

STRUCTURAL EVIL AND
WORLD HUNGER

Come now, you rich, weep and howl for the miseries that are
coming upon you. Your riches have rotted and your garments are moth-eaten. Your gold and silver have rusted, and
their rust will be evidence against you and will eat your flesh
like fire. You have laid up treasure for the last days. Behold,
the wages of the labourers who mowed your fields, which
you kept back by fraud, cry out; and the cries of the
harvesters have reached the ears of the Lord of hosts. You
have lived on the earth in luxury and in pleasure; you have
fattened your hearts in a day of slaughter (Jas. 5:1–5).

I read some time ago that Upton Sinclair, the author, read
this passage to a group of ministers. Then he attributed the
passage to Emma Goldman, who at the time was an anarch-
ist agitator. The ministers were indignant, and their response
was, 'This woman ought to be deported at once!' (unpublished sermon [June 1st, 1975] by Dr Paul E. Toms, former
president of the National Association of Evangelicals).

In the early 1950s Northeast High School in Philadelphia
was famous for its superb academic standards and its
brilliant, long-standing athletic triumphs. The second oldest school in the city, Northeast had excellent teachers and
a great tradition. And it was almost entirely white. Then in
the mid-fifties, the neighbourhood began to change. Black
people moved in. Whites began to flee in droves to the
Greater Northeast, a new, all-white section of Philadelphia. Quite naturally, a new high school became necessary in this developing, overwhelmingly white area.

When the excellent new school was completed in 1957, it took along the name Northeast High School, with its fond memories and traditions and many connotations of academic excellence and athletic triumph. The inner-city school was renamed Edison High. The new school took all the academic and athletic trophies and awards, school colours, songs, powerful alumni, and all the money in the treasury. Worst of all, the teachers were given the option of transferring to the new Northeast High. Two-thirds of them did.[1]

The black students who now attended Edison High had an old, rapidly deteriorating building, frequent substitute teachers, and no traditions. Nor did the intervening years bring many better teachers or adequate teaching materials. The academic record since 1957 has been terrible. But Edison High has one national record. More students from Edison High died in the US Army in Vietnam than from any other high school in the United States.

Who was guilty of this terrible sin? Local, state and federal politicians who had promoted de facto housing segregation for decades? The school board? Parents who had, at best, only a partial picture of what was going on? Christian community leaders? White students at the new Northeast High whose excellent education and job prospects have been possible, in part, precisely because of the poor facilities and bad teachers left behind for the black students at Edison? Who was guilty?

Many would deny any personal responsibility. 'That's just the way things are!' And they would be quite right. Long-standing patterns in jobs and housing had created a system which automatically produced Edison High. But that hardly silences the query about responsibility. Do we sin when we participate in evil social systems and societal structures that unfairly benefit some and harm others?

The Bible and Structural Evil

Neglect of the biblical teaching on structural injustice or institutionalised evil is one of the most deadly omissions in many parts of the church today. What does the Bible say about structural evil, and how does that deepen our understanding of the scriptural perspective on poverty and hunger?

Christians frequently restrict the scope of ethics to a narrow class of 'personal' sins. In a study of over fifteen hundred ministers, researchers discovered that the theologically conservative pastors spoke out on sins such as drug abuse and sexual misconduct.[2] But they failed to preach about the sins of institutionalised racism, unjust economic structures and militaristic institutions which destroy people just as much as do alcohol and drugs.

There is an important difference between consciously willed, individual acts (like lying to a friend or committing an act of adultery) and participation in evil social structures. Slavery is an example of the latter. So is the Victorian factory system where ten-year-old children worked twelve to sixteen hours a day. Both slavery and child labour were legal. But they destroyed people by the millions. They were institutionalised, or structural, evils. In the twentieth century, as opposed to the nineteenth, evangelicals have been more concerned with individual sinful acts than with our participation in evil social structures.

But the Bible condemns both. Speaking through his prophet Amos, the Lord declared, '"For three transgressions of Israel, and for four, I will not revoke the punishment; because they sell the righteous for silver, and the needy for a pair of shoes – they that trample the head of the poor into the dust of the earth, and turn aside the way of the afflicted; a man and his father go in to the same maiden, so that my holy name is profaned"' (Amos 2:6–7). Biblical scholars have shown that some kind of legal fiction underlies the phrase 'selling the needy for a pair of shoes'.[3] This mistreatment of the poor was *legal*! In one breath God condemns both sexual misconduct and legalised oppression of the poor. Sexual sins and economic injustice are equally displeasing to God. God revealed the same thing through his prophet Isaiah:

Woe to those who join house to house,
who add field to field,
until there is no more room,
and you are made to dwell alone in the midst of the
   land.
The Lord of hosts has sworn in my hearing:
'Surely many houses shall be desolate,
large and beautiful houses, without inhabitant . . .
Woe to those who rise early in the morning,
that they may run after strong drink,
who tarry late into the evening
till wine inflames them!' (Isa. 5:8–9, 11)

Equally powerful is the succinct, satirical summary in verses 22 and 23 of the same chapter: 'Woe to those who are heroes at drinking wine, and valiant men in mixing strong drink, who acquit the guilty for a bribe, and deprive the innocent of his right!' Here God condemns in one breath both those who amass large landholdings at the expense of the poor and those who have fallen into drunkenness. Economic injustice is just as abominable to our God as drunkenness.

Some young activists have supposed that as long as they were fighting for the rights of minorities and opposing militarism, they were morally righteous, regardless of how often they shacked up for the night with a man or woman in the movement. Some of their elders, on the other hand, have supposed that because they did not smoke, drink and lie, they were morally upright even though they lived in segregated communities and owned stock in companies that exploit the poor of the earth. God, however, has declared that robbing your workers of a fair wage is just as sinful as robbing a bank. Voting for a racist because he is a racist is just as sinful as sleeping with your neighbour's wife. Silent participation in a company that carelessly pollutes the environment and thus imposes heavy costs on others is just as wrong as destroying your own lungs with tobacco.

God clearly reveals his displeasure at evil *institutions* in Amos 5:10–15. (To understand this passage, we need to

remember that Israel's court sessions were held at the city
gate.) ' "They hate him who reproves in the gate . . . I know
how many are your transgressions, and how great are your
sins – you who . . . take a bribe, and turn aside the needy
in the gate. . . . Hate evil, and love good, and establish
justice in the gate." ' 'Let justice roll down like waters . . .'
(Amos 5:24) is not abstract verbalisation. The prophet is
calling for justice in the legal system. He means, get rid
of the corrupt legal system that allows the wealthy to buy
their way out of trouble, but gives the poor long prison
terms.

Nor are the dishonest and corrupt individuals in the legal
system the only ones who stand condemned. God clearly
revealed that laws themselves are sometimes an abomination to him.

> Can wicked rulers be allied with thee,
> who frame mischief by statute?
> They band together against the life of the righteous,
> and condemn the innocent to death.
> But the Lord has become my stronghold,
> and my God the rock of my refuge.
> He will bring back on them their iniquity
> and wipe them out for their wickedness;
> the Lord our God will wipe them out (Ps. 94:20–3).

The Jerusalem Bible has an excellent rendering of verse 20:
'You never consent to that corrupt tribunal that imposes
disorder as law.' God wants his people to know that wicked
governments 'frame mischief by statute'. Or, as the New
English Bible puts it, they contrive evil 'under cover of
law'.

God proclaims the same word through the prophet
Isaiah:

> Woe to those who decree iniquitous decrees,
> and the writers who keep writing oppression,
> to turn aside the needy from justice
> and to rob the poor of my people of their right . . .

What will you do on the day of punishment,
in the storm which will come from afar?
To whom will you flee for help,
and where will you leave your wealth?
Nothing remains but to crouch among the prisoners
or fall among the slain.
For all this [God's] anger is not turned away
and his hand is stretched out still. (Isa. 10:1–4)

It is quite possible to make oppression legal. Then, as now, legislators devised unjust laws, and the bureaucracy (the scribes or writers) implemented the injustice. But God shouts a divine woe against those rulers who use their official position to write unjust laws and unfair legal decisions. Legalised oppression is an abomination to our God. Therefore, God calls his people to oppose political structures that frame mischief by statute.

The just Lord of the universe will also destroy wicked rulers and unjust social institutions (see 1 Kings 21). God cares about evil economic structures and unjust legal systems – precisely because they destroy people by the hundreds and thousands and millions.

Another side to institutionalised evil makes it especially pernicious. Structural evil is so subtle that one can be ensnared and hardly realise it. God inspired his prophet Amos to utter some of the harshest words in Scripture against the cultured upper-class women of his day: 'Hear this word, you cows of Bashan . . . who oppress the poor, who crush the needy, who say to [your] husbands, "Bring, that we may drink!" The Lord God has sworn by his holiness that, behold, the days are coming upon you, when they shall take you away with hooks, even the last of you with fishhooks' (Amos 4:1–2).

The women involved may have had little direct contact with the impoverished peasants. They may never have realised clearly that their gorgeous clothes and spirited parties were possible partly because of the sweat and tears of toiling peasants. In fact, they may even have been kind on occasion to individual peasants. (Perhaps they gave them 'Christmas hampers' once a year.) But God called these privileged women 'cows' because they profited from social evil. Before God they were personally and individually guilty.[4]

If one is a member of a privileged class that profits from structural evil, and if one does nothing to try to change things, he or she stands guilty before God.[5] Social evil is just as displeasing to God as personal evil. And it is more subtle.

In the first edition of this book, I said that social evil hurts more people than personal evil. That may be true in the Third World, but I no longer believe that it is true in North America and Western Europe. Within the industrialised nations, the agony caused by broken homes, sexual promiscuity, marital breakdown and divorce probably equals the pain caused by structural injustices. That is not to deny or de-emphasise the latter. It is merely to underline the fact that both kinds of sin devastate industrialised societies today.

The prophets told how the God of justice responds to oppressive social structures. God cares so much about the poor that he will destroy social structures that tolerate and foster great poverty. Repeatedly God declared that he would destroy the nation of Israel because of *both* its idolatry *and* its mistreatment of the poor (for example, Jer. 7:1–15).

The *both/and* is crucial. We dare not become so preoccupied with horizontal issues of social justice that we neglect vertical evils such as idolatry. Modern Christians seem to have an irrepressible urge to fall into one extreme or the other. But the Bible corrects our one-sidedness. God destroyed Israel and Judah because of both their idolatry and their social injustice.

Here, however, our focus is on the fact that God destroys oppressive social structures. Amos's words, which could be duplicated from many other places in Scripture, make this divine response clear:

Because you trample upon the poor and take from him exactions of wheat, you have built houses of hewn stone, but you shall not dwell in them. (5:11)

'Woe to those who lie upon beds of ivory, and stretch themselves upon their couches, and eat lambs from the flock . . . but [who] are not grieved over the ruin of Joseph! Therefore they shall now be the first of those to go into exile . . .' (6:4, 6–7)

Hear this, you who trample upon the needy, and bring the poor of the land to an end, saying, 'When will the new moon be over, that we may sell grain? And the sabbath, that we may offer wheat for sale . . . and deal deceitfully with false balances, that we may buy the poor for silver and the needy for a pair of sandals . . . ?' (8:4–6)

'Behold, the eyes of the Lord God are upon the sinful kingdom, and I will destroy it from the surface of the ground. . . .' (9:8)

Within a generation after the time of the prophet Amos, the northern kingdom of Israel was completely wiped out.

Probably the most powerful statement of God's work to destroy evil social structures is in the New Testament – in Mary's Magnificat. Mary glorified the Lord who 'has put down the mighty from their thrones, and exalted those of low degree; [who] has filled the hungry with good things, and the rich he has sent empty away' (Luke 1:52–3). The Lord of history is at work pulling down sinful societies where wealthy classes live by the sweat, toil and grief of the poor.

Institutionalised Evil Today

What does this biblical teaching mean for affluent people today? If Amos were alive, would he deliver the same judgments on us as he did against the unrighteous Israelites of his own day?

The answer, I think, is yes. A former president of World Vision has written of 'the stranglehold which the developed

West has kept on the economic throats of the Third World'. He believes that 'the heart of the problems of poverty and hunger are human systems which ignore, mistreat and exploit man. . . . If the hungry are to be fed . . . some of the systems will require drastic adjustments while others will have to be scrapped altogether.'[6] Together we must examine the evidence for this evaluation.

In citing the disturbing data which follows, I do so neither with sadistic enjoyment of an opportunity to flagellate the affluent, nor with a desire to create feelings of irresolvable guilt. God has no interest in groundless 'guilt trips'. But I do believe the God of the poor wants us all to feel deep pain over the agony and anguish that torment the poor. And I also believe we must call sin by its biblical name.

All developed countries are directly involved. So, too, are the wealthy élites in poor countries. Ancient social patterns, inherited cultural values, and cherished religious and philosophical perspectives in developing countries also contribute in an important way to create and preserve poverty.[7] In some cases, laziness and sinful choices about alcohol, sex and drugs have created poverty. And some poverty results from natural disasters, or lack of the right tools to create wealth. The causes of poverty are complex. It would be naïve to simplify complex realities and isolate one scapegoat.

The affluent North is simply *not* responsible for all the poverty in the world. There are many causes. In fact, even if the rich were not responsible for causing *any* part of global poverty, we would still be responsible to help those in need. The story of Lazarus and Dives (Luke 16:19–31) does not suggest that Lazarus's poverty resulted from oppression on the part of Dives. Dives merely neglected to help. His sin was the sin of omission. And it sent him to hell.

I do believe, however, that affluent nations have played a part in establishing economic structures that contribute to some of today's hunger and starvation. Surely our first responsibility is to understand and change what we are doing wrong.

How then are we a part of unjust structures that contribute to world hunger? We will briefly probe some of the historical origins of the present problem and then examine four current issues: international trade and Third World debt, consumption of natural resources and the environmental crisis, food consumption and food imports, and multinational corporations in the Third World.

Origins and Growth

One quarter of the world's people wallow in the mire of deep poverty. Thirty-five thousand children die each day of malnutrition and related diseases. While one person in five slowly starves, we who have enough resources to end such misery seem strangely indifferent to their plight. In fact, we persist in demanding that our governments preserve and even increase our incredibly high standard of living. The result is an ever-widening gap between the rich and the poor.

How did we get into this situation? One part of the answer – and only one part – can be found if we look briefly at the history of colonialism. Respected development economist Mahbub ul Haq, for years a senior economist at the World Bank, writes that 'the basic reasons for inequality between the presently developed and developing nations lie fairly deep in their history. In most parts of the Third World, centuries of colonial rule have left their legacy of dependency.'[8]

It is now generally recognised by historians that many of the civilisations Europe discovered were not less developed or underdeveloped in any sense. True, the civilisations of Asia, Africa, and the Americas were different from those of Europe and they were not 'Christian'. But their most obvious 'deficiency' was not underdevelopment but their lack of modern military technology.

In his classic of development literature, *Asian Drama*, Gunnar Myrdal places much of the blame for the economic stagnation of South-East Asia at the feet of European colonisers: 'In general, the colonial regimes in South Asia were inimical to the development of manufacturing industry in the colonies. This was even more true when they gradually gave up, after the 1850s and 1870s, the crudely exploitative policies of early colonialism and began to encourage investment and production. It was predominantly or exclusively the production of raw materials for export that was encouraged.'[9]

Most colonising countries used their colonies to enhance their own national status in the world community. Strong nation-states became the ultimate objective, and control over land and wealth around the world was the key to power.[10] The creation of colonies was extremely useful. Preoccupied with the status of the mother country, colonisers seldom exhibited much regard for the economic, social, and cultural conditions of the indigenous peoples.

In his book, *Bread and Justice*, James B. McGinnis cites the example of the town of Potosi, Bolivia. Potosi was a thriving urban area in the seventeenth century when the Spaniards came to mine the area's gold and silver. At first the Spanish miners produced booming economic growth. But:

when the silver ran out, Potosi's boom ended and the area was left to 'underdevelop' . . .

The underdevelopment of Potosi, then, began with the abuse of its people and resources through the European colonial system. The Latin American economy was geared by the Europeans to meet their own needs, not those of the local people. The underdevelopment which is characteristic of this 'ghost' town today, has its roots in the history of military conquests. Underdeveloped countries today are full of 'ghost' towns like Potosi, and nearly all were European colonies at one time.

The arrival of the Europeans in Asia, Africa and Latin America – what is known today as the Third World – fundamentally altered the processes of development which were taking place at the time. In some cases, these societies were more advanced than others; and all, of course, had problems to surmount. But the people in these areas were constructing societies which, although not industrialised, were often highly sophisticated and complex. They were able to meet their physical and psychological needs through their own institutions. The military conquest of Third World people led to the plunder and destruction of some of the world's greatest civilisations.[11]

As McGinnis emphasises, there are other examples. Consider an article in the *Wall Street Journal*. Examining the modern attempt of Gabon to build a transnational railway, it asked why one was not built in colonial days. The author responded:

The French built only what they needed to find and export Gabon's raw materials. In fact, colonials' habit of building only those roads and ports and power plants that served their purposes, while ignoring the rest of the country, still stifles Third World economies. 'They inherited a legacy that condemned them to underdevelopment,' complains the UN's Mr Doo Kingue, whose own country, Cameroon, was colonized by Germans, English and French.[12]

It would be simplistic, of course, to suggest that the impact of colonialism and subsequent economic and political relations with industrialised nations was entirely negative. It was not. One thinks for instance of the spread of literacy and improved health care. Furthermore, I can only thank God for the opportunities to spread the gospel around the world during the colonial period, although I wish missionaries had more often challenged imperial injustice. Christian values often undercut ancient social evils such as the caste system in India. What a tragedy, however, that so much of the impact of the 'Christian' North on the developing political, economic structures of the colonies was shaped by economic self-interest rather than the biblical principles of justice. If the whole biblical message had been shared and lived in social and economic life, developing nations would know less misery today. If Christian attitudes towards property and wealth had ruled the colonisers' actions, if the principles of jubilee, the sabbatical year, and empowerment of the poor had been an integral part of the colonial venture and international economic activity, there would probably be no need for this book today.

Unfortunately, however, they were not. Nor has there been any major sustained effort on the part of the developed nations since then to restore or institute just economic relations with poorer nations. The wealthy nations continue to pursue their own self-interest with only marginal interest in the economic progress (or regress) of the less fortunate.

As a result the legacy lingers. Not surprisingly, many of the injustices perpetuated in the early days of colonialism have become cemented in the institutions that govern contemporary economic activity. In her book *Aspects of Development and Underdevelopment*, Joan Robinson shows how trade structures and land and labour institutions in the Third World, as well as international financial structures, all developed substantially from the foundation which was laid in the colonial era.[13]

It would be silly, of course, to depict colonialism as the sole cause of present poverty in LDCs. Cultural values, widespread corruption, misguided policies chosen by local élites, and overpopulation all play a part. So do present international economic structures. Consider, for example, the patterns of international trade today.

International Trade

The industrialised nations have shaped the patterns of international trade for their own economic benefit. In colonial days, as we have seen, the mother countries regularly made sure that economic affairs were organised to their own advantage.[14] Such advantage was largely achieved through manipulation of commodity trade. Institutions and policies were implemented to increase the quantity of useful goods going to the colonising countries and at the same time to subdue any local efforts to improve manufacturing capacities. As a result, many colonies became heavily dependent on trade with their 'mother' countries.

Even today most of the less developed countries depend highly on international trade for a major share of their livelihood. As a consequence, favourable patterns of international trade are vital to developing nations.

The industrialised countries impose restrictive tariffs and import quotas to keep out many of the goods produced in the less developed countries.[15] Tariff structures and import quotas affecting the poor nations are in fact one fundamental aspect of present injustice in today's international economic structures. Major European countries (members of the EEC) charge four times as high a tariff on cloth imported from poor nations as from developed countries. In fact, the World Bank indicates that the trade barriers imposed by rich nations on goods from poor nations cost poor nations $50–$100 billion a year.[16] No wonder they have trouble repaying their debts. Tragically, the developed world has largely refused to remove these harmful restrictions. In the early 1960s, for instance, the Kennedy round of tariff negotiations lowered the tariffs on goods traded among the rich industrial nations by 50 per cent. But it did little to lower tariffs on goods from poorer countries. The relative situation of the poor countries actually grew worse.[17]

Traditionally, developed countries have allowed many agricultural and other primary products (minerals, cocoa, rubber, sisal, and so on) to enter relatively duty-free. But they have been less lenient with manufactured goods. The more manufacturing and processing done by the poor country, the higher the tariff. The tariff on bars of chocolate, for example, is five times higher than on raw cocoa beans.[18]

The reasons for the imposition of such trade restrictions are clear. In colonial times they were imposed in order to limit the competition with the mother country's own fledgling industrial enterprises and to facilitate the transfer of needed primary products. Britain, for example, in the nineteenth century, allowed British textiles to enter India duty-free, but imposed heavy import duties on those coming from Bengal's then flourishing textile industry. As a result, Britain's textile industry prospered and India's stagnated. Today, restrictions are maintained mainly because their removal would threaten the interests of certain well-organised and politically entrenched groups. Both labour and management in the developed countries want to be able to buy cheap raw materials in order to profit from processing and manufacturing them here.

In the 'eighties, 'voluntary' quotas and other non-tariff barriers to manufactured goods from LDCs became more common. The World Bank's *1987 World Development Report* showed that these non-tariff barriers were increasing and also that all the industrial nations had higher non-tariff barriers for developing nations than for industrial nations.[19] Oxford economist Donald Hay reports that in the 1980s, non-tariff barriers increased substantially and consequently offset any improvements in tariff reductions.[20] The result is fewer jobs in hungry lands and lower export earnings.

'Voluntary' quotas can have a devastating impact. Industrialised countries simply threaten new tariff barriers on certain manufactures exported by poor countries unless they 'voluntarily' limit the volume exported to them. An example from Brazil shows how it works.

Coffee used to provide Brazil with approximately a half of its total export earnings. Brazil's coffee exports increased 90 per cent between 1953 and 1961. But the total revenue earned from coffee dropped by 35 per cent. So in 1966 Brazil decided to process its own coffee in order to supply more jobs and earn more income for its people. But when it seized 14 per cent of the US market, the US coffee manufacturers charged the Brazilians with unfair competition. What did the US government do? It threatened to cut off aid to Brazil, warning that it might not renew the International Coffee Agreement (which until recently kept coffee prices somewhat stable). Brazil eventually was forced to tax its instant coffee exports, and its nascent industry was seriously damaged.[21]

'Voluntary' quotas have become especially common for Third World exports to developed nations in the case of textiles, clothing, leather and footwear. In fact, ailing domestic industries keep demanding more restrictions on imports. Unfortunately, these kinds of labour-intensive manufactured goods are precisely the things that poor nations could most easily export to developed nations.

In his text *Economic Development*, Theodore Morgan summarises the situation as follows:

> The overall pattern is plain. Primary and simple products have low duties, though some have quotas. Simple manufactures have higher duties; and complex manufactures still higher. There are sharp obstacles to major cuts in tariff and nontariff barriers because of the resistance of domestic businessmen, labor groups, and regions, which fear injury from increased imports.[22]

The result is to deprive poor countries of millions of jobs and billions of dollars from increased exports.

By and large the countries of the Third World have been historically bound to produce primary commodities for export. In many cases colonial governments coercively discouraged manufacturing industries and actively encouraged the production and export of certain agricultural products and other raw materials. In other cases powerful landowners were able to squelch local industrialisation efforts so that agricultural export enterprises remained highly profitable.[23] As soon as the developed countries began industrialising, they set up tariffs and quotas to discourage industrialisation in the Third World. For all these reasons LDCs (Less Developed Countries) have specialised in primary products and have tended to import manufactured products from the industrialised nations.

Many Third World economists have charged that their reliance on primary products has destined them to suffer continually declining relative terms of trade. They cite such evidence as Brazil's being able in 1954 to buy one US jeep for fourteen bags of coffee, while in 1968 the same US jeep cost Brazil forty-five bags of coffee.[24] Tanzania could buy a tractor in 1963 for five tons of sisal; in 1970, by contrast, the same tractor cost ten tons of sisal.[25] Tanzania had to export four times the amount of cotton or ten times the amount of tobacco to buy a tractor in 1981 as was needed a mere five years earlier.[26]

The World Development Report 1982 shows how Sri Lanka, which has been dependent on its exports of tea, rubber and coconut products, has suffered severe terms-of-trade losses over the last thirty years.[27] During the 1980s the terms of trade for non-oil-exporting developing countries fell to their lowest level in twenty-five years. 'One estimate has placed the extra costs of deteriorating terms of trade for the LDCs at over $2.5 billion per year during the last decade. As a result, Third World merchandise trade balances have steadily worsened during the 1980s – falling, for example, from plus $55.8 billion in 1981 to minus $1.2 billion in 1985.'[28]

Although some cases are extreme and are surrounded by special intervening circumstances, economists generally recognise that over the last thirty years the low-income developing countries have experienced a serious decline in the relative prices of agricultural commodities.[29] At the same time, middle-income developing countries, which tend to export more minerals (including oil) than agricultural products, have been more fortunate. Prices on these commodities do not show the same unequivocal downward trend.[30]

Sometimes certain agricultural commodities enjoy short surges in prices, such as coffee did in 1977 and sugar does periodically. But in general the declining trend is clear. Hans Singer, a respected economist at the United Nations, argues, 'It is a matter of historical fact that ever since the 'seventies [the 1870s] the trend of prices has been heavily against the sellers of food and raw materials and in favor of the sellers of manufactured articles. The statistics are open to doubt and to objection in detail,

Table 14 Commodity Prices and Third World Debt

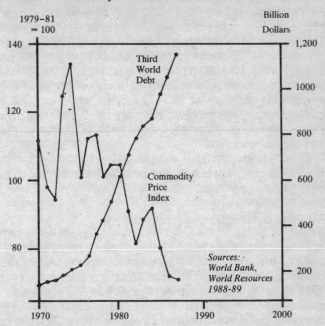

Source: Lester Brown, State of the World 1990, *p. 144.*

but the general story which they tell is unmistakable.'[31]

Table 14 shows the devastating effect. Between 1980 and 1987 alone, the prices of thirty-three commodities exported by heavily indebted developing nations dropped by 40 per cent! In the same period, their debt burden soared. How can we blame them for failing to pay their debts when our trade barriers cost them $50–$100 billion a year?[32]

A second pernicious problem to which primary-product exporters are vulnerable is that prices fluctuate widely. Violent fluctuation in prices of primary products is harmful to the developing countries' economies. It makes planning almost impossible, since they depend on export earnings for the vital foreign exchange needed to buy essential imported goods. Some countries are dependent on just one or two commodities for a great deal of their foreign exchange earnings. For example, Zambia depends on copper (88 per cent of its foreign exchange earnings); El Salvador on coffee (63 per cent); Bolivia on natural gas and tin (74 per cent); Ghana on cocoa (66 per cent).[33] Hence their economies fluctuate violently with the world price of the commodity they export. It is like living perpetually on a roller coaster, one moment enjoying the benefits of high prices, the next enduring a harrowing tumble into the trenches of low prices.

Closely interconnected with the issues of trade and tariffs is another crucial problem: the crushing international debt of developing nations.

The International Debt Crisis

Millions of children have already died to repay debts to affluent nations. UNICEF blames the debt burden for the death of five hundred thousand children each year. From 1970 to 1989, the foreign debt of developing nations increased by 1,846 per cent. Interest payments jumped 1,400 per cent. Today developing nations owe about $1.3 trillion and the annual interest charges alone are more than $160 billion. They cannot pay it all without increasing poverty and starvation.

Seeking repayment, creditors have imposed tough austerity programmes on many debtor nations through the International Monetary Fund (IMF). These austerity programmes along with other factors such as global recession and falling commodity prices have contributed to the worst economic crisis in their histories. Between 1981 and 1988 real per capita income declined in absolute terms in almost every country in South America. In many countries, such as Argentina and Peru, the drop in national income was greater than 20 per cent. Living standards in many countries have fallen to levels of the 1950s and 1960s. Unprecedented inflation has raged in Brazil (934 per cent in 1988), Argentina, and Peru (annual inflation in both reached several thousand per cent in 1988). The region is rife with political instability. Democratic governments are damaged. In February 1989, Venezuelans rioted in Caracas and other cities in protest against austerity measures prompted by Venezuela's debt crisis. Three hundred people died.[34]

In sub-Saharan Africa, per capita gross domestic product declined in this region every year in the 1980s. World Bank projections for the early 1990s indicate *no* per capita growth.[35]

Between 1982 and 1988, the IMF tested its strategy in twenty-eight of the thirty-two countries of Latin America and the Caribbean. The result has been economic stagnation, rising unemployment, and a decline in per capita income of 7 per cent.[36]

Who suffers the most? The poor, naturally, especially the children. A few years ago, former Tanzanian President Julius Nyerere posed a hard question: 'Must we starve our children to pay our debts?' If the actions of international bankers provide the answer, it is: YES. Millions of the developing world's children have given their lives to pay their countries' debts. Even more millions continue to pay the interest with their malnourished minds and bodies.[37]

Forced to slash government programmes dramatically, debtor nations cut spending on human services like education, health care and food subsidies rather than the military.

With few exceptions, severe increases in malnutrition and illness have occurred in poor nations with large foreign debts. Bolivia has been hailed by Northern banks and governments for its new economic programme and fiscal discipline in recent years. Less attention has been given to the health of the Bolivian people. In 1986, in compliance with an IMF stabilisation programme, Bolivia slashed its health budget by 67 per cent – at a time when 67 per cent of Bolivia's people suffered from malnutrition![38]

The link between debt and death among the poor is painfully clear in the Philippines. The Philippine government allocates approximately 44 per cent of its budget per year to service a foreign debt built up primarily during the Marcos dictatorship. Too little is left for vital health care programmes. UNICEF has found that nearly 150,000 Filipino infants under the age of five die each year from malnutrition and related illnesses. One study estimates that if the Philippines were to cut its debt payments to 20 per cent of export earnings, at least 9,200 Filipino children could be saved in one year. That is twenty-five children a day, one child an hour.[39] It is tragic that IMF policies, in effect, encouraged and even rewarded (with new loans) governments that neglected the health of their people for the sake of debt repayment.

Education. Third World debt payments have also deprived children of basic education. In twenty-one out of thirty-three poor debtor countries surveyed by UNICEF, spending per primary school pupil fell, often sharply, in the first half of the 1980s.

With some notable exceptions, poor debtor countries in the 1980s saw falling primary school enrolment rates, rising drop-out rates, and massive losses of qualified teachers. In the Philippines, school completion rates fell from 67 per cent to 63 per cent between 1981 and 1984. Bolivia suffered a rise in school desertion from 2.2 to 8.5 per cent among primary school-age children between 1980 and 1983. Similar drop-out rates are recorded in Barbados and Mexico. In Zaire, seven thousand teachers were dismissed in 1984 for budgetary reasons.[40]

These facts underscore a general pattern. In 70 per cent of developing countries, the 1980s were a time of widespread and sharp reversals in the trend towards improving standards in child education. As in the case of health care, the heaviest burden of debt is falling on those who are least able to bear it. The director general of UNESCO, Federico Mayor, has warned:

If debt repayment is to take precedence over the necessary investment in the social sectors including education, then [we will suffer] a dangerous erosion of human resources that . . . might set back the countries of the South by a whole generation or more.[41]

The adjustment policies imposed by creditors on debtor nations has not only contributed to reduced spending in basic services like education and health care for the poor. It has also helped to create stagnating economies where few jobs and lower wages also crush the poor. In many cases, as we saw, living standards have fallen to levels of the 1950s and 1960s. Examples are numerous.

A World Bank study found that in Sâo Paulo, Brazil, where a large reduction in government spending and wage restrictions had been instituted, real wages of unskilled construction workers fell by over 25 per cent between 1980 and 1985. Between 1983 and 1985, the nominal minimum wage in Brazil fell to only one-fifth to one-seventh the amount necessary to cover a family's basic needs. From 1976 to 1986, workers in Bolivia suffered a 36 per cent reduction in purchasing power. In early 1987, the Bolivian workers' union, COB, fought for a monthly minimum wage of £24.00, the cost of a monthly food 'basket' for a family of four. The government, however, would only agree to £15.00.

The July 1986 issue of *World Bank News* noted that in Zambia, where IMF wage caps had been imposed, incomes in 1986 were less than 60 per cent of their 1974 level.[42] In Chile, the real minimum wage in 1985 had dropped below the 1981 level.[43] The government of Mexico between 1982 and 1986 agreed to contract its budget deficit as part of an IMF adjustment package which was intended to put the economy back in shape. As a result, unemployment in Mexico soared from 4.7 per cent in 1982 to 17.6 per cent in 1987.[44] Real wages in Mexico declined about 50 per cent between 1980 and 1988.[45] Wealthy bankers in business suits may think that this type of adjustment is 'necessary'. But not poor parents who watch their kids die of starvation or malnutrition-related diseases.

The debt problem is not really a banking crisis. It is a development crisis. Huge debt payments not only reduce spending on needed human services. They also prevent essential capital investment that could provide new jobs and new income in the future. Unless there is major change, the future is bleak. Poor debtor economies will continue to shrink, essential social services will be cut even more, and millions of people will be submerged in even greater poverty.

The Background. How did the debt crisis develop? And who is to blame? The truth is that almost everyone must share responsibility except of course the poor who suffer the most.

The fourfold leap in oil prices in 1973–4 triggered a rapid increase in borrowing by developing countries who were eager to continue their growth. Commercial banks overflowing with petro dollars deposited by oil-producing nations made huge loans to Third World governments without asking proper questions about the use of the loans or the possibility of repayment. In the late 'seventies, Citicorp chairman Walter Wriston defended these loans with the optimistic credo, 'countries never go bankrupt'.

But mistaken government policies in poor debtor nations were also helping to prepare the way for disaster. Too much of what was loaned was spent on the latest armaments or wasted because of official corruption. Faced with budget deficits, governments chose to cut education and health programmes rather than their military budgets, and they printed money, which produced surging inflation. High inflation encouraged – and governments tolerated – capital flight by wealthy élites. In 1981 and 1982, the fifteen largest debtor nations received £49 billion in new loans. In the same period, wealthy élites moved £31 billion out of those same countries into Swiss bank accounts, US real estate, or other places.[46]

Rising exports by Third World nations, however, enabled them to meet payments until 1979 when further disaster struck. Oil prices doubled. Then the US decided to curb inflation, which produced a global recession that drastically reduced exports by Third World nations. At the same time, soaring interest rates (produced partly by the

US's huge budget deficit) greatly increased the interest payments on poor nations' foreign loans since they were at variable rather than fixed rates. Short-term loans that debtor nations received in the mid-seventies at approximately 6.5 per cent interest cost as much as 19 per cent when renewed in 1980 and 1981.

The export earnings of the non-oil-producing developing nations dropped sharply as demand in the recession-prone industrialised countries declined, and as the price of their exports dropped a precipitous 20 per cent in glutted world markets. In addition, their export prices, which were concentrated in agricultural goods and raw materials, fell as much as 40 per cent relative to prices of industrial goods, which the developing nations were importing heavily. Table 14 (see p. 139) illustrates the double bind of tumbling commodity prices and rising debt.

Poor debtor nations now faced widening balance-of-payment deficits and increasing trouble meeting their debt-service payments. They also had carried over from the previous period a huge debt obligation, made even more onerous by burgeoning interest rates.

Faced with this situation, Third World borrowers had two options. They could either cut their imports and impose tight spending and credit limits on their own economies, thus impeding their growth and development objectives. Or they could finance their widening deficits through still *more* foreign borrowing. With their resources already stretched to the limit, many countries opted for the latter. Amazingly, the commercial banks still made huge new loans in 1979–81. In fact, in the two years after interest rates soared, commercial banks made as many net loans to major debtor countries as during the entire period of 1973–9.[47] Developing debtor countries now found themselves meeting payments for old debts with newly borrowed money, at much higher interest rates. As a result, their debts piled up even higher, and by the early 1980s they faced severe difficulties in paying even the *interest* on their debts.

In August 1982, Mexico announced that it could no

longer meet the interest payments on its $58 billion foreign debt. Not much later, Venezuela, Brazil, Argentina and the Philippines followed suit. Commercial banks, severely shaken, started cutting back on new lending almost at once. Total gross bank lending to non-oil-developing nations had risen by 24 per cent in 1980 over 1979; but by 1982 that increase fell to 7 per cent.[48] As private lending dried up, developing nations were increasingly forced to finance both their old debts and their economic growth out of their own fragile export earnings. New private lending had largely ended by 1986. Furthermore, developing nations were sending back $11.3 billion *more* to the commercial banks than came to them in new loans. When one includes paybacks to the IMF and World Bank, the net flow of money (new lending minus payments for debts) for all indebted developing nations went from a positive $35.2 billion in 1981 to a *negative* $30.7 billion in 1986.[49] This negative transfer of funds, according to the World Bank's latest annual report, reached $50.1 billion in 1989.

The net flow of resources from the underdeveloped to the developed world is creating a major drain on domestic investment in poor nations. The tragic result is the derailing of Third World development. But development is crucial to the creation of the new wealth which is necessary to pay off the debt in the future. Thus the debt crisis has trapped many developing countries (especially in Africa and Latin America) in a downward spiral of capital outflows, shrinking foreign exchange reserves, and stalled development prospects.

Undoubtedly developing nations made some bad choices and wasted some of the borrowed funds. But the adverse economic conditions faced by the debtor countries have been to a large degree outside their control. One study estimates that nearly 85 per cent of the total increase in the foreign debt of the non-oil-developing nations between 1973 and 1982 resulted from four causes about which they could do almost nothing: OPEC oil price increases, the spurt in dollar interest rates in 1981–2, the reduction of Third World exports because of worldwide recession, and the precipitous drop in the world price of primary exports from developing nations.[50]

It is simply not honest to put all the blame on Third World countries for their debt problems. International bankers, politicians, and voters in industrialised nations also share some responsibility.

But it is the poor who suffer. An international banking system that works well for comfortable folk in industrialised nations helps shape a policy that dooms the weakest and most vulnerable to suffer and die. The Bible says that we are to have a special concern for widows and orphans. Current policies for handling the international debt crisis do exactly the opposite. 'Today, Third World children are the orphans of the debt crisis and their mothers are the widows.'[51]

We have looked briefly at several aspects of present international trade patterns which work to the disadvantage of the developing nations: high tariffs; low quotas and other non-tariff barriers imposed by industrialised nations on goods, especially manufactured goods from developing nations; a long pattern of declining relative terms of trade; wild fluctuations in prices of primary commodity exports; and a crushing foreign debt owed by poor nations.

What has been the developing nations' response?

Proposals from the Developing World

Less developed countries have protested against the unjust patterns of international trade for decades. At the Bandung Afro-Asian Conference in 1955 and at the 1964 UN Conference on Trade and Development, developing nations urged the wealthy nations to support trade patterns that were not so detrimental to them. But the affluent turned a deaf ear. In 1972 the American *Journal of Commerce* reported that Washington was ignoring all the reform proposals from poor nations. The *Journal* concluded: 'In other words, just about every major proposal put forth in the interests of protecting the LDCs from further deterioration in the terms of trade is drawing a negative reaction in Washington.'[52]

In 1974 developing nations introduced into the United Nations proposals for the formation of a New International Economic Order (NIEO). That same year the General Assembly adopted a 'Declaration and Action Programme' and a 'Charter of Economic Rights and Duties of States' for the NIEO. There were eight key proposals:[53]

1. *Prices of primary products and raw materials* The prices, the developing nations insisted, should increase immediately. Furthermore, they should be tied directly to the prices of the manufactured products which the poor nations must import from rich nations. A common fund should be set up which would be used to finance buffer stocks of twenty or thirty key commodities so that wild fluctuations in commodity prices could be ironed out.

2. *Tariffs and other barriers to trade* Developed countries should remove tariffs and other trade barriers to products from the developing nations.

3. *National sovereignty over national resources* Developing nations should have the 'right' to nationalise foreign holdings with fair compensations.

4. *Foreign aid* Rich nations should increase both emergency food aid and grants for long-term development. The UN should achieve its target of 0.7 per cent of GNP on official development assistance by the developed countries (see Table 12, p. 37).

5. *Industry* The developing world should increase its share of world manufactured-goods output from about 10 per cent in 1975 to 25 per cent by the year 2000.

6. *International debt* Debt should be rescheduled for many developing countries, and for the poorest it should be cancelled.

7. *Technology* Arrangements should be made for the transfer of technology from developed to developing countries – other than through multinational companies.

8. *International monetary arrangements* The poor nations should have a larger role in the International Monetary Fund and other international monetary arrangements which affect trade and development.

One should not accept these proposals simply because

Third World leaders made them. Indeed, some valid critisms of them have been made.[54] But, as Oxford economist Donald Hay has argued, the proposals merited careful, sympathetic attention.[55]

Little happened. Initially, the developed countries made it appear that they would grant some concessions. In practice, however, they have been exceptionally stingy with anything but palliative measures. Some of the proposals have been attempted half-heartedly (the commodity fund, for example). But most of them have either been ignored into oblivion or negotiated to death.[56]

Consider item seven. One of the ways for transferring technology and sharing resources was to be through agreements concerning the Law of the Sea. Under the sea lies a wealth of unclaimed resources. Because no nation can justly claim property rights to the oceans, the untapped wealth of the ocean floor seems to offer a chance for the Third World to gain without sacrifice from the wealthy nations. The seabed is a 'common heritage' of humankind whose riches should benefit all. However, the developing nations do not possess the sophisticated technology needed to mine the resources. Hence the possibility for the transfer of technology from rich to poor.

Negotiations began in 1973 and continued steadily until 1981. Then, at the last minute in 1981, when the final details were to be worked out and the treaty signed by all participating nations, the United States, under the direction of President Ronald Reagan, backed out. The reason given was that the administration feared the transfer of technology would jeopardise the economic advantage of US-based mining companies. Britain, too, rejected the treaty, being the only member of the Commonwealth to do so. The Law of the Sea, a mechanism that might have greatly assisted the poorer countries, was scuttled.[57]

A similar fate met the 1980 report of the Brandt commission. An international commission of leaders from both developed and less developed countries issued the report *North-South: A Program for Survival in 1980*.[58] The purpose of the report was to reopen the lines of communication between the rich nations of the North and the poor nations of the South. The report stressed the mutual interdependence of all countries of the globe. It emphasised that the wealthy countries could not expect peaceful international relations while over half of the globe struggles with poverty. It also emphasised that poor countries could not expect to develop without the support of their wealthy counterparts. The report encouraged co-operation instead of confrontation.

The Brandt report did lead to a potentially significant international summit of twenty-two world leaders in Cancun, Mexico, in October 1981. At Cancun, British Prime Minister Margaret Thatcher seemed impressed by an Indian proverb used by Indian Prime Minister Indira Gandhi to compare the economic problems of the West and India: 'I complained of having no shoes until I met a man with no feet.' But the industrialised nations made virtually no concessions, and little happened.

Abstract analysis of unjust trading patterns may seem dull for us in the comfortable North. But experiencing the effects can be sheer agony. In *What Do You Say to a Hungry World?* Stan Mooneyham tells the story of Juan Diaz, a coffee worker in El Salvador, a country which depends on coffee exports for a major share of its earnings.

He and three of his five daughters spend long, hard days in the coffee fields of Montenango. On a good day, Juan picks enough coffee to earn $1.44 [85p]; his daughters make a total of $3.35 [£2]. With $1.24 [75p] of these wages, Juan and his wife Paula are able to feed their family for one day. In bad times, Juan and his daughters make as little as $.56 [34p] a day – less than half the money they need just to eat.

At the end of the six-week coffee season, Juan does odd jobs around the hacienda – provided there is work to be done. He can earn about $.90 [55p] there for an eight-hour day. Paula Diaz supplements her husband's earnings by working in the market. When people have enough money to purchase the tomatoes, cabbages and other home-grown vegetables she sells, Paula can make about $.40 [24p] a day.

The hacienda provides a simple dwelling for the Diaz family, but no modern facilities. Candles are used for light, water has to be hauled from a well and furnishings consist of little more than a table and some chairs. Aside from a dress and shoes for each of the girls during the coffee season, the family has not been able to buy much else in the last five years. Whatever money doesn't go for food is spent for visits to the health clinic ($.40 [24p] each time), the high interest on bills at the company store, expenses for the children in school, and for the burial of Juan's father, who died last year.

'You know, I look forward to a better life for my children,' Juan says. 'I dream that if it is possible – if I can possibly afford it – my children will not follow in my footsteps, that they will break out of this terrible way of life. But the money problems we face every day blot out those dreams. I feel bad, nervous, I don't sleep nights worrying about how I'll get something for them to eat. I think and think but don't find any answers. I work hard; my wife and daughters do, too. We all do. But still we suffer. Why?'[59]

One big reason is that the present distribution of the benefits of international trade is fundamentally unjust. While their genesis was in the colonial period, the trade relations built up since then continue to afflict the LDCs. In chapters 7 to 9 we shall examine proposals for constructive change – in society at large, in the church, and in our personal lifestyles. For the present, it is enough to see that current trade patterns make it impossible to live in affluent nations without being involved in social structures that contain serious injustice and help keep millions of people hungry.

Destroying the Environment and the Poor

Economic life today, especially in industrialised societies, is producing such severe environmental pollution and degradation that the future for everyone – rich and poor alike – is dangerously threatened. We are destroying our air, forests, lands and water so rapidly that we face disaster in the next century unless we make major changes.

Since 1950, global economic growth has been massive. On average, the economic production of every decade in the last forty years equalled the total production of all human civilisation prior to 1950! In the same forty years, however, we have lost one-fifth of the world's topsoil, one-fifth of our tropical rainforests, and tens of thousands of plant and animal species.[60] Scientists warn that we are polluting the atmosphere so badly that global warming may drastically change the world's climate producing floods, drought and famine on a scale never seen before.

Always of course, the poor suffer the most. This is true in two ways. They already suffer from reduced food production, toxic wastes that the rich do not want in their neighbourhoods, unproductive land, and polluted rivers. Furthermore, unless we can redirect economic life in a way that dramatically reduces environmental decay, it will be impossible to expand economic growth enough in poor nations to enable them to enjoy a decent standard of living.

The affluent, of course, produce most of the pollution. One fourth of the world's people produce about 70 per cent of the carbon emissions, through their burning of fossil fuels.[61] Both in absolute numbers and per capita, the US is the worst.[62]

E. F. Schumacher puts it bluntly:

It is obvious that the world cannot afford the U.S.A. Nor can it afford Western Europe or Japan. . . . Think of it – one American drawing on resources that would sustain fifty Indians! . . . The poor don't do much damage; the modest people don't do much damage. Virtually all the damage is done by, say, 15 per cent. . . . The problem passengers on Space-Ship Earth are the first-class passengers and no one else.[63]

How are we destroying our air, land, water and forests?

Table 15   Carbon Emissions from Fossil Fuels (1987)

	(Tons Per Capita)
US	5.03
Canada	4.24
USSR	3.68
West Germany	2.98
UK	2.73
Japan	2.12
South Korea	1.14
Mexico	0.96
Brazil	0.38
India	0.19
Zaire	0.03

Source: State of the World 1990, *p. 19.*

The reality of global warming produced by 'greenhouse gases' has captured newspaper headlines around the world in the last few years. ('Greenhouse gases' such as carbon dioxide, methane, nitrous oxide, and chlorofluorocarbons [CFCs] hold heat in the lower atmosphere of the earth and thus slowly cause the temperature of the earth to rise.) In June 1988, the US National Aeronautics and Space Administration (NASA) released a study of global temperatures over the last century. The report indicated that there had been a gradual long-term warming – and that the four warmest years had all occurred in the 'eighties![64]

Half a dozen computer models have predicted even faster warming – from 2.5–5.5 degrees Celsius (4.5–9.9 degrees Fahrenheit) by the end of the next century.[65] If temperature increases of this order occur, what can be expected are conditions much worse than the heat, droughts and poor harvest experienced in central North America and China in 1988. Those were just a tiny forewarning of a wrenching future. Drastic, rapid changes on the earth's surface would confront our children with terrible new problems. Lester Brown, an internationally renowned specialist on food and environmental issues, says: 'Indeed, it can be compared with nuclear warfare for its potential to disrupt a wide range of human and natural systems, complicating the task of managing economies and coping with other problems. Irrigation works, settlement patterns and food production would be tragically disrupted by a rapid warming.'[66]

Meteorological models suggest that the summer growing season would be much warmer and drier in the North American agricultural heartland and in a large area of central Asia. These are two of the world's largest food-producing regions. Droughts and heat waves would cripple food production and threaten the world's food security. Widespread famine and starvation would probably occur.

Global warming could also put some of the land on which we live under water. As ocean water warms, it expands, increasing water volume. Melting of glaciers and ice caps at the poles would also result. Studies conclude that a temperature rise of 3 degrees Celsius by 2050 would raise the sea level by 50–100 centimetres. By the end of the century, sea level may be up by as much as 2 metres.[67]

Such an increase in sea level would cause floods in much of Asia, including India, China, and Bangladesh. Water would probably cover up to 18 per cent of Bangladesh, displacing more than 17 million people.[68] Coastal cities such as New York, New Orleans and Shanghai, as well as The Netherlands, would also be threatened by rising sea levels. The poor, of course, would find it most difficult to protect themselves from these new dangers.

In spite of this ghastly prospect, we keep adding carbon to the atmosphere at a dangerous rate. In 1988, we dumped 5.5 billion tons of carbon into the atmosphere through the burning of fossil fuels and another .4 to 2.5 billion tons through deforestation.[69] World Watch Institute's *State of the World 1990* suggests that by 2030 this figure must fall to 2 billion tons – i.e., approximately one-third of the present level and a mere one-eighth of current Western European levels. Their more realistic short-term goal for the 'nineties is a 10–20 per cent reduction.[70]

That is possible, but only if industrialised countries accept a major part of the burden. In order to reduce

poverty, developing nations are expanding their economies. Their carbon emissions are expanding rapidly and
will continue to do so for some time even with new, cleaner
technologies. Therefore the wealthy nations who are better
able to afford it must cut carbon emissions drastically so
that in the short run developing economies can expand to
feed the poor without destroying the global ecological
system. 'Unfortunately, no industrial nations have yet
proposed lowering carbon emissions by the needed 20–35
per cent in the next ten years.'[71] Only active, organised
citizens can make that happen.

I have focused on carbon emission. But that is not the
only problem in the atmosphere. We are depleting the
ozone layer in the upper atmosphere, which protects
the planet from ultraviolet rays. A 1988 NASA Ozone
Trends Panel reports documented dangerous ozone losses
around the globe, not just at the poles where depletion was
previously observed.[72] Decreased ozone means greater
exposure to ultraviolet rays which means increased rates
of skin cancer and eye cataracts. Thanks to modern
(expensive!) technology, cataracts are not a serious
problem in industrial countries. But the poor in the
developing world will simply go blind.

Deforestation.   Rapid deforestation represents another
serious problem. It increases flooding, deprives us of potential new medicines and contributes to carbon emissions.
The Food and Agricultural Organization (FAO) of the
United Nations has estimated that, in the early 'eighties,
11.3 million hectares of tropical forests were cleared
annually. But we replanted only 1.1 million hectares of
trees – one hectare of trees planted for every ten cleared.[73]

In the Third World, forests are cleared to provide for
cropland, fuelwood, cattle ranching and tropical hardwood
for industrial countries. Many people clear and farm forest
land because inequitable land distribution, population
growth and an emphasis on export cropping have left them
little land on which to grow their food. Small-scale culti-
vators, denied access to land for subsistence farming elsewhere, 'cause the final elimination of at least 5 million

hectares of forest each year, and gross degradation of another 10 million'.[74] Unfortunately, much of this land is ill-suited for farming and after a few growing seasons is abandoned for more recently cleared forest land, continuing a cycle of poverty, displacement and environmental abuse.

In 1984, Jose Lutzenberger, a Brazilian agronomist and engineer, testified before the US Congress about one such example:

> He told how thousands of poor peasants from agriculturally rich southern Brazil were pouring into Amazonian Rondonia because they had been dispossessed of their land, either by large landowners or by government plantations covering thousands of hectares, all bent on growing soybeans and other cash crops. The Rondonia Rush was needed precisely because the government refused to undertake real land reform and confront the plantation owners. . . . Thus the Polonoreste project – financed one-third by the World Bank – has become an infertile dumping ground for peasants who will never be able to earn a livelihood from poor land, leached of all nutrients, from which the tree cover has been removed. 'It is quite common to see settlers give up their clearing after their first meagre harvest. They have to make new clearings every year. Then, when the whole plot is cleared, they move on again.'[75]

Using live trees for fuel is sometimes a last resort in areas where dead wood and branches have disappeared. In 1980, the FAO found that nearly 1.2 billion people in developing countries were cutting wood for fuel faster than it was being replaced.[76] Boiling water becomes an unaffordable luxury. Where fuelwood is critically scarce, people often have no choice but to divert dried dung and crop residues from fields to cooking stoves. Tragically, that diminishes soil fertility and depresses crop yields.

The demand for cheap beef by wealthy North Americans and Europeans contributes to deforestation in Latin America. Currently, cattle ranchers destroy at least 2.5

million hectares a year of forest in Central America and Amazonia. They use most of this cleared land to raise beef for export to the developed world, particularly the US.[77] Some of the land cleared can support cattle. But much of the land is ill-suited for grazing for more than a few years. Deforested tropical soils often turn to brick after several years of cattle tramping on it. Since there are no trees to hold nutrients, the nutrients are washed and leached from the soil by rains, and the land becomes unable to support 'even the most aggressive pasture grasses'.[78]

Another significant drain on forests comes from the industrialised countries' demand for tropical hardwoods. In logging for commercially valuable trees (which sometimes account for less than 5 per cent of any given hectare), loggers often destroy between 30 and 60 per cent of unwanted trees.[79]

Deforestation produces floods and increased carbon emissions and also deprives us of important potential new medicines. When forests disappear, rainfall runs off much faster, causing soil erosion, immediate floods and subsequent drought (because the water quickly disappears rather than soaking into the soil). In India, a growing number of scientists now blame deforestation for the worsening of droughts and floods.[80]

Deforestation also contributes significantly to the carbon in the atmosphere. Estimates run from 0.4 billion to 2.6 billion tons of carbon per year.[81]

One half of US medicines come from genetic material of wild plants which are found mostly in tropical forests. We have scientifically examined only 1 per cent of the world's plant species to assess their potential beneficial use. But we are destroying them and their natural habitat at a ferocious pace. At current rates a quarter of the world's remaining tropical forests will disappear in the next twenty years.[82]

Misuse of the Land.   Topsoil is currently eroding more quickly than it forms on about 35 per cent of the world croplands.[83] Each year, irreversible desertification (at which point the land is unable to nourish crops or cattle) claims an estimated 6 million hectares. An additional 20 million hectares become so impoverished that farming or grazing them is unprofitable.[84] Overgrazing on rangelands, overcultivation of croplands, waterlogging and salinisation of irrigated lands are exacting a terrible toll.

Our abuse of the soil is probably partially responsible for a disturbing reversal of a long pattern of expanding grain production. Between 1950 and 1984 world grain harvests expanded 260 per cent.[85] Since then, however, there has been no significant increase. The 1989 estimate was only 1 per cent higher than 1984.[86] Meanwhile the world's population kept growing by 88 million a year. In per capita terms, grain production has fallen every year since 1984.

An understanding of how grain production was increased helps us see why production is now decreasing and why land degradation is so serious. Prior to 1950, most increased food output resulted from expanding the area cultivated. From 1950, however, the emphasis has been on increasing land productivity with new technology.[87] The use of fertiliser reduced the practice of crop rotation which served both to fertilise the soil *and* protect the soil from erosion. A study in Missouri in the 1930s showed soil erosion increased from 2.7 tons per acre annually when the land was in a corn-wheat-clover rotation to 19.7 tons per acre when the same land was continuously planted with corn. As the topsoil decreases, so does its productivity.

In the short run, however, reduced fertility of the land is often masked by advances in technology. 'Often the very practices that cause excessive erosion in the long run, such as the intensification of cropping patterns and the ploughing of marginal land, lead to short-term production gains, creating an illusion of progress and a false sense of security.[88] Decreasing grain production is a reminder that careful stewardship of our soil is imperative.

In the Third World, the problem is both poor land management and population pressure. Soil scientists S. A. El-Swaify and E. W. Dangler note that it is in those regions with high population density that 'farming of marginal hilly lands is a hazardous necessity. Ironically, it is also in those very regions where the greatest need exists to protect the rapidly diminishing or degrading soil resources.'[89] Frequently poor people are forced to farm marginal land because the most fertile land is used for export cropping.

> The heavy machinery, fertilizers, and pesticides of export agriculture degrade the fertile land, and overuse by the poor degrades the hillside land.[90]

Frequently such high density areas also lack firewood. Consequently natural fertilisers (such as dung and crop residues) are burned as fuel instead of being used as natural nutrients for the soil.

The final verdict? If we continue present patterns of land abuse, we will not be able to feed the world's growing population. Today we have .28 hectares per person in the world. By 2030, it will be only .19. That means one-third less land per person in forty years![91] Taking good care of our soil is a matter of life and death.

The poor, as always, suffer the most. They are most exposed to the vast array of environmental problems. They are the most likely to drink contaminated water and the most likely to farm marginal land. They certainly will bear the brunt of whatever convulsive changes global warming forces upon everyone.

One striking symbol of this vulnerability is the fact that they are most likely to live near and therefore suffer more from toxic wastes. It is not an accident that the environmental disaster in Bhopal, India, especially impacted the poor. Everywhere around the world, poverty forces many people to live dangerously close to smoke-belching factories and toxic wastes. A study in the US discovered that 'the poorer the neighborhood, and the darker the skin of its residents, the more likely it is to be near a toxic waste dump'.[92]

'The rich get richer and the poor get poisoned.'[93]

We face a painful choice. To maintain and expand our material abundance, we are polluting our air and water, and destroying our lands and forests. We simply cannot continue these present economic patterns, *and* reduce global poverty, *and* preserve a livable planet all at the same time. We could choose both justice for the poor and a livable planet – but only if we give up rampant materialism and make hard choices to reverse environmental destruction. Great efforts are being made by some EEC countries in this direction – notably The Netherlands, Denmark and West Germany. Britain woke up rather late to environmental issues, and will have to cut down sulphur dioxide emissions and other industrial pollution if it is to lose the label of the 'Dirty Man of Europe' – efforts which are now beginning to be made.

Food Consumption Patterns

Our eating patterns – a third area where we are caught in institutionalised sin – may seem to us personal and private. But they are tightly interlocked with complex economic structures, including national and international agricultural policies and the decisions of multinational corporations engaged in agribusiness.

Dr Georg Borgstrom, for many years an internationally known food specialist and professor of food science and human nutrition at Michigan State University, has pointedly underscored the way North Americans consume a disproportionate share of the world's supply of food. He has insisted that we ought to measure the world population not merely in terms of people but also in terms of the total 'feeding burden' of the globe. In a fascinating paper presented in 1974 he pointed out that, if we count livestock as well as people, the earth already had in 1974 not 4 billion but 19 billion 'population equivalents', that is, inhabitants. (He computed the amount of protein required by the livestock and calculated how many people that protein would feed.)[94] So the feeding burden of the United States was not 210 million people in 1974. Rather, the 'U.S. total feeding burden in biological terms was consequently 1.6 billion'.[95]

Though India had three times as many people as the United States, it had far less livestock. Counting livestock, India had only 1.2 billion 'population equivalents'. So who had the sacred cows?

Table 16 Food Exports and Imports (in millions of US dollars)

Year	Food Exports from Developed World to Developing World	Food Imports by Developed World from Developing World	Net Loss of Food by Poor Countries
1970	4,912	10,974	6,062
1975	16,058	20,807	4,749
1984	33,186	38,063	4,877
1985	28,823	36,450	7,627
1986	27,367	42,282	14,915

Source: United Nations, Handbook of International Trade and Development Statistics, *1989, A-8-11.*
Note: Centrally planned economies are not included.

Another indication that something is wrong comes from a review of trade statistics on food imports. Rich countries have regularly imported more food from poor nations than they have exported to them. Poor nations have been feeding the affluent minority. Table 16 shows that in 1986 the developed nations exported $27,367 million worth of food to poor nations; but they imported $42,282 million worth of food. Poor nations sent rich nations $14,915 million more food than they received!

Data about the world fish catch tell the same story. In 1973 the world fish catch was 65.7 million tons. Had the catch been divided evenly, each person in the world would have received thirty-four pounds.[96] Not surprisingly, it was not so divided. The developed nations, with a quarter of the world's people, took about three-quarters of the year's fish catch. Peru has the largest anchovy fisheries in the world, but little of the anchovy protein goes to feed the millions of poor Peruvians; most of it fattens livestock in the United States and Europe. The story with tuna is similar. Professor Borgstrom has pointed out that at one point two-thirds of the total world tuna catch ended up in the United States. One-third of that tuna went for catfood![97] Obviously North Americans do not import so much food because they need it, but because they want it and have enough money to pay for it.

Why is it that countries with a less-than-adequate food supply for their own people willingly send us more food than they get in return? The obvious answer is that food exports by poor nations pay for their imports of high technology, oil, and luxury goods. But poor people are less interested in those things than in food to feed their families. So we still face the question. Why does food needed to end starvation and malnutrition in poor nations get exported to rich nations?

The answer is double-pronged. The first prong is purely economic: Much food grown or gathered in developing nations is not available to their own poor people simply because the poor cannot afford it. They have no land on which to grow their own crops to sell. Nor can they find productive work in the squalid, overpopulated cities.

The second prong of the answer is historical, once again stretching back to the colonial era.[98] In those days export crops were actively promoted – to the detriment of food production for local consumption. Plantations were planned to produce export crops. Local people, frequently dispossessed of their land, were turned into either slaves or poorly paid agricultural workers. Those who managed to keep some land were 'encouraged' to produce foodstuffs desired in the mother countries. Growing food for the 'mother' country was seen as the colony's highest priority. John Stuart Mill, the respected nineteenth-century British economist, 'reasoned that colonies should not be thought of as civilisations or countries at all but as "agricultural establishments" whose sole purpose was to supply the "larger community to which they belong"'.[99]

Colonial days have ended for the most part, but the vestiges remain. The plantations created have not willingly been returned to the descendants of their original owners. New owners (whether the local élite or multinational corporations) of the same large holdings still look to the industrialised countries as their trading partners since the peasant community has little to offer in the way of goods desired by the landowner. Owners of large landholdings could grow beans, corn or rice for the local population, but the local people cannot pay because they do not have the assets to produce anything marketable. So instead the owners look to rich countries for their markets. They send us cotton, beef, coffee, bananas or other agricultural products, and we send them the goods they desire in return. As time goes on, the landowners and other persons of wealth look increasingly to the developed world for economic partnership. Besides withholding land from the peasant community, this relationship leads to the introduction of labour-saving farm technology. Fewer workers are needed to work the large estates, and people are left unemployed with nowhere else to go. In such a way the structures favour the wealthy and oppress the poor.

It is perhaps in this context that the divine wisdom of the jubilee principle is best understood. The jubilee calls for redistribution of society's pool of productive assets so that everyone has the resources to earn their own way. When members of a society lose their assets, by whatever means, it is difficult for them to participate in economic activity. People with no assets can produce no goods. With no goods to trade, they cannot purchase necessities.

In almost all today's poor nations the process of displacing people from the land began many years ago and has continued to the present. Seldom has anything like the jubilee occurred, and so the problems have grown. And the longer they grow, the more impossible they become.

Why are we so perplexed by the existence of hunger and poverty today? Is it really any wonder? People were impoverished a long time ago, and steps have never been taken to right the initial injustices or to restore productive capabilities to the poor. This is why developed countries import far more food from poor nations than they send back to them. Injustice has become deeply embedded in national and international economic and social life.

Consider export agriculture in Central America. Today, the bulk of the staple foods (beans, corn, rice) eaten by the poor in Central America are grown by small farmers on marginal lands. At the same time, as a recent study shows, 'virtually all the fertile, flat agricultural lands in the region [are] used for export oriented crops'.[100]

The story of beef since the 1950s helps one understand.[101] In the 1950s, almost all beef slaughtered in Central America was eaten locally. Then the first beef-packing plant approved by the US Department of Agriculture (USDA) was built in 1957. By the late 1970s, three-quarters of Central America's beef was exported.[102] By 1978, Central America provided the US with 250 million pounds of beef a year. US-backed development programmes built roads, and provided credit to facilitate the expansion of beef exports. From 1960–80, over a half of all the loans made by the World Bank and the Inter-American Development Bank for agriculture and rural development in Central America went to promote the production of beef for export.[103]

Wealthy élites made great profits. But large numbers of poor farmers growing basic foodstuffs were pushed off the land as the ranchers demanded more and more grazing land to grow beef for export. In El Salvador, before the first USDA-approved beef-packing plant was opened, 29 per cent of rural households were landless. By 1980, a half of all El Salvador's beef was going to the US. And 65 per cent of the rural households were landless.[104] The poor protested, but the ranchers succeeded in painting the peasant activists as communists. The national security forces trained by the US often used repressive tactics including torture and murder to repress peasant protesters. 'Local ranchers in this way got free eviction forces, armed and trained at US taxpayers' expense.'[105]

I do not mean to suggest that Central America should not export any beef. It does have a competitive advantage over many areas in producing grass-fed beef. With different policies it might have been possible to expand beef exports in a way that did not oppress the poor or destroy the environment (vast tropical forests were burned to provide the new pasture lands). But it was not done that way.

Instead, the poor suffered to produce cheap hamburgers

for American consumers. Since the 1960s, beef consumption within Central America has declined 20 per cent. The poor cannot compete with us. A study by the Pan American Health Organization showed that between 1969 and 1975 malnutrition rose by 67 per cent among children five years and under. In 1988, about seven times as many children per thousand died by the age of five in most Central American countries as in the United States.[106] You don't need communists to tell you that is a bad deal.

Not all the examples come from Latin America. In 1988, in the Philippines, seventy-three of one thousand infants died before the age of five, and forty-four before the age of one. Between 1977 and 1987, 50 per cent of the urban population and 64 per cent of the rural population was below the absolute poverty level.[107]

Again the tragic story goes back to colonial days. Before the Spanish conquerors in the Philippines arrived in the early 1600s, local villages owned land co-operatively. But the Spanish demand for surplus crops for taxes allowed the better-off Filipinos who collected the taxes for the Spanish colonialists to amass larger and larger holdings. After the United States replaced Spain in 1898, export cropping (and land concentration) increased still further. After 1960 export cropping grew even faster, as American pineapple producers moved from Hawaii to the Philippines to take advantage of cheaper wages. (They saved 47 per cent in production costs.) From 1960 to 1980 the amount of land devoted to export crops increased from 15 to 30 per cent.

The government of President Ferdinand Marcos promoted a national development policy based on export crops by ruthlessly suppressing movements of workers who pressed for higher wages or land reform. (The average wage for a sugar-cane labourer working thirteen to fourteen hours a day was $7.00 or £4.25 a week.) Both Amnesty International and the International Commission of Jurists documented the existence of thousands of political prisoners. Electric-shock torture, water torture, extended solitary confinement and beatings were widespread. Meanwhile, American military aid to Marcos continued.[108]

In February 1986, a non-violent revolution overthrew Marcos.[109] Hope surged through the Philippines. President Cory Aquino promised both democracy and justice for the poor. Unfortunately, there has been very little land reform and the majority of the people continue to live in poverty.

Who is responsible for the children dying in Central America or the Philippines? The wealthy national élites who want to increase their affluence? The American companies that work closely with the local élite? The Americans who eat the beef needed by hungry children in Central America?

Once again we dare not make the simplistic assumption that if we stop eating food imported from the poor nations, hungry children there will promptly enjoy it. Ending all food imports is not the answer. What *is* needed is the economic empowerment of the poor masses so that they can be productive and earn a decent living. Chapter 9 examines some of the ways we can promote such changes. My purpose here is simply to show that our eating patterns are interlocked with destructive social and economic structures that leave millions hungry and starving.

Multinationals in Developing Countries

Multinational corporations (MNCs) are children of the affluent North. Most of them began years ago as small, localised firms. Slowly, they expanded into sprawling corporations. For the most part their growth has been gradual and they have evolved alongside the economy as a whole. Consequently the developed world, although at times exasperated at the apparent indifference of large corporations to wider social goals, has learned, at least to a degree, to work constructively with them.

After World War 2 these big corporations moved in droves to set up overseas operations. Most of their activity went to other developed countries, but increasingly they moved into less developed countries as well. Development economist Michael Todaro notes that in 1962 private investment in these countries was $2.4 billion. By the mid-seventies it was around $9 billion[110] and by 1985 over $13 billion.[111] By a different calculation the book value of foreign investment in non-OPEC developing countries in 1967 was about $21 billion; by 1975 the figure had increased to around $44 billion.[112] Unfortunately, serious problems can arise when a large technologically advanced, managerially sophisticated firm, whose goal is to create profit for shareholders back home, goes to do business in a materially poor, technologically less sophisticated country.

Positive arguments can be made for MNCs. Their proponents view them as a major engine of economic development and growth in developing nations. It is argued that MNCs help in a number of ways: (1) by providing access to scarce capital resources; (2) by increasing the flow of foreign exchange; (3) by providing developing governments with healthy businesses from which to generate the tax revenues needed for development projects; and (4) by introducing technology, and training workers in technical and managerial skills.[113]

On paper the possibilities look promising. If the developing nations were equally powerful bargaining and trading partners, this might work. Unfortunately, increasing evidence shows that MNCs also have a negative impact counterproductive to the true progress and development of poor nations.

This should really not surprise people with a biblical view of sin. Powerful agents regularly dominate and take advantage of weaker ones. Interested primarily if not exclusively in profits for themselves, MNCs took advantage of the developing countries they courted.

We often overlook the extent of their power. The two largest MNCs have gross sales that are greater than the GNPs of all but the five largest developing nations. The six largest MNCs have combined sales greater than the total GNP of countries like Canada, Sweden or Switzerland. In 1985, 159 MNCs each had gross sales of more than $5 billion. Of Africa's 37 countries, 27 had total GNPs of less than $5 billion.

As development economist Professor Todaro points out,

this kind of power results from and increases oligopolistic market positions. By manipulating prices and profits, dominating new technologies and restricting potential competition, they avoid the qualification of their power that a freer market would impose.[114] Anyone concerned with the dangers of centralised power should be concerned with the way huge MNCs have concentrated economic and political power.[115]

What is the case against MNCs? One analyst answers the question this way: 'If we take as the development priority the requirement that minimum basic needs in food, shelter, health, water and education must be met early in the development process, then the contribution of the multinationals based on the record is almost certain to be negative.'[116] In evaluating this claim, three dimensions are important: economic effects, political effects and ideological effects.

First, *the economic effects*. Oxford economist Donald Hay outlined three problems in his paper at the International Consultation on Simple Lifestyle sponsored by the World Evangelical Fellowship and the Lausanne Committee for World Evangelization. First, MNCs do not really contribute the amount of capital they usually profess to.[117] Instead they borrow heavily from the banks in host countries, thereby reducing the funds available to local entrepreneurs and diminishing the level of indigenous business involvement. Second, MNCs are naturally more concerned about their own profit than the welfare of the host countries. This sometimes results, for example, in the shutting down of an entire subsidiary operation, an action that is devastating in impact on a small, poor nation while only marginally significant for the MNC. MNCs may also artificially vary their profit picture to avoid local taxes by selling their finished product to the parent company at below-market prices. A third problem Hay finds is that MNCs frequently promote 'the wrong sort of development' in developing nations. He argues that MNCs usually produce highly differentiated products for the wealthy instead of necessities for the poor. They also bring along capital-intensive, labour-saving technology inappropriate for poor countries with vast numbers of unemployed. By so doing, MNCs reinforce the dualistic structures that keep the majority in poverty and a minority in the mainstream of developed world economics.[118]

On *the political side*, MNCs may work to ensure political stability even though political change may be essential for widespread social and economic development. MNCs are often not interested in the basic needs of the poor, but rather in ensuring stable markets so that profits are not jeopardised.[119] As a result MNCs all too often end up staunchly supporting oppressive military regimes that are not interested in the basic needs of the poor.

In addition, MNCs have built up a strong bargaining position both because of their size and the fact that over the years developing countries have become increasingly more dependent on their presence. By threatening to leave and thereby throwing a dependent economy into chaos, MNCs can often extort one-sided agreements on such issues as tax concessions, profit-repatriation limits, indigenous training requirements, and so on. Once MNCs are established, they become pressure groups 'lobbying' for preferred treatment for foreign firms. They can divert government spending away from development projects for the poor and towards expenditures on 'roads, harbors, [and] subsidies for high technology, to develop the infrastructure to support profitable private investment'.[120]

Finally, *ideological issues*. By default, MNCs happen to be on the cutting edge of First World contact with the people of Third World nations. MNCs thus communicate to a poverty-stricken world what life is like in affluent nations. But not only do they impress on the poor how affluent Northerners live; they also encourage them, through lavish advertising campaigns, to try and live the same way.

The result is that many poor people are enticed into spending a disproportionate share of their incomes on goods that do them no good. Soft drinks are an example of unnecessary but frequently purchased goods.[121] Even more outrageous are the aggressive advertising campaigns of US tobacco companies in poor nations. They seduce the poor into destroying their lungs with US cigarettes.

Perhaps the most well-known and pernicious case involves the Nestlé Corporation and its persistence in marketing powdered milk for babies to Third World women who were better off nursing their children. Company representatives were dressed to look like nurses and recommended to mothers that they feed their infants powdered milk. Nestlé routinely handed out free samples, frequently by donating supplies to hospital maternity wards. (The use of bottled milk can cause a mother's milk to dry up, rendering her incapable of nursing even if she wanted.) Parents were then forced to buy milk powder. They were often unable to read the instructions, lacked access to sanitary water with which to mix it, or overdiluted it in order to make it last longer.

Prepared improperly, powdered milk can lack the nutrition babies require; and even under the best of circumstances, it lacks the immunological protection breast milk provides.[122] Frequently the result is 'Bottle Baby Disease', severe malnutrition, and diarrhoea. In 1990, UNICEF reported that bottle-fed infants are much more likely to get sick and are as much as twenty-five times more likely to die in childhood than infants exclusively breast-fed for the first six months of life.[123]

Promotion like that of Nestlé has drastically reduced the number of breast-fed babies in the Third World. In its 1982–3 report UNICEF noted that the percentage of breast-fed infants in Brazil declined from 96 per cent in 1940 to 40 per cent in 1974. In Chile it fell from 95 per cent in 1955 to 20 per cent in 1982–3.[124] In 1990, UNICEF reported that breast-feeding has continued to decline. The World Health Organization has estimated that the promotion of breast-feeding alone could reduce diarrhoea mortality in the first six months of life by 10 per cent.[125]

While an international boycott of Nestlé ended in 1984 after Nestlé agreed to abide by the World Health Organization's Code of Marketing for Breast-Milk Substitutes, the boycott was renewed in October 1989 after it was discovered that Nestlé has continued to donate powdered milk to hospitals and maternity clinics for distribution to new mothers.[126]

In a moment of candour, H. W. Walter, chairman of the board of International Flavors and Fragrances, put it bluntly:

> How often we see in developing countries that the poorer the economic outlook, the more important the small luxury of a flavored soft drink or smoke. . . . To the dismay of many would-be benefactors, the poorer the malnourished are, the more likely they are to spend a disproportionate amount of whatever they have on some luxury rather than on what they need. . . . Observe, study, learn. . . . We try to do it at IFF. It seems to pay off for us. Perhaps it will for you.[127]

Development economist Todaro sums up the ideological argument: 'MNCs typically produce *inappropriate products* (those demanded by a small minority of the population), stimulate *inappropriate consumption patterns* through advertising and their monopolistic market power, and do this all with *inappropriate* (capital-intensive) *technologies of production*.'[128] The judgment of Oxford economist Donald Hay is that 'multinational companies, themselves the creations of developed countries, are on balance detrimental to less developed countries'.[129]

I do not know if Hay is correct. A careful, comprehensive judgment on whether MNCs finally do more harm than good is beyond my technical competence and the space requirements of this book. But we do not need to settle that vast, technical question in order to see one fact clearly: specific MNCs do inflict significant damage on developing nations.

Once again we must ask who is at fault? Is it the host governments, for letting in multinationals? Is it the MNCs, for not taking a more charitable stance towards the poor? Is it the people in the developed world, for unknowingly supportng MNCs by purchasing their products or owning their stock? The answer is, all three. All three share some responsibility for the negative impact of MNCs on developing countries.

We are all implicated in structural evil. International trade patterns are unjust. Current patterns of economic life severely threaten the world environment and the long-term development opportunities of the Third World. Food consumption patterns are interlocked with past and present injustices that have never been rectified. And multinational corporations often hinder rather than promote meaningful development in less developed nations. Every person in developed countries is involved in these structural injustices. Unless you have retreated to some isolated valley and grow or make everything you use, you participate in unjust structures which contribute directly to the desperate poverty of over a billion suffering neighbours.

We cannot, of course, conclude that international trade or investment by multinational corporations in poor countries is necessarily immoral. Nor would the economies of the developed world be destroyed if present injustices in the system were corrected. The proper conclusion is that injustice has become deeply embedded in some of our fundamental economic institutions. Biblical Christians – precisely to the extent that they are faithful to Scripture – will dare to call such structures sinful.

The reader without a degree in economics probably wishes international economics were less complex or that faithful discipleship in our time had less to do with such a complicated subject. But former UN Secretary-General Dag Hammarskjöld was right: 'In our era, the road to holiness necessarily passes through the world of action.'[130] To give the cup of cold water effectively in the Age of Hunger frequently requires some understanding of international economic and political structures. The story of bananas helps clarify these complex issues.

The Story of Bananas

On April 10th, 1975, North Americans learned that United Brands, one of three huge US companies that grow and import bananas, had arranged to pay $2.5 million (only $1.25 million was actually paid) in bribes to top government officials in Honduras. Why? To persuade them to impose an export tax on bananas that was less than half of what Honduras had requested.[131] In order to increase profits for a US company and to lower banana prices, the Honduran government agreed, for a bribe, to cut drastically the export tax, even though the money was desperately needed in Honduras.

The story actually began in March 1974. Several banana-producing countries in Central America agreed to join together to demand a one-dollar tax on every case of bananas exported. Why? Banana prices for producers had not increased in the previous twenty inflation-ridden years. But the costs for manufactured goods had constantly escalated. As a result the real purchasing power of exported bananas had declined by 60 per cent. At least half the export income for Honduras and Panama came from bananas. No wonder they were poor.

What did the banana companies do when the exporting countries demanded a one-dollar tax on bananas? They adamantly refused to pay. Since three large companies (United Brands, Castle and Cooke, and Del Monte) controlled 90 per cent of the marketing and distribution of bananas, they had powerful leverage. In Panama the fruit company abruptly stopped cutting bananas. In Honduras the banana company allowed 145,000 crates to rot at the docks. One after another the poor countries gave in. Costa Rica finally settled for twenty-five cents a crate; Panama, for thirty-five cents; Honduras, thanks to the large bribe, eventually agreed to a thirty-cent tax.[132]

One can easily understand why a UN fact-finding commission in 1975 concluded, 'The banana-producing countries with very much less income are subsidizing the consumption of the fruit, and consequently the development of the more industrialized countries.'[133]

Why don't the masses of poor people demand change? They do. But too often they have little power. For much of the last thirty years, dictators representing tiny, wealthy élites working closely with American business interests ruled many Latin-American countries.

The history of Guatemala, also a producer of bananas for United Brands, shows why change is difficult. In 1954 the CIA helped overthrow a democratically elected government in Guatemala. Why? Because it had initiated a modest programme of agricultural reform that seemed to threaten unused land owned by the United Fruit Company (the former name of United Brands). The US Secretary of State in 1954 was John Foster Dulles. His law firm had written the company's agreements with Guatemala in 1930 and 1936. The CIA director was Allen Dulles, brother of the Secretary of State and previous president of United Fruit Company. The assistant Secretary of State was a major shareholder in United Fruit Company.[134] In Guatemala and elsewhere change is difficult because US companies work closely with wealthy, local élites to protect their mutual economic interests.

In the past, the world knew little about the injustice in Central America. That began to change in the early 1980s. With radical guerrilla movements gaining ground in El Salvador and Guatemala, President Reagan launched a vigorous military response. Front-page headlines on Central America became a regular feature of the newspapers. In 1981 Reagan authorised secret CIA military support for right-wing guerrillas attacking the new socialist government of Nicaragua. The stated goal was to stop alleged arms shipments from the Soviet Union and Cuba through Nicaragua to the guerrillas in El Salvador.[135] Later, however, when the contra army numbered over ten thousand fighters and the US offered no convincing evidence of any substantial arms flow to El Salvador, the administration admitted that it had embarked on an effort to 'overthrow' the Sandinista government and make it 'say Uncle'. The result has been enormous suffering and massacre in Nicaragua. In its brief to the World Court, Nicaragua claimed that contra violence had killed 2,600 persons; maimed, raped or kidnapped 5,500; and displaced 150,000 civilians.[136]

The civil wars that raged in Central America in the 'eighties undoubtedly had many roots.[137] Certainly the fact that some of the guerrilla movements turned in despair to Marxist countries for support and supplies complicated the problems. Soviet shipments of arms must be condemned. One of the last things we need is another ghastly Marxist-Leninist experiment in the world. But the US attempt in the 'eighties to solve the problems primarily via a military response was both immoral and foolish. The root causes of the violence and war were the long-standing economic injustice and desperate poverty of the masses of poor people in the region. If seven times as many of your children per thousand are dying from malnutrition as in the U.S., you do not need Marxist-Leninists to tell you something needs to change.[138]

Tragically there will always be those eager to provide plausible rationalisations. Andrew M. Greeley, a prominent sociologist at the University of Chicago, has mocked those who try to make people in the industrialised North feel guilty about their economic relationships with the developing nations: 'Well, let us suppose that our guilt finally becomes too much to bear and we decide to reform. . . . We inform the fruit orchards in Central America that we can dispense with bananas in our diets. . . . Their joy will hardly be noticed as massive unemployment and depression sweep those countries.'[139]

One wonders if Greeley is naïve or perverse. The point is not – and Greeley surely knows this – that we should stop importing bananas. It is rather that multinational firms and huge agribusinesses, in complicity with all the buyers of bananas in the developed world, are engaged in a sordid business which keeps the poor from escaping their poverty trap. The point is further that we should encourage the reorganisation of economic structures and promote programmes here and in Central America that will help poor people in producing countries share in the benefits of agricultural production and trade.

The example of bananas shows how all of us are involved in unjust international economic structures. The words of the apostle James seem to speak directly to our situation.

> Come now, you rich, weep and howl for the miseries that are coming upon you. . . . Your gold and silver have rusted, and their rust will be evidence against you. . . . Behold, the wages of the labourers who mowed your fields, which you kept back by fraud, cry out; and the cries of the harvesters have reached the ears of the Lord of hosts. You have lived on the earth in luxury and in pleasure; you have fattened your hearts in a day of slaughter (Jas. 5:1–5).

The Repentance of Zacchaeus

What should be our response, brothers and sisters? For biblical Christians the only possible response to sin is repentance. Unconsciously, to at least some degree, we have become entangled in a complex web of institutionalised sin. Thank God we can repent. God is merciful. He forgives. But only if we repent. And biblical repentance involves more than a hasty tear and a weekly prayer of confession. Biblical repentance involves conversion. It involves a whole new lifestyle. The One who stands ready to forgive us for our sinful involvement in terrible economic injustice offers us his grace to begin living a radically new lifestyle of identification with the poor and oppressed.

Sin is not just an inconvenience or a tragedy for our neighbours. It is a damnable outrage against the Almighty Lord of the universe. If God's Word is true, then all of us who dwell in affluent nations are trapped in sin. We have profited from systematic injustice – sometimes only half knowing, sometimes only half caring, and always half hoping not to know. We are guilty of an outrageous offence against God and neighbour.

But that is not God's last word to us. If it were, honest acknowledgment of our involvement would be almost impossible. If there were no hope of forgiveness, admission of our sinful complicity in evil of this magnitude would be an act of despair.[140] But there is hope. The One who writes our indictment is the One who died for us sinners.

John Newton was captain of a slave ship in the eighteenth century. A brutal, callous, man, he played a central role in a system which fed thousands to the sharks and delivered millions to a living death. But eventually, after he gave up his career as captain, he saw his sin and repented. His familiar hymn overflows with joy and gratitude for God's acceptance and forgiveness.

> Amazing grace! How sweet the sound,
> that saved a wretch like me;
> I once was lost, but now am found,
> was blind but now I see.
> 'Twas grace that taught my heart to fear,
> and grace my fears relieved;
> How precious did that grace appear
> the hour I first believed.

John Newton became a founding member of a society for the abolition of slavery. The church which he pastored, St Mary Woolnoth in the City of London, was a meeting place for abolitionists. William Wilberforce frequently came to him for spiritual counsel. Newton delivered impassioned sermons against the slave trade, convincing many people of its evil. He campaigned against the slave trade until he died in the year of its abolition, 1807.

We are participants in a system that dooms even more people to agony and death. If we have eyes to see, God's grace will also teach our hearts to fear and tremble, and then also to rest and trust.

But only if we repent. Repentance is not coming forward at the close of a service. It is not repeating a spiritual law. It is not mumbling a liturgical confession. All of these things may help. But they are no substitute for the kind of deep inner anguish that leads to a new way of living.

Biblical repentance entails conversion; literally the word means 'turning around'. The Greek word *metanoia*, as Luther insisted so vigorously, means a total change of mind. The New Testament links repentance to a transformed style of living. Sensing the hypocrisy of the Pharisees who came seeking baptism, John the Baptist denounced them as a brood of vipers. 'Bear fruit that befits repentance', he demanded (Matt. 3:8). Paul told King Agrippa that wherever he preached, he called on people to 'repent and turn to God and perform deeds worthy of . . . repentance' (Acts 26:20).

Zacchaeus should be our model. As a greedy Roman tax collector, Zacchaeus was enmeshed in sinful economic structures. But he never supposed that he could come to Jesus and still continue enjoying all the economic benefits of that systematic evil. Coming to Jesus meant repenting of his complicity in social injustice. It meant publicly giving reparations. And it meant a whole new lifestyle.

What might genuine, biblical repentance mean for affluent Christians entangled in their society's sinful structures? And would not deep joy flow from obedient sharing that empowered others? Part 3 examines these questions.

Study Questions

1. What is the difference between personal sin and social sin?

2. How would you respond to someone who rejected the idea of structural evil?

3. Were you convinced that present international economic structures involve us all in structural evil? How, specifically, does that happen?

4. How do tariffs and import quotas of industrialised countries hurt the poor? And how are they related to the debt crisis?

5. What are the connections between environmental pollution and poverty?

6. What are the advantages and disadvantages of multi-national corporations in reducing poverty?

7. How does the original setting of 'Amazing Grace' parallel the problems described here?

8. What were your strongest emotions as you read this chapter? Why?

Part 3

Implementation

Where should we change?

A prominent Washington think tank once assembled a large cross-section of distinguished religious leaders to discuss the problems of world hunger. The conferees expressed deep concern. They called for significant structural change. But their words rang hollow. They were meeting at an expensive, exclusive resort in Colorado!

Simpler personal lifestyles are essential. But personal change is insufficient. A friend of mine has forsaken the city for a rural community. He grows almost all his own food, lives simply and places few demands on the poor of the earth. This person has considerable speaking and writing talents which could promote change in church and society, but unfortunately he uses them less than he might because of the time absorbed by his 'simple' lifestyle.

We need to change at three levels. Simple personal lifestyles are crucial to symbolise, validate and facilitate our concern for the hungry. The church must change so that its common life presents a new model for a divided world. Finally, the structures of secular society, both here and abroad, require revision.

7

THE GRADUATED TITHE AND OTHER MODEST PROPOSALS: TOWARDS A SIMPLER LIFESTYLE

Before God and a million hungry neighbors, we must rethink our values regarding our present standard of living and promote more just acquisition and distribution of the world's resources[1] (The Chicago Declaration of Evangelical Social Concern [1973]).

Those of us who live in affluent circumstances accept our duty to develop a simple life-style in order to contribute more generously to both relief and evangelism[2] (Lausanne Covenant [1974]).

The rich must live more simply that the poor may simply live[3] (Dr Charles Birch [1975]).

I once heard a politician argue that his constituents were so nearly poor that they simply could not afford to pay another penny in taxes. He cited a letter from an irate voter as proof. This woman had written to him announcing that her family could not possibly pay any more taxes. Why, she said, they already paid the government income taxes and VAT – and besides that they bought licences for their two cars, caravan, houseboat and motorboat!

We affluent Westerners have a problem. We actually believe that we can just barely get along on the fifteen, twenty, or twenty-five thousand pounds a year that we make. We are in an incredible rat race. When our income goes up by another £500, we convince ourselves that we need about that much more to live – comfortably.

The politician was not joking. He agreed that more taxes would have threatened his constituent with poverty and destitution.

How can we escape this delusion? How will we respond to the desperate plight of the world's poor? Over thirty-five thousand children died today because of inadequate food and easily preventable diseases. Over a billion people live in desperate poverty. Another two billion are poor. The problem, we know, is that the world's resources are not fairly shared. North Americans and Western Europeans live on an affluent island amid a sea of poverty-stricken people.

How will we respond to this gross inequality? Former President Richard Nixon enunciated one response in a speech on June 13th, 1973 to the American nation: 'I have made this basic decision: in allocating the products of America's farms between markets abroad and those in the United States, we must put the American consumer first.'[4] Such a statement may be good politics, but it certainly is not good theology.

But how much should we give? Should we congratulate the Christian millionaire who tithes faithfully?

John Wesley gave a startling answer. One of his frequently repeated sermons was on Matthew 6:19–23 ('Lay not up for yourselves treasures upon earth . . .' AV).[5] Christians, Wesley said, should give away all but 'the plain necessaries of life' – that is, plain, wholesome food, clean clothes and enough to carry on one's business. One should earn what one can, justly and honestly. Capital need not be given away. But Wesley wanted all income given to the poor after bare necessities were met. Unfortunately, Wesley discovered, not one person in five hundred in any 'Christian city' obeys Jesus's command. But that simply demonstrates that most professed believers are 'living men but dead Christians'. Any 'Christian' who takes for himself anything more than the 'plain necessaries of life', Wesley insisted, 'lives in an open, habitual denial of the Lord'. He has 'gained riches and hell-fire!'[6]

Wesley lived what he preached. Sales of his books often

earned him fourteen hundred pounds annually, but he spent only thirty pounds on himself. The rest he gave away. He always wore inexpensive clothes and dined on simple food. 'If I leave behind me ten pounds,' he once wrote, 'you and all mankind bear witness against me that I lived and died a thief and a robber.'[7]

One need not agree with Wesley's every word to see that he was struggling to follow the biblical summons to share with the needy. How much should we give? Knowing that God disapproves of great extremes of wealth and poverty, we should give until our lives truly reflect the principles of Leviticus 25 and 2 Corinthians 8. Surely Paul's advice to the Corinthians applies even more forcefully to Christians today in the Northern Hemisphere: 'I do not mean that others should be eased and you burdened, but that as a matter of equality your abundance at the present time should supply their want . . . that there may be equality' (2 Cor. 8:13–14).

The God of the Affluent North and Its Prophet

Why are we so unconcerned, so slow to care? We learn one reason from the story of the rich young ruler. When he asked Jesus how to obtain eternal life, Jesus told him to sell his goods and give to the poor. But the man went away sad because he had great possessions. Now, as we are usually told, the point of the story is that if we want to follow Christ, he alone must be at the centre of our affections and plans. Whether the idol be riches, fame, status, academic distinction or membership in some in-group, we must be willing to abandon it for Christ's sake. Riches just happened to be this young man's idol. Jesus then is not commanding us to sell all our possessions. He is only demanding total submission to himself. This interpretation is both unquestionably true and unquestionably inadequate. To say no more is to miss the fact that wealth and possessions are the most common idols for us rich citizens of industrialised nations. Jesus, I suspect, meant it when he added, '"Truly, I say to you, it will be hard for a rich man to

enter the kingdom of heaven. Again I tell you, it is easier
for a camel to go through the eye of a needle than for a rich
man to enter the kingdom of God"' (Matt. 19:23–4).

We have become ensnared by unprecedented material
luxury. Advertising constantly convinces us that we really
need one unnecessary luxury after another. The standard
of living is the god of twentieth-century affluent nations,
and the adman is their prophet.

We all know how subtle the materialistic temptations are
and how convincing the rationalisations. Only by God's
grace and with great effort can we escape the shower of
luxuries which has almost suffocated our Christian compassion. All of us face this problem. Some years ago I spent
about fifty dollars on an extra suit. That's not much, of
course. Besides, I persuaded myself, it was a wise investment (thanks to the 75 per cent discount). But that
money would have fed a starving child in India for about a
year. In all honesty we have to ask ourselves: dare we care
at all about current fashions if that means reducing our
ability to help hungry neighbours? Dare we care more
about obtaining a secure economic future for our family
than for living an uncompromisingly Christian lifestyle?

I do not pretend that giving an honest answer to such
questions will be easy. Our responsibility is not always
clear. One Saturday morning as I was beginning to prepare
a lecture (on poverty!), a poor man came into my office and
asked for five dollars. He was drinking. He had no food, no
job, no home. The Christ of the poor confronted me in this
man. But I didn't have the time, I said. I had to prepare a
lecture on the Christian view of poverty. I did give him a
couple of dollars, but that was not what he needed. He
needed somebody to talk to, somebody to love him. He
needed my time. He needed me. But I was too busy.
'Inasmuch as you did it not to the least of these, you did it
not . . .'

We need to make some dramatic, concrete moves to
escape the materialism that seeps into our minds via the
diabolically clever and incessant radio and TV commercials. We have been brainwashed to believe that bigger

houses, more prosperous businesses, more luxurious gadgets, are worthy goals in life. As a result, we are caught in an absurd, materialistic spiral. The more we make, the more we think we need in order to live decently and respectably. Somehow we have to break this cycle because it makes us sin against our needy brothers and sisters and, therefore, against our Lord. And it also destroys us. Sharing with others is the way to real joy.

The Graduated Tithe

The graduated tithe is one of many models which can help break this materialistic stranglehold. I share it because it has proved helpful in our family. Obviously it is not the only useful model. Certainly it is not a biblical norm to be prescribed legalistically for others. It is just one family's story.

I tell our story here partly to underline how much our 'graduated tithe' has evolved! When we hit the secondary school and college years in the family life cycle, we were astounded with how much more seemed right to spend on our family. I don't claim that we always got it right. But we tried to be more concerned with persons (specifically our children's changing needs) than some abstract 'rule' or theoretical framework. Hopefully our personal pilgrimage will underline the point that the graduated tithe is merely a framework for every family to adapt to their unique situation. (Obviously factors such as geography, family size, health, etc., all make a great difference.)

When Arbutus and I decided to adopt a graduated scale for our giving in 1969, we started by sitting down and trying to calculate honestly what we would need to live for a year. We wanted a figure that would permit reasonable comfort but not all the luxuries. We decided that we would give a tithe (10 per cent) on our base figure and then give a graduated tithe (15 per cent plus) on income above that. For each thousand dollars above our base, we decided to increase our giving by another 5 per cent on that thousand. Somehow we arrived in 1969 at a base of $7,000. By 1973 we had increased it to $8,000. And in 1982 we increased it again to $10,000. (This time we had decided to use an approximation of the 1982 federal poverty level: $9,862 for a family of four.)

Then the secondary school and college syndrome hit! We decided that in our situation a Christian school was important. That added major costs. College expenses soon followed. We discovered that we simply could not continue with our original scheme. So we added costs for Christian education and college to our base.

What about taxes? At first we did not deduct taxes. Obviously one would have to do that beyond a certain income or the graduated tithe and taxes would eat up all one's money. So in 1979 we added taxes to our base.

Eventually we stumbled into the following pattern. We give 10 per cent on a base that includes: (a) the current US poverty level ($12,100 in June 1990 for a family of four)[8]; plus (b) Christian education and college/university expenses; plus (c) taxes; plus (d) genuine emergencies. On the income above that base, we apply the graduated tithe (see Table 17). We don't always quite make it! But that is what we aim at. Trying to compare US incomes with incomes in the UK is difficult, but a figure of $3 to £1 might give a more accurate purchasing power equivalence, since most goods and services in the US are more expensive than in the UK if the official parity of $1.64 = £1 (May 1990) is used. (Petrol is one of the few goods that is actually cheaper in the US.)

Every family's situation is unique. Housing costs vary enormously in different parts of the country and city. Probably the single most important decision on family expenses is where you decide to live. Our choice to live in a lower-income, inter-racial city neighbourhood where housing and related expenses are vastly less than in the suburbs has helped us immensely. (It has also lowered the children's sense of what they 'needed'.)

There are a near limitless set of variations. Some families will have special expenses arising from disabilities. Some children need special dental work. Some people with

Table 17   Graduated Tithe

Total Income		Per Cent Given Away		Total Given Away	
Base		10% of Base		10% of Base	
Base + £	1,000	15% of last £1,000		10% of Base + £	150
Base +	2,000	20% of last	1,000	10% of Base +	350
Base +	3,000	25% of last	1,000	10% of Base +	600
Base +	4,000	30% of last	1,000	10% of Base +	900
Base +	5,000	35% of last	1,000	10% of Base +	1,250
Base +	6,000	40% of last	1,000	10% of Base +	1,650
Base +	7,000	45% of last	1,000	10% of Base +	2,100
Base +	8,000	50% of last	1,000	10% of Base +	2,600
Base +	9,000	55% of last	1,000	10% of Base +	3,150
Base +	10,000	60% of last	1,000	10% of Base +	3,750
Base +	11,000	65% of last	1,000	10% of Base +	4,400
Base +	12,000	70% of last	1,000	10% of Base +	5,100
Base +	13,000	75% of last	1,000	10% of Base +	5,850
Base +	14,000	80% of last	1,000	10% of Base +	6,650
Base +	15,000	85% of last	1,000	10% of Base +	7,500
Base +	16,000	90% of last	1,000	10% of Base +	8,400
Base +	17,000	95% of last	1,000	10% of Base +	9,350
Base +	18,000	100% of last	1,000	10% of Base +	10,350

special entrepreneurial skills require substantial sums of capital for investment and may choose to count that as part of their base. What do you do about untaxed employer contributions to a pension fund? (We don't count it at all – but will when it appears as income during retirement.) What about employer-paid medical insurance?

Every family must work out its own answers to these questions. Our story is not a law for everyone – not even one other person! Each person or family will need to develop his or her own plan.

But the basic pattern is easy. All you need to do is decide through prayer, study, and conversation with sympathetic friends what you should consider your base on which you will give 10 per cent. Then for every additional £1,000 above the base, you give an additional 5 per cent. Table 17 shows you how to do the calculations.

Here are a few suggestions if you feel God leading you to adopt the graduated tithe.

First, discuss the idea with the whole family. Everyone needs to understand the reasons so that the family can come to a common decision. Second, spell out your plan in writing at the beginning of the year. It is relatively painless, in fact exciting, to work it out theoretically. After you commit yourself to the abstract figures, it hurts less to dole out the cash each month! Third, discuss your proposal with a committed Christian friend or couple who share your concern for justice. Fourth, discuss major expenditures with the same people. It is easier for slightly more objective observers to spot rationalisations than it is for you. They may also have helpful hints on simple living. Fifth, each year see if it is possible to reduce your basic figure and total expenditures. (That does not mean you have no understanding of the need for capital investment to increase productivity. It simply means that you give more via Christian organisations for capital investment among the poor.)

As the perceptive reader has already noticed, this proposal for a graduated tithe is really a modest one. In fact, the proposal is probably so modest that it verges on unfaithfulness to Saint Paul. But it is also sufficiently radical that its implementation would revolutionise the ministry and life of the church.

Some Christians are experimenting with far more radical attempts to win the war on affluence.

Communal Living

The model which permits the simplest standard of living is probably the commune. Housing, furniture, appliances, tools and cars that would normally serve one nuclear family can accommodate ten or twenty people. Communal living releases vast amounts of money and people-time for alternative activities.

Some Christian communes have been initiated as conscious attempts to develop a more ecologically responsible, sharing standard of living. Others simply emerged as a spontaneous response to human need. Jerry Barker, a member of a Texas community, put it this way:

> It soon became obvious that the needs we were faced with would . . . take lots of resources and so we began to cut expenses for things we had been accustomed to. We stopped buying new cars and new televisions and things of that sort. We didn't even think of them. We started driving our cars until they literally fell apart and then we'd buy a used car or something like that to replace it. We began to turn in some of our insurance policies so that they would not be such a financial drain on us. We found such a security in our relationship with the Lord that it was no longer important to have security for the future. . . . We never have had any rule about it, or felt this was a necessary part of the Christian life. It was just a matter of using the money we had available most effectively, particularly in supporting so many extra people. We learned to live very economically. We stopped eating steaks and expensive roasts and things like that and we began to eat simple fare . . . We'd often eat things that people would bring us – a box of groceries or a sack of rice.[9]

The standard of living of Christian communities varies. But almost all live far more simply than the average Western family. For many years at Chicago's Reba Placc, for example, eating patterns were based on the welfare level of the city (see chapter 8). In the last few decades, Christian communes have had a symbolic importance out of all proportion to their numbers. They quietly question society's affluence. And they offer a viable alternative.

Communal living, of course, is not for everyone. In fact, I personally believe that it is the right setting for only a small percentage of Christians. We need many more diverse models.

Other Models

In her delightful book *Living More with Less*, Doris Long-acre gives us quick glimpses of several hundred Christians who are learning the joy of sharing more.[10] Some still live in what I would consider substantial affluence. Others live far more simply than I do. But everyone is trying to spend less on themselves in order to share more.

That is what Robert Bainum did. Bainum was a successful Christian businessman – in fact, a millionaire. But in a personal conversation he told me that as he read the first edition of *Rich Christians in an Age of Hunger* God called him to share more with the poor of the earth. He gave away half of his wealth and then devoted a major portion of his creative energy and organisational abilities to relief and development programmes among the poor, both at home and abroad.[11]

In the mid-1970s Graham Kerr was the Galloping Gourmet for two hundred million TV viewers each week. He was rich and successful, but his personal life was falling apart. Since he came to Christ in 1975, his family life has been miraculously restored. He has abandoned his gourmet TV series and given away most of his money.

For more than a decade Graham devoted his time and used his knowledge of nutrition to develop a new kind of agricultural missionary who both shares the gospel and helps poor Third World people develop a better diet with locally available products.

Very recently, Graham has returned to national television and again earns a big salary. But he and his wife Treena still live simply – but not because they are ascetics. They live simply because they want to share as much as possible to evangelise the world and reduce poverty.[12]

Are Graham and Treena happy? They are immeasurably happier than before. Every time I see them I see joy and contentment flooding through their lives. They are having the time of their lives living more simply.

Biblical Christians are experimenting with a variety of simpler lifestyles. An Age of Hunger demands drastic change. But we must be careful to avoid legalism and self-righteousness. 'We have to beware of the reverse snobbery of spiritual one-up-manship.'[13]

No one model is God's will for everyone. Our God loves

variety and diversity. Does that mean, however, that we ought to fall back into typical Western individualism, with each person or family doing what is good in its own eyes? By no means.

Two things can help. First, we need the help of other brothers and sisters – in our local congregation, in our town or city, and around the world. We need to develop a process for discussing our economic lifestyles with close Christian friends in our congregation. We also need new ways to exchange ideas about the shape of a faithful lifestyle with poor Christians.[14]

Second, certain criteria can help us determine what is right for us. I offer six – as suggestions, not as norms or laws.

1. We ought to move towards a personal lifestyle that could be sustained over a long period of time if it were shared by everyone in the world.

2. We need to distinguish between necessities and luxuries, and normally we need to reject both our desire for the latter and our inclination to blur the distinction.

3. Expenditures for the purpose of status, pride, staying in fashion and 'keeping up with the Joneses' are wrong.

4. We need to distinguish between expenditures to develop our particular creative gifts and legitimate hobbies and a general demand for all the cultural items, recreational equipment, and current hobbies that the 'successful' of our class or nation enjoy. Each person has unique interests and gifts. We should, within limits, be able to express our creativity in those areas. But if we discover that we are justifying lots of things in many different areas, we should become suspicious.

5. We need to distinguish between occasional celebration and normal day-to-day routine. A Harvest Supper to celebrate the good gift of creation is biblical (Deut. 14: 22–7). A Christmas turkey for the family is legitimate. Unfortunately, many of us overeat every day, and that is sin.

6. There is no necessary connection between what we earn and what we spend on ourselves. We should not buy things just because we can afford them.

Some Practical Suggestions

The following are hints, not rules. Freedom, joy and laughter are essential elements of simple living. (See the Appendix for addresses and information about groups and organisations named.)

1. Question your own lifestyle, not your neighbour's.
2. Reduce your food budget by:
   - gardening: try hoeing instead of mowing
   - substituting vegetable protein for animal protein. Cookbooks like *Recipes for a Small Planet* and *More with Less Cookbook* tell how to prepare delicious, meatless meals. Our daily requirement of protein costs more than five times as much via veal cutlets as it does via peanut butter[15]
   - fasting regularly
   - opposing (by speech and example) the flagrant misuse of grain for making beer and other alcoholic beverages (the United States annually uses 5.1 million tons of grain in the production of alcoholic beverages, enough to feed 25 million people in a country like India)[16]
   - setting a monthly budget and sticking to it.
3. Lower energy consumption by:
   - keeping your thermostat (at the home and office) at 68°F, or lower during winter months
   - supporting public transport with your feet and your vote
   - using bicycles, shared or hired cars and, for short trips, your feet
   - making washing-up a family time instead of buying a dishwasher.
4. Resist consumerism by:
   - laughing regularly at TV commercials
   - developing family slogans like: 'Who Are You Kidding?' and 'You Can't Take It With You!'
   - making a list of dishonest ads and boycotting those products

- using the postage-paid envelopes of direct-mail advertisers to object to unscrupulous advertising.
5. Join up with other Christian friends to buy or rent a property together, forming a small Christian community in the process.
6. Reduce your consumption of non-renewable natural resources by:
   - resisting obsolescence (buy quality products when you must buy)
   - sharing appliances, tools, lawnmowers, sports equipment, books, even a car (this is easier if you live close to other Christians committed to simple living)
   - organising a 'things closet' in your church for items used only occasionally – edger, clippers, cots for unexpected guests, lawnmowers, camping equipment, ladder.
7. See how much of what you spend is for status and eliminate it.
8. Refuse to keep up with clothing fashions. (Very few readers of this book need to buy clothes – except maybe shoes – for two or three years.)
9. Enjoy what is free.
10. Live on a welfare budget for a month. (Ron Jones's *Finding Community* will tell you how to calculate it.)[17]

    Examine *Alternatives Celebrations Catalog*, published by Alternatives, which provides exciting, inexpensive, ecologically sound alternative ideas for celebrating Christmas and other holidays.
11. Give your children more of your love and time rather than more things.

That's enough for a beginning.

Criteria for Giving

If 10 per cent of all Christians in the affluent North adopted the graduated tithe, huge sums of money would become available for kingdom work. Where would that money do the most good?

Obviously Christians should not give all their money to relieve world hunger. Christian education and evangelism are extremely important and deserve continuing support.

Give approximately as much to support evangelism as you do for social justice activities. (Holistic programmes that combine both are ideal.)[18]

It is important to seek a balance between emergency relief, development and broad structural change. Emergency food is important when people are starving. But more money needs to go for long-term community development so folk can feed themselves. It is especially crucial to give to organisations that increase understanding and promote public policy and structural change for justice (especially since so few Christians understand this last area). Part of one's graduated tithe might very appropriately go to political campaigns to promote justice for the poor.

Which relief and development agencies are doing the best job? This issue is important, but you must decide for yourself. Here are some general criteria for deciding where to channel your giving for development in hungry lands:

1. Do the funds support holistic projects in the Third World, working simultaneously at an integrated programme of evangelism, social change, education, agricultural development and so on?

2. Do the funds support truly indigenous projects? That involves several issues: (a) Are the leaders and most of the staff of the projects in the developing nations indigenous persons? They should be. (b) Do the projects unthinkingly adopt Western ideas, materials and technology, or do they use materials suited to their own culture? (c) Did the project arise from the felt needs of the people rather than from some outside 'expert'?

3. Are the projects primarily engaged in long-range development (that includes people development), or in emergency aid only?

4. Are the programmes designed to help the poor masses understand that God wants sinful social structures changed and that they can help effect that change?

5. Do the programmes work through and foster the growth of the church?

6. Are the programmes potentially self-supporting after an initial injection of seed capital? And do the programmes from the beginning require commitment and a significant contribution of capital or time (or both) from the people themselves?

7. Do the programmes aid the poorest people in the poorest developing countries?

8. Is agricultural development involved? (It need not always be, but in many cases it should be.)

9. Is justice rather than continual charity the result?[19]

10. Several crucial questions pertain to the international agency through which one channels funds. (a) Does the organisation spend more than 10 or 15 per cent of total funds on fund-raising and administration? (b) Are Third World people, minority people and women represented among the board and top staff? (c) Is the organisation audited annually by independent accountants? (d) Are the board members and staff of known integrity? Is the board paid? (It should not be.) (e) Are staff salaries consistent with the biblical call for jubilee among all God's people? (f) Does the organisation object to answering these questions?[20]

An example will help clarify the kind of holistic programme which meets most of the above criteria.

Elizabeth Native Interior Mission [is] in southern Liberia. ENI is headed by Augustus Marwieh who became a Christian under Mother George, one of the first black American missionaries to Africa. Ten years ago Gus went to work at the struggling mission where he had been saved. The young people were leaving the villages to go to the capital city of Monrovia; there, most found only unemployment, alcohol and prostitution. Local skills like log sawing, blacksmithing, and making pottery were dying out as the people became dependent on outside traders (usually foreigners) and became poorer and poorer. At least 90 per cent of the people were illiterate, and many suffered from protein deficiency.

Today 160 churches have been started, and 10,000 people have become Christians. Eleven primary schools are operating, and they stress locally usable skills instead of the usual Liberian fare of Spot and Jane in English. A vocational school is forming that will help revive local trades and encourage new skills; and steps are being taken to form co-operatives which will avoid middlemen, replace foreign merchants, provide capital, etc.

One crucial element, especially in view of their protein shortage, is agriculture, and in the last ten years the people have made great strides. But they are so poor that often the only farming tool they have is a machete (a heavy knife). So Gus is burdened to start a revolving loan fund from which people can borrow to buy a hoe, a shovel, a watering can, spraying equipment, a pick, or an axe. You and I buy tools like that on a whim for our gardens, but for these people such purchases are completely out of reach even though they need them to fight malnutrition. So next time you start feeling poor, remember Gus's people.[21]

There are scores of similar holistic programmes operated by biblical Christians in developing countries. And they desperately need additional funds. Organisations that enable us to share with them represent a contemporary way for God's people to live the jubilee.

Maranatha Trust is one such organisation. It was founded by David Bussau, an evangelical businessman from Australia, who now gives his life to promote credit-based income generation among the poor.[22] Working through local Christian organisations, Maranatha makes small loans of £60–£600 to individuals who can then purchase better tools to increase their productivity and thereby improve their standards of living. The loans are almost always repaid, usually within a few months, and the money returns to the revolving fund to help someone else. Almost always, the poor person quickly and dramatically increases his or her earnings.

In 1990, Maranatha is creating ten thousand jobs on a budget of less than five million dollars.[23] The average loan is a mere $380 (about £230!). With an average of five people per family, those ten thousand jobs will substantially improve the life of fifty thousand people.

Think of what one billion dollars could do! Counting overheads and training programmes in entrepreneurship, NGOs (non-governmental organisations) like Maranatha can create one new job for a poor person for every $500 (£300) invested. So $1 billion given through such organisations would create two million jobs and have a dramatic impact on ten million people. Thirteen billion dollars would fundamentally change the lives of one-tenth of all the people living in near absolute poverty!

The gulf between what affluent Christians give and what they could give is a terrifying tragedy. *Christianity Today* reported that in 1971 a mere tithe from the fifty-two largest US denominations would be $17.5 billion annually. Instead they gave only $4.4 billion in total church giving that year.[24] (Only a tiny fraction of that $4.4 billion, of course, went to help poor people.) Even if another $4.4 billion in charitable contributions were given through non-church channels, the combined total of $8.8 billion still would be less than 5 per cent. We ought to quadruple that.

And it does make a difference. Northern private voluntary organisations (PVOs) have tripled in the last decade. PVOs now provide 20 per cent ($4 billion in 1984) of the total assistance given by the North to the South.[25] That does not mean that working for increased governmental foreign aid is unimportant. But it does mean that church contributions to developing nations are extremely significant.

I have focused on monetary giving in most of this

chapter. But that is not the only way. Giving oneself is equally important. Some Christians choose low-paying jobs because the opportunity for service is great. Others decline overtime to permit more volunteer activity. Thousands of Christians have given two or more years to serve in developing countries.

There is a great need for sensitive persons who will live with people in rural villages, showing the poor that God wants them to have both the tools to earn a decent living and the knowledge and power to change the unjust structures which oppress them. Agricultural workers who can share intermediate technological skills are in high demand. 'One person with practical skills who's prepared to work and live in a remote village is generally worth a dozen visiting university professors and business tycoons.'[26] Time is money. Sharing time is just as important as sharing financial resources.

I am convinced that simpler living is a biblical imperative for contemporary Christians in affluent lands. But we must remain clear about our reasons. We are not committed to a simple lifestyle. We have only one absolute loyalty and that is to Jesus and his kingdom. But the head of this kingdom is the God of the poor! And hundreds of millions of his poor are starving.

An Age of Hunger summons affluent people to a lower standard of living. But a general assent to this truth will not be enough to escape the daily seductions of London's West End. Each of us needs some specific, concrete plan. The graduated tithe and communal living offer two models. The examples of Robert Bainum, David Bussau and Graham and Treena Kerr suggest others. There are many more. By all means the Christian must avoid legalism and self-righteousness. But he or she needs courage to make a commitment to some specific method for moving towards a just personal lifestyle.

Will we dare to measure our living standards by the needs of the poor rather than by the lifestyle of our neighbours? Will we have the faith to believe Jesus's word that joy and happiness flow from sharing?

Study Questions

1. How does the graduated tithe work? How would you want to adapt it if you chose to use it in your life?

2. What other specific mechanisms could help Christians avoid materialism? Which ones do you think are: (a) most biblical; (b) most workable?

3. Which practical suggestions for consuming less did you find most helpful? Can you add others?

4. In the light of the criteria for giving, how do you evaluate your own giving, your church's giving?

5. In what ways do you feel called to change your spending patterns?

6. How did this chapter make you feel?

8

WATCHING OVER ONE ANOTHER
IN LOVE

Extra ecclesiam, nulla salus.

Somehow the pressures of modern society were making it increasingly difficult for us to live by the values we had been taught. We thought our church should constitute a community of believers capable of withstanding these pressures, yet it seemed to go along with things as they were instead of encouraging an alternative. The 'pillars' of the church seemed as severely trapped by material concerns and alienation as most non-Christians we knew[1] [Dave and Neta Jackson].

The church should consist of communities of loving defiance. Instead it consists largely of comfortable clubs of conformity. A far-reaching reformation of the church is a prerequisite if it is to commit itself to Jesus's mission of liberating the oppressed.

If the analysis in the preceding chapters is even approximately correct, then the God of the Bible is calling Christians today to live in fundamental nonconformity to contemporary society. Affluent North American and European societies are obsessed with materialism, sex, economic success and military might. Things are more important than people. Job security and an annual salary increase matter more than starving children and oppressed peasants. Paul's warning to the Romans is especially pertinent today: 'Don't let the world around you squeeze you into its own mould' (Rom. 12:2 Phillips). Biblical revelation summons us to defy many of the basic values of our materialistic, adulterous society.

But that is impossible! As individuals, that is. It is hardly possible for isolated believers to resist the anti-Christian values which pour from our radios, TVs, and billboards. The values of our affluent society seep slowly and subtly into our hearts and minds. The only way to defy them is to immerse ourselves in Christian fellowship so that God can remould our thinking as we find our primary identity with brothers and sisters who are also unconditionally committed to biblical values.

That faithful obedience is possible only in the context of powerful Christian fellowship should not surprise us. The early church was able to defy the decadent values of Roman civilisation precisely because it experienced the reality of Christian fellowship in a mighty way. For the early Christians, *koinōnia* was not the frilly 'fellowship' of church-sponsored, bi-weekly bowling parties. It was not tea, biscuits and sophisticated small talk in Fellowship Hall after the sermon. It was an almost unconditional sharing of their lives with the other members of Christ's body.

Christian fellowship meant costly, sweeping availability to and liability for the other sisters and brothers – emotionally, financially and spiritually. When one member suffered, they all suffered. When one rejoiced, they all rejoiced (1 Cor. 12:26). When a person or church experienced economic trouble, the others shared without reservation.[2] And when a brother or sister fell into sin, the others gently restored the straying person (Matt. 18:15–17; 1 Cor. 5; 2 Cor. 2:5–11; Gal. 6:1–3).[3] The sisters and brothers were available to each other, liable for each other, accountable to each other.

The early church, of course, did not always live out the New Testament vision of the body of Christ. There were tragic lapses. But the network of tiny house churches scattered throughout the Roman Empire did experience their oneness in Christ so vividly that they were able to defy and eventually conquer a powerful, pagan civilisation.

John Wesley's early Methodist class meetings captured

something of the spirit alive in the early church. These assembled in houses weekly, bringing together people 'united in order to pray together, to receive the word of exhortation, and to watch over one another in love, that they may help each other to work out their salvation'.[4] The overwhelming majority of churches today, however, do not provide the context in which brothers and sisters can encourage, admonish and disciple each other. We desperately need new structures for watching over one another in love, new settings that will help us become truly one.

A Sociological Perspective

The sociology of knowledge underlines the importance of Christian community for biblical nonconformists. Sociologists of knowledge have studied the relationship between ideas and the social conditions in which ideas arise. They have discovered that the plausibility of ideas depends on the social support they have. 'We obtain our notions about the world originally from other human beings, and these notions continue to be plausible to us in a very large measure because others continue to affirm them.'[5] An Amish youth who migrates to New York City will soon begin to question earlier values. The sociological reason for this change is that the 'significant others' who previously supported his ideas and values are no longer present.

The complicated network of social interactions in which one develops and maintains one's view of reality is called a plausibility structure. This plausibility structure consists of ongoing conversation with 'significant others' as well as specific practices, rituals and legitimations designed to support the validity of certain ideas. As long as these social processes continue, we tend to accept the corresponding beliefs as true or plausible. But if the supportive structures disappear, doubt and uncertainty arise.

Hence the difficulty of a cognitive minority. A cognitive minority is a small group of people who hold a set of beliefs that differ sharply from the majority view in their society.

Because they constantly meet people who challenge their fundamental ideas, members of a cognitive minority find it difficult to maintain their distinctive beliefs. According to well-known sociologist Peter Berger, a cognitive minority can maintain its unpopular ideas only if it has a strong community structure:

> Unless our theologian has the inner fortitude of a desert saint, he has only one effective remedy against the threat of cognitive collapse in the face of these pressures. He must huddle together with like-minded fellow deviants – and huddle very closely indeed. Only in a countercommunity of considerable strength does cognitive deviance have a chance to maintain itself. The countercommunity provides continuing therapy against the creeping doubt as to whether, after all, one may not be wrong and the majority right. To fulfill its function of providing social support for the deviant body of 'knowledge', the countercommunity must provide a strong sense of solidarity among its members.[6]

Berger's analysis relates directly to contemporary Christians determined to follow biblical teaching on the poor and possessions. Berger analysed the problem of orthodox Christians who defy the dominant 'scientific' ideas of contemporary secularism and maintain a biblical belief in the supernatural. But his analysis pertains just as clearly to the problem of living the ethics of Jesus's kingdom in a world that follows different standards. Most of our contemporaries – both inside and outside the churches – accept the dominant values of our consumption-oriented, materialistic culture. Genuine Christians, on the other hand, are committed to the very different norms revealed in Scripture. It should not surprise us that only a faithful remnant continues to cling to these values. But the fact that genuine Christians are a cognitive minority alerts us to the need for strong Christian community.

That does not mean that Christians should retreat to isolated rural solitude. We must remain at the centre of contemporary society in order to challenge, witness against, and, it is to be hoped, even change it. But precisely as we are in the world but not of it, the pressure to abandon biblical norms in favour of contemporary values will be intense. Hence the need for new forms of Christian community today.

The ancient Catholic dictum *extra ecclesiam, nulla salus* ('outside the church there is no salvation') contains a significant sociological truth. Certainly it is not impossible for individual Christians to maintain biblical beliefs even if a hostile majority disagrees. But if the church is to consist of communities of loving defiance in a sinful world, then it must pay more attention to the quality of its fellowship.

What are some promising models of Christian community for our time?

New Patterns of Christian Community

When one speaks of Christian community, some people instantly think of Christian communes. That is unfortunate. Communes are only one of many forms for genuine Christian fellowship today. House churches or mission groups within larger congregations, individual house churches, and small traditional churches, all offer excellent contexts for living out the biblical vision of the church.

I am thoroughly convinced, however, that the overwhelming majority of Western churches no longer understand or experience biblical *koinōnia* to any significant degree. As mentioned earlier, the essence of Christian community is open accountability to and far-reaching liability for our sisters and brothers in the body of Christ. That means that our time, our money and our very selves are available to the brothers and sisters.

That kind of fellowship hardly ever happens in large churches of one hundred or more persons. It requires small communities of believers like the early Christian house churches. The movement which conquered the Roman Empire was a network of small house churches. Frequently Paul speaks of 'the church that meets in the house of . . .'

(Rom. 16:5, 23; 1 Cor. 16:19; Col. 4:15; Philem. 2; see also Acts 2:46; 12:12; 20:7–12). It was only in the latter part of the third century that the church started to build sanctuaries. The structure of the early church fostered close interaction and fellowship.[7]

What happens when God grants the gift of genuine Christian fellowship? Deep, joyful sharing replaces the polite prattle typically exchanged by Christians on Sunday morning. Sisters and brothers begin to discuss the things that really matter to them. They disclose their inner fears, their areas of peculiar temptation, their deepest joys. And they begin to challenge and disciple each other according to Matthew 18:15–17 and Galatians 6:1–3.

In that kind of setting – and perhaps only in that kind of setting – the church today will be able to forge a faithful lifestyle for Christians in an Age of Hunger. In small house-church settings, brothers and sisters can challenge each other's affluent lifestyles. They can discuss family finances and evaluate each other's annual budgets. Larger expenditures (like those for houses, cars, and long vacations) can be evaluated honestly in terms of the needs of both the individuals involved and God's poor around the world. Tips for simple living can be shared. Voting patterns that liberate the poor, jobs that are ecologically responsible, and charitable donations that build self-reliance among the oppressed – these and many other issues can be discussed openly and honestly by persons who have pledged themselves to each other as brothers and sisters in Christ.

What models of the church foster that kind of Christian community?

A Congregation of House Churches

Congregations composed of clusters of house churches make up, in my opinion, the most exciting, viable alternative to the typical congregation today. Living Word Community in Philadelphia and the Church of the Savior in Washington, DC, are two variations on this theme.

Twenty years ago Living Word (then called Gospel Temple) was a typical, successful Pentecostal church. There was a large, growing congregation of several hundred people from the greater Philadelphia area. The church had a young dynamic pastor, a packed schedule of meetings, a full repertoire of church organisations and, according to the pastor, little real Christian fellowship.

In 1970 it decided to change drastically. The church jettisoned all existing activities except the Sunday morning worship service. Everyone was urged to attend 'home meetings', where twelve to twenty people met weekly for study, prayer, worship and shepherding. For a couple of years they wondered if they had made a gigantic mistake. 'To move from a pew to a living-room chair and look at people face to face was terrifying.'[8] But a breakthrough occurred when the leaders of the home meetings realised that most people did not know how to meet each other's needs. The leaders started making suggestions: 'You two ladies go to Jane Brown's house and make dinner for her because she is sick.' 'You three people paint Jerry's apartment on Saturday.'

Oneness and caring began to develop. These weekly gatherings became the centre of spiritual activity in the church. Counselling, discipling, even evangelistic outreach all began to happen primarily in the home meetings. One result was rapid growth. As soon as a home meeting reached twenty-five, it was divided into two home meetings.

In 1974 growth had already led to division into two weekend services. By 1976 thirteen to fourteen hundred people were attending weekend services. There were fifty different home meetings and four separate 'Sunday' services.

Several new congregations have evolved. One still occurs on Sunday morning in the original downtown sanctuary. Often the others rent space from various churches and hold the weekend service on Saturday or Sunday evening. As a result they have avoided costly building programmes and kept financial resources available for more important matters.

Genuine Christian community has emerged from this drastic restructuring. Because of the small home meetings, the leaders confidently assert that all eight hundred members of Living Word receive personal, pastoral care. Each individual's burdens and problems are known in his or her small home meeting.

Financial sharing was not part of the original vision. But it has begun to happen in a significant way. Members of home meetings have dug into savings and stocks to provide interest-free loans for two families who purchased mobile homes to live in. When members went to sign the papers for an interest-free mortgage for another family's house, secular folk present for the transfer were totally perplexed! If a member of a home meeting needs a small amount of financial assistance (£30 or £60), the other members of his home meeting help out. A congregational fund meets larger needs. A food co-op and a store for used clothing and furniture supply basic needs inexpensively. A sizeable portion of total congregational giving is used for economic sharing in the church.

Living Word has begun to develop an extensive concern for justice and the poor. The leaders preach about social justice. The church has worked in a major way with refugees from South-East Asia. The church's relief fund contributes several thousand dollars each year to relieve world poverty.

Living Word has been successful in working with black and Hispanic Americans. The interracial subcongregation of 150 people is growing rapidly. In the summer of 1982, Living Word began an evangelistic outreach in the poorest Hispanic section of the city. Drug rehabilitation, job counselling, emergency food distribution, and ministry to battered women are all part of this holistic outreach. Some church members are relocating in this needy area and evangelistic efforts continue.

Living Word has demonstrated that a traditional congregation can be transformed into a cluster of house churches. And the result has been not decay but growth – in discipleship, Christian community and numbers.

The Church of the Savior in Washington, DC, pioneered the small-group model at the end of World War 2.[9] All members must be in one of its many mission groups. Prospective members must take five classes over a period of about two years. The membership covenant, renewed annually, commits every member to four disciplines: daily prayer, daily Bible study, weekly worship, and proportionate giving, beginning with a tithe of total gross income.

Consisting of five to twelve people, the mission groups are the heart of the Church of the Savior. They are not merely prayer cells, Bible study gatherings, encounter groups or social action committees (although they are all of these). Gordon Cosby, pastor of Church of the Savior, emphasises that it is in the mission groups that the members experience the reality of the body of Christ: 'The mission group embodies the varied dimensions of church. It is total in scope. It is both inward and outward. It requires that we be accountable to Christ and to one another for the totality of our lives. It assumes that we share unlimited liability for one another.'[10] Via verbal or written reports, each member of a mission group reports weekly on failure or success in following the covenanted disciplines, on new scriptural insight and on the problems and joys of the week.

Economics figures prominently in the membership commitment. Part of the membership covenant reads, 'I believe that God is the total owner of my life and resources. I give God the throne in relation to the material aspect of my life. God is the owner. I am the ower. Because God is a lavish giver, I too shall be lavish and cheerful in my regular gifts.'[11]

The church has held out the goal of accountability of brothers and sisters to each other in the use of personal finances. Some mission groups regularly share income tax returns as a basis for discussing each other's family budgets and finances. Concern for more simple lifestyles is growing at Church of the Savior.

The goal of many of the mission groups is liberation for

the poor. Members of the mission group called Jubilee Housing have renovated deteriorating housing in inner-city Washington. Along with other mission groups (Jubilee jobs, Columbia Road Health Service, Family Place), they are bringing hope of genuine change to hundreds of people in the inner city. For Love of Children has fought for the rights of neglected children through court action, legislation, and monitoring of local and federal governmental activity.

In recent years several of the church's mission groups have dedicated themselves to peace and justice in the international arena. World Peacemakers has worked to develop peace-and-justice groups in churches throughout the United States, modelling them after their own group structure. COSIGN (The Church of the Savior International Good Neighbors) has made it possible for several hundred Americans to serve in the Thailand refugee camps. Now this mission group, along with the Central American Peace Institute and the Dayspring Refugee Mission, is providing direct relief to Central American refugees driven by violence from their homes into neighbouring countries and the United States. At the same time these missions are working to change US foreign policy which exacerbates the Central American refugee problem.

The Dunamis concept emerged in one of the mission groups. Different task forces select specific public policy issues and build relationships of love, prayer, pastoral concern and prophetic witness with senators and congress members. In 1983, Henri Nouwen travelled across the United States promoting local Dunamis groups' work on US policy in Central America. The Dunamis approach of forming a pastoral/prophetic relationship with persons in political office could be applied at the local or state level.[12]

By 1976 increasing size seemed to threaten genuine community at Church of the Savior. (There were one hundred members plus fifty intern members.) As a result the church divided into seven fully autonomous sister communities. Gordon Cosby's hope was that these new communities would have a wide economic mix so that economic sharing and simple living could increase. Like Living Word in Philadelphia, Church of the Savior prefers to subdivide into small congregations rather than run the risk of diluting Christian community.

Thousands of churches today have small groups – encounter groups, biweekly fellowship groups, serendipity groups, prayer cells, and an infinite variety of action groups that aim at fellowship. Do these small groups fulfil the same function as Living Word's home meetings and Church of the Savior's mission groups? Hardly ever.

Though the numerous small groups flourishing in the churches today are useful and valuable, they seldom go far enough. Participants may agree to share deeply in one or two areas of life, but they do not assume responsibility for the other brothers' and sisters' growth towards Christian maturity in every area of life. Hardly ever do they dream that truly being sisters and brothers in Christ means costly, sweeping economic liability for each other or responsibility for the economic lifestyles of the other members. The crucial question is, have the participants committed themselves to be brothers and sisters to each other so unreservedly that they enjoy nearly total liability for and accountability to each other?

Almost everyone expects most small groups to dissolve in six months or two years. Life will then continue as before. They are 'limited liability' small groups, and they have genuine importance. But what people desperately need today is the church. From the biblical perspective, being the church means accepting liability for and availability and accountability to the other members of the local expression of Christ's body.

Various efforts in this direction have been made in the UK as well. One of the best known was at St Cuthbert's, York, where for some years several 'nuclear' families were extended to include single people who benefited from the sense of belonging in a Christian home.

The same idea was one of the reasons for the formation of the Community of the Word of God in Hackney, East London, in 1972. Prebendary John Pearce, an Anglican clergyman, and his wife saw many Christian people, mainly single women, finding themselves unable to cope as Christians in the East End without close supporting fellowship, and consequently having to leave the area. Wondering how to prevent this exit of the Christian presence in Hackney, the Pearces' original concept was a community of women. Later, it became clear that men wished to join and, later still, married couples.

The other basic strand in their thinking was the community concept of the early church (as related in Acts 2.44: 'All who believed were together and had all things in common'). Commitment to God and to each other means, for them, the sharing of all monetary income, homes, food and friendship. Not a church in itself, this community is linked very closely with the local Anglican church.

The Community of Celebration is interesting too. Following the development of the community lifestyle in Houston (see chapter 7), the Rev. Graham Pulkingham founded the Community of Celebration in the UK in the early 1970s. People from many countries joined the community and in 1975–6 it divided into two groups: one, which included the International Fisherfolk, moved to the Cathedral of the Isles on the island of Cumbrae, Scotland. The other joined the Post Green Community in Dorset. They have lived and taught the principles of corporate life and worship over recent years, and since 1984 the Cumbrae Community has moved to a base near Pittsburgh, Pennsylvania, and the other to Bletchingley, Surrey, in the Anglican Diocese of Southwark. At Bletchingley the members hold ordinary jobs. They aim to be a presence, offering God's love and the signs of the Kingdom wherever he has placed them.

The Individual House Church

Another structure where true Christian community can happen is the individual house church. Virtually no expenses are involved. When it is impossible to find genuine Christian community in any other way, small groups of

Christians should begin meeting in their own homes. (But they should promptly seek a relationship with other bodies of Christians. Lone rangers are not God's will for his church!) In his book on church structures, Howard A. Snyder proposed that denominations adopt the house church model for church planting, especially in the city. This structure is flexible, mobile, inclusive and personal. It can grow by division, is an effective means of evangelism, and needs little professional leadership.[13]

An ideal house church arrangement is to have several families or single people purchase homes within a street or two of each other. In many inner-city locations, especially in changing neighbourhoods, inexpensive houses and flats change hands rapidly. Living round the corner from each other greatly facilitates sharing cars, washing machines, driers, freezers and lawnmowers (or gardening equipment). Living close together also encourages Christian community. It quickly creates open relationships which foster honest mutual searching for a less unjust standard of living.

The Christian Commune

Thousands of communal experiments have occurred in the last decade. Many have been explicitly Christian. The Christian commune represents an alternative model for persons dissatisfied with our consumer-oriented society.

Reba Place Fellowship in Evanston, Illinois, began in 1957 with three people.[14] By 1990, there were about sixty people living with a common treasury. A small percentage of these live in large households, but most have their own homes. They all live close to each other in the same neighbourhood.

In addition to the sixty who share a common treasury, another two hundred and fifty are part of Reba Place Church. These have their own private budgets, but share the community's commitment to a simple lifestyle and generous sharing with each other and the poor.

The sixty who share a common treasury place their

earnings in a central fund. The central fund pays directly for large expenditures like housing, utilities and transport. Each month, every family and single person receives an allowance for food, clothing, and incidentals. The food allowance is the same as that for people on food stamps in Chicago. Because of the size and permanence of the community, no insurance is necessary (except that required by law). Not channelling cash into the rich insurance industry frees considerable money for other things. Community living also requires fewer cars, washing machines and lawnmowers.[15] The simple lifestyle at Reba Place enables this community to share generously with the poor in the immediate community and around the world.

One incident suggests the character of their availability to one another. One day a man with a serious drinking problem dropped in to talk with Virgil Vogt, one of the elders. When Virgil invited him to accept Christ and join the community of believers, the man grew uncomfortable and hastily insisted that he simply wanted money for a bus ticket to Cleveland.

> 'Okay,' Virgil agreed, 'we can give you that kind of help too, if that's all you really want.' He was quiet a moment, then he shook his head. 'You know something?' he said, looking straight at the man. 'You've just really let me off the hook. Because if you had chosen a new way of life in the kingdom of God, then as your brother I would have had to lay down my whole life for you. This house, my time, all my money, whatever you needed to meet your needs would have been totally at your disposal for the rest of your life. But all you want is some money for a bus ticket. . . .' The man was so startled he stood up and shortly left, without remembering to take the money. The next Sunday he was sitting next to Virgil in the worship service.[16]

Although not for everyone, Reba Place and other Christian communes offer one setting in which widespread liability for and accountability to other brothers and sisters can become a reality.[17]

Glass Cathedrals in an Age of Hunger?

In early 1976, Eastminster Presbyterian Church in suburban Wichita, Kansas, was planning an ambitious – and expensive – church construction programme. Their architect had prepared a $525,000 church building programme. Then a devastating earthquake struck in Guatemala on February 4, destroying thousands of homes and buildings. Many evangelical congregations lost their churches.

When Eastminster's board of elders met shortly after the Guatemalan tragedy, a layman posed a simple question: 'How can we set out to buy an ecclesiastical Rolls-Royce when our brothers and sisters in Guatemala have just lost their little Volkswagen?'

The elders courageously opted for a dramatic change of plans. They slashed their building programme by nearly two-thirds and settled instead for church construction costing $180,000. Then they sent their pastor and two elders to Guatemala to see how they could help. When the three returned and reported tremendous need, the church borrowed $120,000 from a local bank and rebuilt twenty-six Guatemalan churches and twenty-eight Guatemalan pastors' houses.

I talked with Eastminster's pastor, Dr Frank Kirk. Eastminster stays in close touch with the church in Central America and has recently pledged $40,000 to an evangelical seminary there. The last few years have seen tremendous growth – in spiritual vitality, concern for missions, and even in attendance and budget, in the Wichita church. Dr Kirk believes that cutting their building programme to share with needy sisters and brothers in Guatemala 'meant far more to Eastminster Presbyterian than to Guatemala'.

The Eastminster Presbyterian congregation asked the right questions. They asked whether their building programme was justified at this moment in history given the particular needs of the body of Christ worldwide and the mission of the church in the world. The question was not, are Gothic (or glass) cathedrals ever legitimate? It was rather: is it right to spend millions on church construction when over 2.5 billion people have not yet heard of Jesus Christ and when a billion people are starving or malnourished?

The Bible and the daily newspaper issue the same summons. Faithful people in an Age of Hunger must adopt simple lifestyles and change unjust economic structures. But that is not a popular path to tread in an affluent society. Unless Christians anchor themselves in genuine Christian community, they will be unable to live the radical nonconformity commanded by Scripture and essential in our time. Our only hope is a return to the New Testament vision of the body of Christ. If that happens, the Lord of the church may again create communities of loving defiance able to withstand and conquer the powerful, pagan civilisations of East and West worshipping at the shrine of Mammon.

Study Questions

1. What is Christian community? Why is it so important?
2. What specific structures encourage closer Christian community? Which ones are (a) most biblical; (b) most workable?
3. How close is your local church to the ideal of Christian community? What do you feel led to do about that?

9

STRUCTURAL CHANGE

The present social order is the most abject failure the world has ever seen. . . . This great civilisation of ours has not learned so to distribute the product of human toil that it shall be equitably held. Therefore, the government breaks down[1] (C. I. Scofield, author of the Scofield Bible Notes, 1903).

A group of devout Christians once lived in a small village at the foot of a mountain. A winding, slippery road with hairpin bends and steep precipices without guardrails wound its way up one side of the mountain and down the other. There were frequent fatal accidents. Deeply saddened by the injured people who were pulled from the wrecked cars, the Christians in the village's three churches decided to act. They pooled their resources and purchased an ambulance so they could rush the injured to the hospital in the next town. Week after week church volunteers gave faithfully, even sacrificially, of their time to operate the ambulance twenty-four hours a day. They saved many lives, although some victims remained crippled for life.

One day a visitor came to town. Puzzled, he asked why they did not close the road over the mountain and build a tunnel instead. Startled at first, the ambulance volunteers quickly pointed out that this approach, although technically quite possible, was not realistic or advisable. After all, the narrow mountain road had been there for a long time. Besides, the mayor would bitterly oppose the idea. (He owned a large restaurant and service station half-way up the mountain.)

The visitor was shocked that the mayor's economic

interests mattered more to these Christians than the many human casualties. Somewhat hesitantly, he suggested that perhaps the churches ought to speak to the mayor. After all, he was an elder in the oldest church in town. Perhaps they should even elect a different mayor if he proved stubborn and unconcerned. Now the Christians were shocked. With rising indignation and righteous conviction they informed the young radical that the church dare not become involved in politics. The church is called to preach the gospel and give a cup of cold water, they said. Its mission is not to dabble in worldly things like changing social and political structures.

Perplexed and bitter, the visitor left. As he wandered out of the village, one question churned round and round in his muddled mind. Is it really more spiritual, he wondered, to operate the ambulances which pick up the bloody victims of destructive social structures than to try to change the structures themselves?

Ambulance Drivers or Tunnel Builders?

An Age of Hunger demands compassionate action and simplicity in personal lifestyles. But compassion and simple living apart from structural change may be little more than a gloriously irrelevant ego trip or proud pursuit of personal purity.

Eating less beef or even becoming a vegetarian will not necessarily feed one starving child. If millions of North Americans and Europeans reduce their beef consumption but do not act politically to change public policy, the result will not necessarily be less starvation in the developing world. To be sure, if people give the money saved to private agencies promoting rural development in poor nations, then the result will be less hunger. But unless one also changes public policy, the primary effect of merely reducing one's meat consumption may simply be to persuade farmers to plant less corn. What is needed is a change in public policy. Our Age of Hunger demands structural change.

Many questions promptly arise. What specific structural changes would be consistent with biblical principles and economic facts? Are biblical principles pertinent to secular society? Israel, after all, was a theocracy. Can we really expect unbelievers to live according to biblical ethics?

The Bible does not directly answer all these questions. Although biblical revelation tells us that God and his faithful people are always at work liberating the oppressed, we do not find a comprehensive blueprint for a new economic order in Scripture. We do find, however, some principles about justice in society.

Certainly the first application of biblical truth concerning just relationships among God's people should be to the church. As the new people of God, the church should be a new society incarnating the biblical principles regarding justice in society through its common life (Gal. 3:6–9; 6:16; 1 Pet. 2:9–10). Indeed, only as the church itself is a visible model of transformed socio-economic relationships will any appeal to government possess integrity. Much recent Christian social action has been ineffective because Christian leaders were calling on the government to legislate what they could not persuade their church members to live.

Biblical principles, however, are also relevant to secular societies as well as the church. We must be careful, of course, to remember that church and state are two distinct institutions with different tasks and roles. The state should not legislate every item of Christian ethics. Therefore a carefully developed political philosophy is essential.[2] But biblical principles of justice are not arbitrary rules relevant only for believers. The Creator revealed basic principles about social justice because he knew what would lead to lasting peace, social harmony and happiness for his creatures.

The biblical vision of the coming kingdom suggests the kind of social order God wills. And the church is supposed to be a model now (imperfect, to be sure) of what the final kingdom of perfect justice and peace will be like. Thus as the church models the coming kingdom, it exercises a powerful leavening influence in society. Furthermore, the more faithfully and appropriately any *secular* society applies the biblical norms on justice in society, the more peace, happiness and harmony that society will enjoy. Obviously, sinful people and societies will never get beyond a dreadfully imperfect approximation. But social structures do exert a powerful influence on saint and sinner alike. Christians, therefore, should exercise political influence to implement change in society at large.

That the biblical authors did not hesitate to apply revealed norms to people and societies outside the people of God supports this point. Amos announced divine punishment on the surrounding nations for their evil and injustice (Amos 1–2). Isaiah denounced Assyria for its pride and injustice (Isa. 10:12–19). The book of Daniel shows that God removed pagan kings like Nebuchadnezzar in the same way that he destroyed Israel's rulers when they failed to show mercy to the oppressed (Dan. 4:27). God obliterated Sodom and Gomorrah no less than Israel and Judah because they neglected to aid the poor and feed the hungry (Ezek. 16:49). As the Lord of the universe, Yahweh applies the same standards of social justice to all nations.

This last principle bears directly on the issues of this chapter. Some countries, like the United States, the Soviet Union, Canada, and Australia, have a bountiful supply of natural resources within their national boundaries. Do they therefore have an absolute right to use these resources as they please solely for the advantage of their own citizens? Not according to the Bible. If we believe Scripture, then we must conclude that the human right of all people to earn a just living clearly supersedes the right of the developed nations to use resources exclusively for themselves. We are only stewards, not absolute owners. God is the absolute owner, and he insists that the earth's resources be shared.

Before sketching specific steps for applying these principles, I must register one disclaimer and one clarification.

We must constantly remember the large gulf between revealed principles and contemporary application. There are many valid ways to apply biblical principles. The application of biblical norms to socio-economic questions today leaves room for creativity, and honest disagreement among biblical Christians.[3] Objecting to *my application* of biblical ethics to contemporary society is not at all the same as rejecting biblical principles. Of course, not all applications are equally valid; but humility and tolerance of each other's views are imperative. We can and must help each other see where we are unfaithful to biblical revelation and biased by our economic self-interest. Scripture, as always, is the norm.

One clarification is also necessary. To argue that Christians should work politically to change those aspects of our economic structures that are unjust is not to call for a violent revolution that would forcibly impose a centralised, state-controlled society. I believe that the way of Jesus is the way of non-violent love, even for enemies. I therefore reject the use of lethal violence.[4] The exercise of political influence in a democratic society, of course, involves the use of non-lethal pressure (or force). When we legislate penalties for drunken driving or speeding, we use an appropriate kind of non-lethal 'force'. The same is true when we pass legislation that changes foreign policies towards poor nations, makes trade patterns more just, restricts the oppressive policies of multinational corporations or increases foreign economic aid. In a democratic society, of course, such changes can occur only if a majority freely agrees or at least quietly acquiesces.

As we work to correct unjust economic structures, it is important constantly to promote decentralised, democratic decision-making and control.[5] Both Marxist totalitarianism and multinational corporations centralise power in the hands of a tiny group of individuals. Often, the choices of these powerful élites reflect their own self-interest, not what is good for the majority. It should be possible to work both for a decentralisation of economic power and a more just economy built on the basic biblical affirmation that God is on the side of justice for the poor and oppressed.

What then are some practical steps we can take?

Who Will Be Helped?

We face a complex question: Given the present situation in the less developed countries, who would benefit from changes such as increased economic foreign aid or more just patterns of international trade?

Foreign aid and free trade would not necessarily benefit the poorest half of the developing countries one iota. North Americans and Europeans are not to blame for all the poverty in the world today. Sin is not just a White European phenomenon. Many of the developing countries are ruled by wealthy élites, many of whom are largely unconcerned about the suffering of the masses in their lands. They often own a large percentage of the best land, on which they grow cash crops for export to earn the foreign exchange they need to buy luxury goods from the developed world. Meanwhile, the poorest 30 to 70 per cent of the people face grinding poverty.

That is why more foreign aid and improved trading patterns for developing countries would not necessarily improve the lot of the truly poor. Such changes might simply enable the wealthy to strengthen their repressive regimes.

But that does not mean that North Americans and Europeans can wash their hands of the whole problem. In many cases over the past few decades, the wealthy élites continued in power partly because they received massive military aid and diplomatic support from the United States and other industrial nations.[6] The United States has trained large numbers of police who have then tortured thousands of people working for social justice in countries like Chile and Brazil.[7] Western-based multinational corporations have worked closely with repressive governments. Events in Brazil, Chile, El Salvador, and the Philippines demonstrate that the United States will support dictatorships that use torture and do little for the poorest half as long as these regimes are friendly to US investments and foreign policy objectives.[8]

A Change in Foreign Policy

What can be done? Citizens of industrialised countries could demand a major reorientation of foreign policy. We could insist that our nations unequivocally side with the poor.

If we truly believe that all people are created equal, then our foreign policy must be redesigned to promote the interests of all people and not just the wealthy élites in developing countries or our own multinational corporations. We should use our economic and diplomatic power to promote democracy and justice for all, especially the poorest.

Insisting on ethical norms in the operations of our multinational corporations is difficult, of course, precisely because MNCs are large and international. But, the United States and Britain are the countries of origin for fifty-four of the hundred largest multinational corporations and, with West Germany and France, control over 75 per cent of all MNCs. Citizens in those nations have a particular responsibility to see that the impact of MNCs on poor nations is positive rather than negative.[9]

Unfortunately, US foreign policy has usually supported the economic interests of US MNCs rather than the poor in the developing nations. In May 1981, for instance, the United States was the only nation of 119 to vote in the World Health Organization against a code to control the advertising and marketing of powdered baby milk by MNCs in the Third World. In spite of worldwide documentation of the evil effects of the marketing activities of Nestlé and other MNCs[10] the Reagan administration voted no because it said the code might damage 'free enterprise'.[11]

A foreign policy which seeks biblical justice for the poor will have to be willing to place ethical controls on the operations of MNCs, even if that is not in the short-term economic interest of the MNC and its US shareholders. Both by political activity and by well-designed citizen boycotts like the Nestlé boycott, Christian citizens can help reduce the negative impact of MNCs on the poor of the earth.[12]

We should also insist that foreign aid goes primarily to countries seriously committed to Basic Needs Development strategies. Aid to countries whose governments care little about improving the condition of the poor will likely end up in the pockets of the rich. A nation's foreign policy ought to encourage justice rather than injustice. Only then will proposed changes in international trade and foreign aid programmes actually improve the lot of the poorest billion.

Social Change and Conversion

A fundamental change in Western policy towards the developing nations is imperative. But it is not enough. In addition, the poor masses in developing nations must be encouraged to demand sweeping structural changes in their own lands. We should actively promote non-violent movements working to empower the poor.

Such changes, however, can only happen if a fundamental transformation of values occurs. In a scholarly book on land tenure in India, Robert Frykenberg of the University of Wisconsin lamented the growing gulf between rich and poor. 'No amount of aid, science, and/or technology,' he concluded, 'can alter the direction of current processes without the occurrence of a more fundamental "awakening" or "conversion" among significantly larger numbers of people. . . . Changes of a revolutionary character are required, changes which can only begin in the hearts and minds of individuals.'[13]

At precisely this point the Christian church – and missionaries in particular – can play a crucial role. Two things are important: first, evangelism; and second, the whole message of Scripture. Evangelism is central to social change. Nothing so transforms the self-identity, self-worth and initiative of a poor, oppressed person as a personal, living relationship with God in Christ. Discovering that the Creator of the world lives in each of them gives new worth and energy to people psychologically crippled by centuries of oppression.

The second important component is sharing the whole biblical perspective. Some religious worldviews tend to create a fatalistic attitude towards poverty. Hinduism, for instance, teaches that those in the lower castes (and they usually are also the poorest) are there because of sinful choices in prior incarnations. Only by patiently enduring their present lot can they hope for a better life in future incarnations. In addition, Eastern religions de-emphasise the importance of history and material reality, considering them illusions to be escaped.

Biblical faith, on the other hand, affirms the goodness of the created, material world and teaches that the Creator and Lord of history demands justice now for the poor of the earth. As missionaries share this total biblical message, they can make a profound contribution to the battle against hunger, poverty and injustice.[14] To be sure, missionaries cannot engage directly in political activity in foreign countries. But they can and must teach the whole Word for the whole person. Why have missionaries so often taught Romans but not Amos to new converts in poor lands? If it is true, as we argued in Part 2, that Scripture constantly asserts that God is on the side of the poor, then missionaries should make this biblical theme a central part of their teaching. If we accept our Lord's Great Commission to teach 'all that I have commanded you', then we dare not omit or de-emphasise the biblical message of justice for the oppressed, even if it offends ruling élites.

Cross-cultural missionaries need not engage directly in politics. But they must carefully and fully expound for new converts the explosive biblical message that God is on the side of the poor and oppressed. The poor will learn quickly how to apply biblical principles to their own oppressive societies. The result will be changed social structures in developing countries. Thus far we have looked at two things: a fundamental change in foreign policy of rich nations and a mass movement of social change rooted in new religious values in the poorer countries. Christians should promote both. But what else needs to happen?

Basic Needs Development

The most obvious structural solution to the tragedy of world hunger is to foster rapid economic development in poorer nations. These countries would then be able either to produce all their own food and basic necessities, or to trade for them on the world market.

Throughout the 'fifties and 'sixties and into the 'seventies, this was the main focus of people concerned about the condition of the developing world. Many economists advocated and many Third World governments implemented economic programmes that were designed to produce economic growth, which at that time was thought to be synonymous with economic development. As the GNP of a country grew, people expected the forthcoming benefits eventually to 'trickle down' to the poor masses so that the entire society would benefit. The poor would obtain jobs in a growing economy and poverty would vanish.

Over the years, however, it became evident that, even when the GNP increased, the conditions of the poor did not automatically improve.[15] Instead, the gap between the wealthy and the poor often increased and the poor remained hungry. In light of the experience of the last several decades, it is now widely recognised that this trickle-down approach to development benefits the middle and upper classes, but does much less, if anything, to help the poor.[16] Mahbub ul Haq, an economist with the World Bank, speaks for the growing consensus: 'Growth in the GNP often does not filter down. What is needed is a direct attack on mass poverty.'[17]

In the past decade, therefore, a new approach to the development of the Third World has emerged. It is often called 'growth with equity'. Development certainly includes economic growth, but economic growth must happen in such a way that the benefits of growth are equitably distributed. In other words, the poor must participate in economic progress.

There are several variants of the growth-with-equity approach to development, but the one most popular and perhaps most consistent with Christian principles is referred to as Basic Needs Development. Basic Needs Development focuses on the situation of the poor. It holds that all people have in common certain basic needs and that the highest priority of any economic programme is to meet those needs for all people. Denis Goulet, Christian author of many books on development and development ethics, outlines these three basic needs: (1) life sustenance, (2) self-esteem, and (3) freedom to choose one's own course of action.[18]

It is really no surprise that basic needs go beyond the purely physical items of food, clothing, shelter and health care needed for life sustenance. Physical goods, for instance, could be generously supplied by some foreign agent in a paternalistic fashion. But while short-term aid is necessary and appreciated in some situations of desperate need, long-term reliance on handouts reduces self-esteem and motivation. Similarly, a totalitarian society that meets all physical needs is not God's will for us. Persons should be free to shape their lives and societies.

According to Paul Streeten, editor of the prestigious journal *World Development*, basic needs include not just the need for material goods but also 'the need for self-determination, self-reliance, political freedom and security, participation in making the decisions that affect workers and citizens, national and cultural identity, and a sense of purpose in life and work'.[19] Goulet's categories of self-esteem and freedom move in the same direction.

Because of this new focus on Basic Needs Development, the watchword in recent years in many circles (although not, unfortunately, in the US government in the 1980s) has become *self-reliant development*. Self-reliant development does not mean sealing the borders, refusing to trade with other countries or isolating the country from the world. Self-reliant development means basically that each country will to a significant degree be economically independent so that its people can provide for their own needs. According to McGinnis, self-reliant development is 'a model of development that emphasizes meeting the basic needs of a people in a country through strategies geared to the particular human and natural resources, values and traditions of the country, and through strategies maximizing the collective efforts of people within each country and among Third World countries'.[20]

Such a concept of development is necessarily broad. It means that few specific development measures will be applicable in all places at all times. Rather, an appropriate Basic Needs Development strategy for any country must take into account that country's unique context.[21] Much of what must be done to implement this strategy, naturally, can come only from the people in their respective countries. Therefore much of the burden rests squarely on the shoulders of the people in developing countries. This is as it should be. Self-esteem and freedom do not arise from Northern development experts or political figures who tell poor nations exactly what to do and how to do it.

Still, people from the developed world have much they can do in addition to changing the basic direction of their foreign policy and promoting basic values that foster social change. First, we should make international trade more fair. Second, we need to adopt new attitudes towards economic growth and the protection of the environment. And finally, we must be willing to help with economic foreign aid which will help prevent starvation during emergencies and empower the poor to earn their own way.

Making International Trade More Fair

In chapter 6 we saw how under colonialism, 'mother' countries often discouraged industrial development in the colonies. Instead, they encouraged the export of agricultural products and raw materials. Since the colonial period, the developed nations have continued to manipulate international trade relations to their economic advantage. The most frequently used strategy has been the erection of tariffs and other trade restrictions that have successfully kept many exports from developing nations from entering the markets of the developed countries. As a result of such policies, many poor nations have become over-dependent on one or just a few primary commodities. The prices of most of these commodities run through periods of wide fluctuation, and some of them have undergone a long-term decline relative to the prices of manufactured goods coming from the developed countries.

Two things need to be done in the short run. First, developed nations should drastically reduce or eliminate trade barriers on imports from the developing countries. Second, we must deal with the problem that some commodities exported by Third World nations have experienced a long-term decline of relative prices.

First, *trade barriers*. The long-standing Northern policy of increasing import duties in proportion to the amount of processing and manufacturing the product has undergone has hindered industrial growth in the South.

An ironic aspect of trade barriers is that economic theory suggests that both the developing and the industrialised nations would be better off after their removal. Developed nations would benefit because we could buy many imported goods more cheaply than before. Indeed, Guy Erb, writing in the *Columbia Journal of World Business*, estimated that trade restrictions in 1971 cost US consumers an extra $10 to $15 billion. That amounted to $200 to $300 for every US family.[22] The World Bank's *World Development Report 1987* cites a variety of studies which estimate costs to Northern consumers created by trade barriers. One study from 1986 estimated that barriers to clothing imports alone cost US consumers $18 billion in 1984.[23] Of course the developing nations would be better off because they would increase both their production and income if they could increase exports. As we saw in chapter 6, trade barriers in rich nations cost poor countries $50 to $100 billion a year. (Whether the poorest 50 per cent would be better off is another issue, and one which foreign policies focused on justice would have to address.)[24]

Still, it is not politically easy to remove such trade restrictions because the people employed in the businesses protected by them would suffer. Although the numbers would be relatively small when we consider the size of our total economy, some people would lose their jobs. But there is a remedy for this problem. It is called *adjustment assistance*.[25] Adjustment assistance is a government programme designed to facilitate the movement of unemployed workers into new areas of employment. It compensates workers for the period during which they are unemployed, and it helps them to relocate and find jobs with comparable pay.

All this talk about free trade and adjustment may seem abstract and boring. But statistics on how many jobs in poor nations result from just one job lost in the rich nations underline how important it is. Careful studies have shown that if Northern countries reduced trade barriers on manufactured goods from the South, they would directly create 4.6 jobs in low-income countries for every one lost in the European Economic Community, and 6.5 jobs in poor nations for every one lost in the US. And indirectly through multiplier effects, the impact would be two to five times greater! Oxford economist Donald Hay concludes: 'Thus in a very poor country, the effect could be as high as twenty additional jobs for one worker displaced in Europe or the U.S.A.'[26]

A relatively modest sacrifice by rich Northerners would produce major benefits in the South. And in the long run, economists expect, the North would not even lose any jobs. As developing nations returned to industrialised countries to spend their new income, the businesses they patronised would need to hire the displaced workers to meet the new demand.

Some attempts have been made in the past to reduce trade barriers on products produced by developing countries. Unrestricted access to Northern markets for textiles would be especially beneficial to developing countries. Unfortunately both the US and Western Europe have major barriers.[27]

The Multi-Fibre Agreement (MFA) governs international trade in textiles and clothing – one of the most significant areas of export for developing countries.[28] The

MFA's alleged purpose is to provide developing countries (who have a comparative advantage in this labour-intensive industry) with growing access to Northern markets. In practice, unfortunately, both Western Europe and the US have managed to impose major barriers to textiles from developing nations. In one ironic case, developed nations actually financed the development of a textile industry in Sri Lanka through the World Bank and then promptly imposed such severe import restrictions that they threatened the survival of this new Sri Lankan industry!

Economists generally agree that it would be very helpful to developing economies if industrialised nations revised the MFA and removed the trade barriers to textiles produced in developing nations. The only thing lacking is political will!

Tragically, protectionist sentiment is increasing in developed countries. In both 1984 and 1988, there were strong voices in the Democratic party calling for more protection from the 'cheap imports' from developing countries.

Will Christian voters be more concerned about hungry people abroad or economic convenience at home? In his book *Economic Development*, Theodore Morgan emphasises that removing tariff barriers would be helpful to developing nations. But he concludes on a pessimistic note: 'Experience to date suggests that domestic pressure in MDCs [more developed countries] from firms and worker organisations will make concessions as modest in the future as they have been in the past.'[29] Those who believe that God is on the side of the poor, however, must defy such pessimism and vested interests, and try to effect the necessary political changes.

Merely removing restrictions on imports, however, does not guarantee that the poor masses in the Third World will enjoy the benefits. If local governing élites seize the land of peasants so that they and multinational corporations can grow crops for export, only the rich benefit. If local governing élites suppress labour unions so that the workers who manufacture the goods for export receive low wages, only the rich benefit. How then can we remove our trade barriers in such a way that the poorest people will benefit?

The law on the Generalised System of Preferences (GSP) governs all US trade incentives with other nations. In spite of some good rhetoric, the GSP was never implemented in a way that adequately opened US markets to Third World goods. That should happen. At the same time, the GSP could also promote justice within those countries so that the poorer 50 per cent benefit significantly from exports sent to us.

Two important provisions could be written into the GSP to do this. The law could require that countries that export agricultural products under the GSP have a Stable Food Production Plan. Such a plan would be designed to make sure that production of food for export does not undercut the need to grow food for domestic consumption. A second set of provisions could demand that countries exporting goods to us under the GSP have fair labour practices and respect human rights. These stipulations would encourage labour unions and other movements which would enable the workers to benefit from the economic growth stimulated by our trade preferences.

Trade – fair trade – could reduce hunger and starvation abroad.

Second, *the problem of long-term decline of relative prices of some commodities must be faced squarely*. In 1982 the International Monetary Fund reported that the gap between the purchasing power of raw commodities exported by the developing nations and the price of imports of manufactured goods was the greatest in twenty-five years.[30] As table 14 in chapter 6 demonstrates, the purchasing power of developing countries' exported commodities continued to drop rapidly through 1987. Unfortunately, the suggestion that developed nations pay higher prices will probably not do much good. The only lasting solution is to assist economies severely affected by declining prices to move into the production of other goods.

But Third World countries cannot do this by themselves. They need economic aid from the developed countries to foster the development of their economies and to move their people, land and other resources into the production of other goods. As can be seen, this ties in closely with the reduction in trade barriers, which creates incentive to move into other areas of manufacturing. The goal, of course, is to aid the Third World to move towards self-reliant development.

What else can we do to help them reach that goal?

Debts and Development

In chapter 6, we saw that the crushing burden of foreign debt hinders sustainable economic growth in developing nations. How can this problem be resolved?

The following principles will help:

1. One central goal must be to foster sustainable, healthy economies where poor people can participate and improve their quality of life.
2. Both creditor and debtor countries contributed to the problem and therefore both should share the cost of solving it.
3. The poor, who had virtually nothing to do with obtaining the loans, should not be asked to bear a major part of the burden of repayment.
4. When debt is adjusted (i.e., cancelled or reduced) the debtor countries' record on human rights, democratic process, capital flight and military expenditures should be taken into account.[31]

Debt Cancellation Some of the debt, especially that of the poorest nations (including most of sub-Saharan Africa), simply needs to be cancelled. Many creditor countries have already started to cancel government loans to the poorest countries. The US Congress granted the President this authority in 1989. President Bush has already cancelled some concessional debt owed to the US government by countries in sub-Saharan Africa.[32] Citizens need to urge further cancellation of debt (including non-concessional official debt).

Reducing Commercial Bank Loans   Since commercial banks did not exercise proper discretion in their loans, they rightly must accept considerable losses. In 1989, the Bush administration proposed the 'Brady Plan'. This plan hoped to produce a 20 per cent reduction of loans owed to commercial banks in three years through a variety of voluntary measures. But it has not worked well, partly because each bank hopes that other banks will write off enough bad loans and thus reduce a given country's debt to the point where its own loans can then be collected in full. Harvard economist Jeffrey Sachs puts it bluntly:

If an individual banker learns that everyone else is going to write off 50 per cent of their Third World loans, that individual would say publicly: 'Wonderful, great idea, absolutely realistic.' While all the other guys join the bandwagon, he would hold out on all his loans and then, when the debtor country has such a reduced burden that it can pay everything on remaining debt, the hold-out banker plans to collect in full.[33] As the British 'In Whose Interest?' campaign (details n. 39) comments: 'In a few isolated cases, banks – including the Midland – have actually cancelled all the loans which they are owed by a few of the poorest countries in return for the debtor country's funding development projects. These gestures, though welcome, have not as yet made any significant impact on the overall level of debt.'

It is probably necessary for the International Monetary Fund and the World Bank to adopt an official policy that penalizes banks that do not join a comprehensive debt reduction package.[34] That, of course, would require political will since any loss borne by the IMF or the World Bank would finally have to be made up by taxpayers in creditor nations. But risking that cost is undoubtedly wiser than risking increasing economic stagnation and chaos in poor debtor nations.[35]

Free Trade   We saw in chapter 6 that trade barriers imposed by industrialised nations reduce the export earnings of developing nations by $50–$100 billion a year. If the industrialised world greatly reduced these barriers to goods from developing nations, debtor nations would be able to increase their export earnings substantially and thus be able to repay a major portion of their debts. As development economist Michael Todaro insists, unless developing nations can find more markets for their exports, they will not escape from the debt trap.[36] But that again demands political will that can only come through vigorous activity by voters who care more about the poor than short-term economic self-interest.

Reducing Debt and Military Expenditures Unfortunately, industrialised nations are not the only ones wasting excessive money on guns. In the early 'eighties when the financial crisis became severe, developing nations slashed their health and education budgets more deeply than their military outlays.[37] In 1986, developing nations devoted more than 30 per cent more dollars to the military than to education and health combined.

Greater debt reduction could be offered to developing nations that reversed these mistaken priorities. Nor would this demand seem so hypocritical if it were linked to the recent proposal for a global reduction of 50 per cent for military expenditures by all countries by the year 2000 (see p. 254). If industrialised nations are willing to share the cost of reducing the crushing debt load, then it is reasonable to ask that developing countries spend more money on the basic needs of their poor majorities rather than on further military hardware whose primary purpose is national prestige or the protection of entrenched élites.

Debt Swaps 'Debt Swaps' reduce Third World debt by trading a certain amount of discounted loans for local currency. That is then used to do (allegedly) useful things in the debtor country. Not all swaps are wise. In fact some may evoke reminders of colonialism. But some swaps are helpful.

'Debt-for-nature' swaps seek to reduce both the debt crisis and environmental destruction at the same time. International environmental organisations have worked out schemes that increase the local funds available to conserve and maintain tropical forests. In 1987, Conservation International bought £400,000 of Bolivia's debt owed to Citibank. Since the loan was discounted by 85 per cent, Conservation International only had to pay £60,000. Conservation International then cancelled the full £400,000. In exchange, the Bolivian government added 3.7 million acres of tropical forests and grasslands to be protected for sustainable usage and gave £150,000 in local currency to do it. No foreign group acquired any control over Bolivian land.

Both private agencies and governments in the North should do more debt-for-nature swaps. Since Northern countries are responsible for so much of the world's environmental destruction, it is particularly appropriate that we pay to preserve tropical ecosystems that are essential to the global climate.

'Debt-for-development' swaps enable private charities to purchase discounted debt in similar ways to do development work in debtor countries. Sometimes a bank holding Third World loans makes a direct donation. Sometimes, the charity purchases heavily discounted loans. Then they forgive the loans in exchange for more local currency than they could have purchased at regular exchange rates for the same dollars. The debtor country gets both a reduced debt load and also increased economic growth through the expanded work of the development agency.[38]

Adjustment Policies They require adjustment! In chapter 6, we saw that the IMF imposed severe adjustment policies on poor debtor nations who then slashed government spending for the poor. As a result half a million children have died each year to pay the debts. Voters in Northern nations that control IMF policy could demand revised IMF adjustment policies for debtor nations. We should insist on policies grounded in God's special concern for the poorest and weakest.

In early 1990, a unique British coalition emerged to do this and more. A coalition of environmental and development groups joined together in a campaign called 'In

Whose Interest?'. They seek to (1) persuade British banks to cancel some loans, and (2) demand adjustment policies that favour the poor and protect the environment.[39] This approach merits sister groups in all major nations.

It will cost some money. But we can solve the debt crisis in a way that enables poor debtor countries to develop sustainable, economic growth that benefits everyone, especially the poorest. That in turn will slow down their population explosion. Debt cancellation, debt swaps, and revised adjustment policies are all important. Most important perhaps is an end to hypocritical Northern trade barriers that prevent debtor nations from carrying their share of the debt burden.

Preserving the Earth and Empowering the Poor

In chapter 6, we saw that we have polluted the environment so severely that everyone, especially the poor, faces grave dangers in the next century. What can be done?

The Environment   Restoring environmental integrity is a-task for individuals and governments, children and adults, churches and businesses. It can be worked on at every level. Each family can make a difference by deciding to recycle rubbish formerly dispatched to the growing mountains of urban waste sites. Churches can teach a new set of values essential if we are to develop a sustainable society. Business must prepare to shoulder more costs and politicians must dare to adopt demanding public programmes.

The basic direction we need to travel is fairly clear. We want to create a decent sustainable life on this planet so that our grandchildren and their grandchildren can continue to rejoice in the earth's goodness and splendour. Therefore we must end the pollution of our environment by recycling, energy efficiency, reforestation, and switching from non-renewable fossil fuels to non-polluting renewable energy from sun, wind and water. Making those changes, however, will be difficult.

Government action is essential. Without it, businesses

Table 18 Sulphur Pollution in Selected European
Countries (1988)

Country	Total Emissions	Total Deposition	Share of Emissions Exported	Share of Deposition Imported
	(thousand tons)		(per cent)	
Norway	37	210	76	96
Austria	62	181	74	91
Sweden	110	302	69	89
Switzerland	37	65	81	89
Netherlands	145	104	80	72
France	760	622	67	59
West Germany	750	628	63	56
Czechoslovakia	1,400	659	75	47
Poland	2,090	1,248	68	46
Soviet Union	5,150	3,201	61	38
Italy	1,185	510	72	36
East Germany	2,425	787	75	22
Spain	1,625	590	72	22
United Kingdom	1,890	636	71	15

Used with permission from Brown, *State of the World 1990*, p. 115.

that invest in pollution control will suffer a competitive
disadvantage from callous competitors who continue
dumping pollution on everyone. In the short run, the
market ignores environmental costs. Therefore legislation
that justly compels all businesses to end pollution places all
competitors on an even playing-field.

The same logic leads to international standards and
regulations. Table 18 demonstrates that for many countries, a great deal of the pollution devastating their nation
comes from abroad. And they in turn export much of the
pollution they produce. So if one country decides to spend
the money to reduce pollution and surrounding nations
refuse, one's investment largely improves the life of selfish
neighbours.

International co-operation and agreement are essential.
An international climate treaty is being drafted in 1990 and

may be adopted in 1992.[40] The United Nations is probably
the best place to locate the crucial task of verification. One
way both to assist developing nations and provide an
incentive to implement international environmental agreements would be to establish a major global environmental
fund (see the discussion of a carbon tax below). Only
developing countries working seriously on programmes to
increase energy efficiency, slow population growth (in ways
that respect the sanctity of human life), reduce pollution of
air and water and switch to renewable energy sources
would be eligible to receive funds.

It would be unwise to centralise vast power in any one
global agency. (Centralised power in a fallen world is
always dangerous.) But that does not mean that we can
ignore the need for a strengthened United Nations to deal
with our inextricably interrelated countries on planet earth.
While we do that, however, we must be careful to do all that
we can at as local a level as possible and make sure that
there are careful checks and balances for new centralised
global institutions which the environmental crisis requires.

What specifically should we do? We can reduce the
likelihood of drastic global warming if we act quickly to
reduce and then reverse the emission of 'greenhouse gases'
into the atmosphere. Reducing the ever escalating disper-
sal of carbon into the air is especially crucial. That in turn
requires greater energy efficiency, public transport and
cycling, reversing deforestation and recycling disposable
wastes. Above all, perhaps, it means switching to energy
sources that produce far less carbon.

Renewable Energy   The two alternative energy possibilities are nuclear energy or renewable energy sources
such as the sun, water and wind. Unfortunately, nuclear
power plants are dangerous: even forty years into the
nuclear age, nobody knows how to dispose of nuclear waste
safely. Renewable energy from sun, wind and water is the
better alternative.

Realistic possibilities exist. Currently, water produces 21
per cent of the world's electricity. If we used fossil fuels for
that, we would annually burden the atmosphere with

another 539 million tons of carbon. In the Third World, there are still major untapped sources of hydropower.[41]

The technology for harnessing wind power to produce electricity is now commercially competitive (6–8¢ per kilowatt hour). Some twenty thousand wind machines already operate – mostly in California and Denmark. Northern Europe, North Africa, India and the Soviet Union have great potential to produce electricity from the wind.[42]

Increasingly, solar energy is becoming commercially viable. Southern California has solar thermal systems producing at a rate of 8¢ per kilowatt hour. Solar photovoltaics uses semiconductor materials to convert the sun's rays directly into electricity. Small solar cells are already in use in six thousand Indian villages. The US Solar Energy Institute reports that solar photovoltaics will be able to supply a half of all US energy needs by 2030.[43] Government policies that encourage the necessary research now are an essential investment.

One very attractive side benefit of solar technology is that the tiny units can be installed in every farm and house. The result is a democratisation of economic power that breaks the monopoly of vast utility companies. Precisely for this reason, of course, we can expect the monopolies to fight decentralised solar power.

Public Transport and Cycling A public policy that fostered greater use of public transport on the one hand and cycling on the other would also reduce pollution from cars burning fossil fuels. Motor vehicles create more air pollution than any other human activity. They produce ground-level ozone that lowers crop yield ($54 billion a year in the US alone).[44] Citizens need to insist that government policy switches more resources from road construction for private cars to safer, more accessible public transport systems. Using high taxes on private cars and very expensive drivers' licences, the Japanese encourage large numbers of people to travel by train rather than by car. Los Angeles's ghastly air pollution has prompted the region to undertake a bold plan to discourage car use and improve public transport. They even plan to limit the number of cars per family![45]

Even bicycles make a difference! In a fascinating essay, 'Cycling in the Future', Marcia Lowe shows how public policy even in very rich nations can encourage widespread use of bicycles.[46] China leads the way in bicycle use. In 1987, more bicycles were purchased in China than cars in the whole world. But the other three leaders in bicycle transport are very wealthy nations – the Netherlands, Denmark, and Japan.

Public policy decisions were crucial in achieving a greater dependence upon bicycling by the public. Government decided that bicycles for short distances and rail transport for longer trips would be the basic pattern for Japan. Legislation enabled localities to require railways and businesses to install facilities for parking bicycles. The Netherlands cut highway funds and invested more in direct, uninterrupted cycling roads.

Bicycles are obviously a more possible mode of transport for larger numbers of people in small, densely populated places like Japan than for the vast distances of the United States. But China is hardly small. And large North American cities could encourage much more cycling by installing interconnected networks of safe cycleways and bike lanes on streets.

Cycling is admittedly good for one's health; and it is better for the planet than the private car. So is the use of public transport. Government should provide economic incentives for switching to both of these by insisting that car owners pay the real costs (including the hidden costs) of cars. Some estimate that the total hidden cost of cars is $300 billion a year in the US. Even those who cannot afford to own cars help subsidise car owners through public taxes that build and maintain highways and cover costs for accident-produced illness and air pollution. The US is last among all nations in taxing car sales and petrol.[47]

We should tax ownership and use and invest the money in mass transit and in building cycle routes. Studies clearly show that driving decreases when car owners have to pay more of the real costs. And think of the extra joy of relaxed reading on the train, commuting to work, or the exhilaration of the warm wind blowing through one's hair and the satisfied awareness of a healthy body able to pedal to work!

Saving Energy   Energy efficiency is also crucial. Simply using currently available technology, we could double our petrol mileage of cars, triple the output of electric lights and cut typical heating requirements by 75 per cent.[48] Super-insulated houses in Canada require only a tenth of the US average to heat them. We now have compact fluorescent bulbs that produce the same amount of light using eighteen watts as regular bulbs produce with seventy-five watts.[49]

We obviously do not want government to legislate every new cost-saving device. The market provides the basic incentive. But there is a significant place for appropriate legislation that provides parameters, incentives and research to increase energy efficiency. Energy-saving appliance standards passed by the Congress in 1986 have already saved the US $28 billion in electrical and gas bills and spared the atmosphere 340 million tons of carbon.[50]

Recycling Waste   At a time when city governments despair of finding adequate waste disposal sites, it is astonishing that the US Congress cannot even pass a simple national bottle recycling bill. The statistics on waste are dumbfounding. After just one usage, we throw away about two-thirds of all aluminium, three-quarters of all steel and paper, and even more of the plastic. We do this in spite of the fact that it takes only 5 per cent as much energy to recycle aluminium as to smelt new bauxite ore. It takes only one-third as much energy to produce new steel from scrap as from iron ore. Newsprint from recycled paper requires 25–60 per cent less energy than from pulp.

Equally important, recycling spares the planet. Steel from scrap results in 85 per cent less pollution than steel produced directly from iron ore. And it also reduces water pollution by 76 per cent. Recycling paper reduces air pollution by 74 per cent and water pollution by 35 per cent.[51] And more forests stay alive to take carbon out of the air. In fact, every ton of recycled paper saves seventeen trees. In the UK many local councils now provide bottle-banks and other recycling facilities for paper and for aluminium cans.

We can all work at recycling: at home as we teach our children by separating tin, glass and paper for recycling; at work as we push our employers to recycle; at the polls as we elect politicians who will resist special interests and vote for public policy that fosters recycling; and at church as we develop a recycling ethic for a sustainable world.

Reversing Deforestation Annually, we lose enough trees to increase the carbon in the atmosphere by one billion tons.[52] Industrialised nations have just begun to ask seriously how they can provide economic incentives to countries with large tropical forests to encourage them to slow down and reverse their destruction.[53] Obviously it is the height of hypocrisy for industrialised nations producing most of the world's carbon pollution to ask poor nations to bear the cost of saving the world from global warming via carbon dioxide in the upper atmosphere. We cause the problem and we need to pay for it.

The task is vast and we can all work at it – by planting a few trees in our gardens, by voting for politicians who will plant a few billion, and by purchasing timber from companies that get their timber from replanted forests. As we do it, we can reflect on the fresh air our grandchildren will enjoy.

A Carbon Tax There are many promising steps for improving our environment. But they all cost money! In the short run, therefore, the temptation is to continue old patterns even though they pollute our cities, destroy our forests and lakes and lead to likely disaster in the next century.

An international carbon tax is one possible step forward.[54] The calculations would not be exact, but we could attempt to estimate the real costs of fossil fuels – including all the negative environmental results of present pollution and the future costs of global warming. Since coal produces the most carbon, the tax on coal would be highest – then oil, then gas. Renewable energies, such as that from the sun and wind, produce no carbon emissions and therefore would suffer no tax. A carbon tax would mean that the market would then work to apply the real costs of pollution. And government could use the tax revenues to encourage energy efficiency.

In the US it is estimated that such a tax would produce $60 billion ($240 per person) a year. The cost of petrol would go up approximately 17¢ (about 10p) a gallon. Electrical costs would increase about 28 per cent. Introduced gradually, such a tax would spur new research and result in greatly expanded energy efficiency.

A global agreement on such a tax would be important. Otherwise countries imposing the tax would suffer a competitive disadvantage. Again, poor developing countries will feel that they cannot afford the luxury of a clean environment while their people starve. But a global agreement on a carbon tax could include a provision that a certain percentage of all global revenues from the carbon tax would go to an international environmental fund solely for environmental improvements in developing countries. Ten per cent of this fund would produce approximately $28 billion a year. That much money would go a long way to enable developing nations to plant trees, slow population growth, encourage use of renewable energies and improve energy efficiency. Doing those things would not only help reduce the likelihood of environmental disaster. It would also help the poor.

New Attitudes Towards Growth and Resource Use

The basic changes just discussed are crucial. But they are not enough. We also need a new set of values and attitudes.

Economic growth has been a catchword in the developed world for years. With hardly a second thought, almost everyone assumes that economic growth is desirable. We usually equate a growing economy with a healthy economy – one that provides jobs, opportunities for advancement, and a rising standard of living. But now we see that our kind of industrialisation plus the population explosion seriously threaten the stability of the world environment.

Environmental decay decreases prospects for the continued development of poor nations even though their economic growth is much more important at this point in history than expanding the wealth even more in rich nations. What then must we do?

The obvious answer is that the developed world should consume less and pollute less. This is essentially correct; but, there are problems. As MIT economist Lester Thurow points out, given today's economic structures, environmental crusades that reduce growth and advocate greater pollution control may well benefit the middle and upper classes at the expense of the poor. Under current structures reducing growth may lead to a rise in unemployment which hits the poor (both here and abroad) harder than the rich. Increased pollution control equipment may raise the prices of goods needed by the poor. Furthermore, a cleaner environment may well raise the standard of living of the wealthier classes who retain their jobs and have enough money to get out and enjoy the enhanced environment.[55]

Few economists doubt the validity of this analysis. But it would be wrong to conclude that it is misguided to use limited non-renewable resources sparingly and end pollution. Rather, Thurow's warning illuminates the size and complexity of the obstacles that we must overcome.

The pervasive notion that increased consumption leads to greater happiness is at the heart of our dilemma. When we use the term *standard of living*, it is commonly thought to refer exclusively or primarily to the level of material consumption. Christians know, however, that a person's standard of living is 'high' when he or she lives in proper relationship with God, other people and the earth. Right relationships with others and the earth certainly include an adequate supply of material resources. But constantly increasing material affluence in no way guarantees an improved standard of living. Unfortunately, this Christian perspective disappeared long ago in the historical development of industrialised societies.[56]

Ironically, even by a secular definition of happiness, economic growth and rising affluence do not generate greater happiness. In a highly acclaimed but little implemented study, economist Richard Easterlin has shown that a highly affluent person is no happier on the whole than someone less affluent (provided basic needs are largely met). The reason is that people tend to measure their happiness by how much they consume relative to their neighbours. As all try to get ahead, most tend to rise together so everyone is frustrated by their unsuccessful efforts to achieve happiness by getting ahead of the others! Easterlin concludes: 'To the outside observer, economic growth appears to be producing an ever more affluent society, but to those involved in the process, affluence will always remain a distant, urgently sought, but never attained goal.'[57] Growth occurs, the earth is used and abused – but no perceptible benefit results.

To Christians this should be no surprise. We should be the first to reject this rat race in which everyone is trying to surpass each other. Knowing that material goods are not what bring ultimate happiness, we should be the first to experiment with simpler lifestyles. As we reduce our demand for dwindling resources that pollute the environment, we witness to others that happiness is not found primarily in material possessions.

As we move in this direction, we need to be alert to Thurow's warnings. If, in our advanced state of technology, significant numbers of people consume less, there will be less need for production. Declining demand will signal a decline in the need for workers. So we need long-term structural changes if displaced workers are to find other jobs. Because of the monumental proportions of the changes needed, they must be slow and gradual. Therefore I offer suggestions both for the immediate future and for the more distant future.

In the short run, a simpler lifestyle lived by Christians will mean more money *not being spent* on consumer goods. If large numbers of people save rather than spend this income, severe unemployment will probably ensue. If, however, we donate the income we have saved to agencies doing development work in poor nations, a major reduction in employment is unlikely. Recipients of the aid will spend the money on goods they need for wealth creation and on attaining an adequate level of material well-being. As they do, the money spent on these goods will eventually return to buy things from businesses in industrialised nations. As the developed nations consume less and share more, we also spur indigenous development in the Third World, thus making for a more just distribution of goods and assets.

As we adopt this short-run approach, Christians all over the world ought to re-examine priorities at a still deeper level. Suppose that by a miracle of God's grace we succeeded in ending the scandal of a world where billions live in grinding poverty while the affluent live like kings. Even if we reached the biblical norm of distributional justice, we would have to ask ourselves the next question: should we once again pursue the same sort of economic growth we formerly did? The obvious answer is no. As we saw earlier, the carrying capacity of the earth is ultimately threatened. Redistributing the earth's burden does not lessen the full load. Shifting a heavy load from one side of the wagon to a more even spread may ease excessive pressure on certain points, but the total poundage of the load will not diminish.

Christians must seek to change the demand for goods and services away from heavy resource usage and environment-damaging goods towards the goods and services that make less demand on the earth's carrying capacity.[58] One suggestion is that people spend more of their time and money creating vibrant, active Christian churches. Another is to spend more money on the arts (drama, music and other creative arts), thus creating an incentive for more people to engage in these activities instead of in the production of more material goods. People could work fewer hours at their jobs, and in their new leisure they could serve the community or spend more time with their families or in constructive hobbies.

In the long run, then, sweeping changes will come. It is hoped that, through increasingly faithful Christian witness, the Spirit will work in the hearts of others so that our society will abandon the heretical notion that happiness comes through ever-expanding material abundance. In the long run there must be the kinds of relationship between persons on the one hand and peoples and the earth on the other, which are discussed in the book *Earthkeeping*, produced by a group of scholars under the auspices of the Calvin Center for Christian Scholarship. We do not have the right, *Earthkeeping* argues, to use and abuse God's creation for selfish purposes. God has put the whole earth, including its land, rivers, mountains, animals and plants, under our care. We are to be stewards of the creation. We should not, therefore, pursue economic and technological growth that unnecessarily damages creation. Instead, God commands us to live in harmony with himself, with people *and* with creation.[59]

Does Foreign Aid Help?

Many critics want to reduce or eliminate foreign aid. Considering American foreign aid conservatives have argued that it has failed to reduce anti-American hostility or to promote US foreign policy and that it has often been wasted by corrupt, inefficient governments. Radicals have argued that the purpose was never the reduction of hunger, but rather the promotion of US foreign policy objectives; that it never gets to the real problem, which is the powerlessness of the poor; and that in fact aid strengthens the power of oppressive Third World élites.[60]

Sometimes these problems and the news stories about waste and corruption tempt us to abandon foreign aid. But that would be a hasty response. Fundamental changes are imperative. But wisely targeted economic foreign aid can make a difference. In 1967 smallpox killed two million people in the world. By 1981 smallpox had totally disappeared. The reason? A massive programme to eradicate this killer. Millions of dollars in foreign aid helped defeat this annual destroyer of two million people.[61]

Two questions are especially pertinent if we want to

provide aid wisely: What would make our aid more effective? How much aid is needed?

1. *Focus on the Poorest of the Poor* First of all, most economic foreign aid should be designed to enable the poorest of the poor people in the poorest nations to meet their own basic needs. Since most poor people live in rural areas, the focus must be on integrated rural development. That will usually mean land reform; agricultural extension services including credit, improved seeds, and fertiliser; rural public-works programmes such as irrigation projects; agricultural research; introduction of appropriate technology; and the development of light industry located in rural areas to complement the agricultural development.

It is particularly important that basic, minimal health care, education, and a secure food supply be available to the rural masses.[62] Only then will the population explosion slow down. A study by the World Bank concluded, 'In all developing countries, policies which succeed in improving the conditions of life for the poor, and in providing education and employment opportunities for women, are likely to reduce fertility. An improvement in the welfare of the poor appears to be essential before fertility can fall to developed country levels.'[63]

Such a conclusion should not surprise the Christian. If, as the Bible teaches, God is at work in history liberating the poor and oppressed, then we should expect that an effective development strategy would be one that brings justice to the poor masses. At the same time this approach to development focused on the poorest of the poor provides a decisive answer to 'lifeboat' theorists. Foreign aid to promote rural development is not a foolish gesture which sustains millions now only to doom even more later. Rather, foreign aid which encourages agricultural production as well as (at the least) minimal education and health care among the rural masses is probably the only way to check the population explosion in time to avoid global disaster. Justice and effectiveness coincide.

Tragically, the bulk of economic assistance has not gone to the truly poor in America. There have been various efforts like the 'New Direction' reforms in 1973 and the legislation in 1982 directing 40 per cent of US development assistance to the poorest. A recent study, however, concludes that the bulk of US foreign aid has gone to 'Third World institutions that have no links to the poor'. Instead, we have channelled 'billions of dollars through unresponsive, ineffective bureaucracies of often corrupt and repressive governments or through private structures controlled by these countries' wealthy élites'. The result? Further concentration of wealth and power.[64]

What can be done?

2. *Support Participatory, People-directed Development* The authors of this critical study point out that in the last four decades, a large number of effective, grass-roots organisations empowering the poor have sprung up in developing countries. Created by or with the poor, they know better than outside experts how to meet their own needs. The US Congress should create a new aid agency independent of the State Department that can forge a new partnership with these local, successful grass-roots organisations representing poor people such as small farmers, urban poor, women and the landless. Two programmes funded by the US Agency for International Development (USAID) – the Inter-American Foundation working in Latin America and the African Development Foundation – have already demonstrated major success with this participatory approach.[65] Other countries should do the same. Our aid will be far more effective when channelled to these and similar grass-roots organisations rather than through central bureaucracies controlled by wealthy élites.

3. *Focus on Empowerment* Development assistance should empower the powerless. Empowerment of the poor will often mean land reform and an end to the political corruption by which the powerful maintain oppressive systems. It will also mean an end to the violation of human rights and the promotion of unions and other organisations that enable the poor to exercise influence in shaping their societies. Obviously, empowering the poor will threaten some oppressive corrupt élites currently in power – in the

local village, the state, the nation and the globe. But only if development assistance empowers the poor so that they can shape their own destiny will it foster justice rather than dependence.

When we do give government-to-government assistance, it ought to go primarily to countries that agree to an overall development strategy to empower the absolutely poor by means of land reform, secure human rights and the democratic process. We could offer such countries trade preferences and reduced tariffs on their exports to us. We could also forgive a portion of their crippling foreign debts.

4. *Adopt a Long-range Approach*   Short-term economic and political considerations have hindered the effectiveness of foreign aid. Too much aid continues to go to nations because they are currently of geopolitical interest to the donor.[66] We should give more aid through multilateral channels such as effective United Nations programmes like UNICEF and the International Fund for Agricultural Development. Multilateral aid rather than bilateral agreements between the donor countries and individual developing countries tends to reduce the influence of short-term political considerations.

The United States has unfortunately 'tied' a good portion of its aid, demanding that the money be used to purchase US goods and services. Since US prices are often higher than global market prices, the aid provides fewer goods and services than it could otherwise. The long-range goal of a global society free of widespread hunger and poverty, rather than immediate political or economic concerns, should govern the granting of aid.

5. *Economic Sustainability*   We dare not continue destroying the world's soil, water and forests. Northern capital-intensive farming, for instance, is not a model to promote in developing nations. Our aid should promote appropriate technology and a labour-intensive approach that is sensitive to preserving a sound global ecosystem. We must also insist that the World Bank implement its new environmental criteria for its projects.[67]

6. *Creating Wealth Through Tiny Loans*   A wide variety

of organisations have discovered that tiny, interest-bearing loans to very poor entrepreneurs is one of the most effective ways to reduce poverty.

The Grameen Bank in Bangladesh was a pioneer. Tiny loans of as little as $65 (about £40) to landless peasants to buy a cow or a rice huller produced dramatic new wealth. By 1989, half a million borrowers (mostly women) earned approximately 43 per cent more than villagers without these loans.[68]

In chapter 7, we saw that David Bussau's Maranatha Trust will create 10,000 new jobs in 1990 transforming the lives of 50,000 people. Cost? A mere $5 million or £3 million. Since very poor people have no securities, banks will not give them loans. Private agencies like Maranatha are stepping into this gap.

Not surprisingly, people are asking how we can channel government economic aid to this kind of micro-income generation project. In 1988, the US Congress designated $50 million to be used wherever possible for tiny loans of less than $300 to the poorest 20 per cent of the people in developing nations. Unfortunately, as a recent study shows, USAID has done a very poor job of implementing this legislation.[69] Congress must correct AID's failures and mandate more investment of economic aid in credit-based micro-income generation projects.

At the Oxford Conference on Christian Faith and Economics in January 1990, participants from around the world enthusiastically endorsed this approach. Recognising that private agencies do a more efficient job of delivering economic assistance to the poorest, they urged governments in industrial nations to consider granting tax credits to those who make donations to approved, private voluntary organisations engaged in credit-based micro-income generation programmes in developing nations.[70] A tax credit of 50 to 80 per cent would mean that a donation of £1000 would reduce the donor's federal taxes by £500–£800. The result would be greatly increased money for loans to enable the poorest to help themselves.

7. *Separating Development Aid from Military Aid*   US

citizens are sometimes confused because four different categories of aid all appear in the annual US foreign aid bill authorising money for developing countries. Military aid provides weapons and training for Third World militaries and the Economic Support Fund (ESF) provides economic aid to promote US security and political interests. (In the 'eighties, most of it went to Israel, Egypt, Pakistan and El Salvador.) Food aid provides food on either easy terms or as grants. Development aid is supposed to help the poor escape poverty.[71]

Unfortunately, all four types of aid appear together in the same foreign aid bill. Military and Security (ESF) aid should be authorised separately from development aid. A new aid agency totally independent of the departments of state and defence should be in charge of all development aid. In the UK development aid is administered by the Overseas Development Administration which is a part of the Foreign Office.

8. *Improving Food Aid*   Far too often, US food aid has been used for political purposes and promotion of US grain sales. At one point during the Vietnam War, fully one half of all US food aid went to the tiny countries of South Vietnam and Cambodia. In the 'eighties, a good deal went to El Salvador. In 1989, Egypt, with an annual per capita GNP of $680, received $177 million in food aid while nine countries in sub-Saharan Africa with a per capita GNP of $378 received only $91 million.

Food aid would be far more effective in reducing poverty if we could agree that its primary goals are emergency food in times of crisis and support for long-term sustainable agricultural development in poor nations. Eligibility standards that focus food aid on the poorest and that provide for the phasing out of food aid as local agricultural output increases are also important.[72]

9. *Reversing Misguided Priorities*   From 1979 to 1988, US military and security aid increased dramatically, and development and food aid decreased. In 1979, the former two received $7.82 billion and the latter two $8.07 billion. By 1988, this had been reversed: political/military aid got

$9.35 billion while development/food aid dropped to $5.17 billion. Poor nations don't need more tanks and bullets. They need more help to win an effective war on poverty. If we improve the way we give foreign aid, it can help reduce hunger, poverty and injustice. But how much aid is needed?

Bombs versus Bread

The world faces a crucial choice. Substantial steps to help the poor and hungry on the scale needed require major sums of money. World expenditures on armaments spiral upward each year. Do the people of the world want to spend as much on arms each year (about $1,100 billion in 1988) as the poorest half of humanity receives in total annual income? Do we want the annual budget of the World Health Organization to equal about five hours of world military spending? Between 1947 and 1952, the United States poured $23 billion ($108.3 billion in terms of 1989 dollars) into Western Europe under the Marshall Plan.[73] One has only to look at the material prosperity of Western Europe today to realise that it was the most successful aid programme the world has ever seen. The plight of over a billion poor people today is more desperate than that of the people of war-ravaged Europe in the late 1940s. And yet, we give a vastly smaller percentage of our wealth to today's needy even though our wealth has grown enormously.[74] The developed world, led by committed Christians in those countries, could lead the fight for greater aid for the developing world.

Government budgets reflect fundamental priorities and values in the same way that the budgets of churches and families do. In the 1980s, the US vastly expanded both its own military expenditures (to $2.2 trillion) and its foreign military aid. At the same time, it reduced development assistance to poor developing nations. These priorities are not biblical. Nor, I believe, do they reflect the deepest values of the American people.

Ironically, such priorities are also bad for our economy.

Careful studies have demonstrated that spending tax money on military equipment is the *least efficient* way of producing jobs. Building military equipment requires high technology and therefore relatively few workers. One billion dollars spent on training nurses creates eighty-five thousand new jobs; the same money spent for military equipment produces only forty-five thousand new jobs.[75]

Fortunately we stand at a moment in history when there is realistic hope for a substantial reduction in military expenditures worldwide. President Gorbachev's sweeping changes in the USSR and the astonishing revolutions in Eastern Europe in the autumn of 1989 have led the top leaders in North America and Western Europe to project major cuts in military spending. Even if Mr Gorbachev is replaced, it will be impossible to return to the past. With leaders as conservative as Prime Minister Margaret Thatcher announcing that the cold war is over, it is genuinely possible to think in terms of a dramatic re-allocation of dollars from arms to empowering the poor and protecting the environment.

In early 1990, Senators Mark Hatfield and Dale Bumpers introduced the Harvest of Peace Resolution into the US Senate. Supported by Bread for the World,[76] Evangelicals for Social Action and a broad range of other organisations, this resolution calls on the US to negotiate a 50 per cent reduction of military spending with the USSR and the other nations worldwide to take effect by the year 2000. Since the world now spends over $1 billion on arms each year, that would free $500 million a year to reduce debt burdens, protect the environment and empower the poor.

We dare not assume, however, that just because reduced international tensions have greatly reduced the danger of war, the military-industrial complex will willingly agree to release 50 per cent of its income. In a powerful speech in the Senate on August 2nd, 1989, Republican Senator Hatfield warned that harvesting the peace dividend would be difficult:

Mr President, from the Revolutionary War to the Civil War to the Spanish-American War through World War 1, through World War 2, through Korea, through Vietnam, and through the cold wars in between, at no time did the spending for military purposes reduce or diminish after those wars. They reached a peak during a war, and then remained at that peak following the war. No build down – only a build up. And no peace dividend, Mr President. None at all.[77]

Reducing military spending worldwide by the year 2000 would be a fantastic gift to the poor. But it will only happen if millions of citizens worldwide work hard to demand it of their political leaders. As we engage in that battle, President Eisenhower's ringing words will help:

Every gun that is made, every warship launched, every rocket fired signifies, in the final sense, a theft from those who hunger and are not fed, those who are cold and are not clothed.[78]

The tasks outlined in this chapter seem overwhelming. Only as individuals join with other concerned citizens can they effectively promote the necessary structural changes. Here are a few organisations working to change public policy.

Bread for the World

Bread for the World (BFW) is a Christian citizens' movement in the United States whose goal is to change governmental policy on all issues that affect hungry people. BFW has members in every congressional district across the country and has organised local chapters at the grass-roots level in many of those. A monthly newsletter keeps members up to date on current administrative and legislative activity. Members influence legislation by calling, writing or visiting government officials, especially their own congressional representatives.

Bread for the World is an explicitly Christian

organisation. Worship is a regular part of the meetings of
local chapters. Art Simon, the director, is a devout
Missouri Synod Lutheran. BFW makes a conscious effort to
involve Catholics, evangelicals and mainline Protestants, at
every level, including the staff and board of directors. This
organisation practises what it preaches. Salaries are based
primarily on need, not position. For many years, the salary
of the executive director was less than that of the packager!
Volunteers carry out most of BFW's local activities, and
income comes largely from the $25 annual membership fee.

BFW has been very successful in affecting public policy.
In 1981 it developed, helped introduce and greatly facili-
tated the passage of the Hunger and Global Security bill.
This bill was based on the belief that 'a major worldwide
effort to conquer hunger and poverty, far from being a
gesture of charity to be offered or withheld according to
temporary political whims, holds the key to both global and
national security'.[79] The bill declared 'that the U.S. [will]
make the elimination of hunger the primary focus of its
relationships with the developing countries, beginning with
the decade of the 1980s'.[80] Its provisions increased funding
for health programmes in developing nations and
reoriented the aid given to multilateral development banks
so that it would reach the people most in need.

Founded in 1974, BFW is a rapidly growing movement.
Membership has increased from fourteen thousand in 1976
to over forty thousand in 1990. BFW offers Christian
citizens an effective way to help shape the public policies
which will mean life or death for millions of people in the
next few decades. (See Appendix B for the BFW address
and the addresses of the organisations which follow.)

Evangelicals for Social Action

Evangelicals for Social Action (ESA) is an evangelical
organisation devoted to promoting justice, liberty and
peace from a biblical perspective. ESA believes that prayer
and radical dependence on the Holy Spirit must be central
to any major contemporary movement to bring structural

change in society. ESA also believes that a consistent biblical stance cuts across ideological stereotypes of left and right. Concerned to strengthen the family and oppose abortion on demand, ESA also believes a biblical position means working against racism and the nuclear arms race.

Reducing hunger and economic injustice is one of ESA's central concerns. It offers its members a regular newsletter, the *ESA Advocate*, which includes my regular column analysing current politics, and a 'Washington Update' section that keeps members informed on the most important developments in Washington so they know when a strategic call or letter to their representatives will make the most difference. ESA also has local chapters, college chapters (each called World Christian Fellowship, promoting evangelism and social action), a Musician's Task Force, regional conferences and Tracts for Justice.

Membership in ESA ($20 a year) enables a person to link arms with other Christians across the US in order to make an effective impact on public policy.

Numerous other organisations attempt to change public policy. The following are among the more important.

Interfaith Action for Economic Justice is a coalition of thirty-four religious denominations and organisations which analyses issues, testifies before Congress and monitors legislation on all hunger-related matters. Interfaith Action also sponsors conferences and meetings to bring affected people into Washington to lobby for themselves. The organisation mails regular legislative update information, *Networkers*, on each of its four issue areas – food and agriculture policy, domestic human needs, international debt and development, and the Churches' Committee for Voter Registration/Education. Other publications are available on specific issues.

The Interfaith Centre on Corporate Responsibility examines the relation of multinational corporations to world hunger. Although not a membership organisation, the Interfaith Centre provides information on request.

Other citizen lobbies include Network, an organisation staffed by Catholic sisters who publish a monthly newsletter, a quarterly, and a hunger packet; and Friends' Committee on National Legislation, which also issues a monthly newsletter. Details of British organisations concerned with development can be found on p. 271.

In this book I have called for the reform of present economic structures. Many Christians have sharply criticised capitalism.[81] Some have called for democratic socialism.[82] Others have articulately defended capitalism.[83] Examination of this growing debate, however, would carry us beyond the space limitations of this chapter.[84]

A new consensus, however, may be emerging. In January 1990, over a hundred Christians from a wide range of professions, countries and ideological perspectives met at Oxford University to discuss the relationship between Christian faith and economics. The resulting Oxford Declaration on Christian Faith and Economics represents significant consensus on the importance of both democracy and market economy and also on the centrality of God's demand for justice and the need to correct the injustices of present-day capitalism.[85]

At a time when Marxism has collapsed and democratic capitalism is in danger of an overconfident neglect of its own failures, it is essential to re-examine economics from a thoroughly biblical perspective. We need economists immersed in biblical faith who will rethink economics as if poor people mattered. I have only an incomplete idea of what a modern version of the year of jubilee would look like. But at the heart of God's call for jubilee is a divine demand for socio-economic structures that provide all people with the means to produce wealth and thus earn their own way. We must discover new, concrete models for applying this biblical principle in our interdependent world. I hope and pray for a new generation of economists and political scientists who will devote their lives to formulating, developing and implementing a contemporary model of jubilee.

The Liberty Bell, which was made in Great Britain and now hangs in historic Philadelphia, could become a powerful symbol for citizens of the industrialised North working to share resources with the poor of the world. The inscription on the Liberty Bell, 'Proclaim liberty throughout the land', comes from the biblical passage on jubilee (Lev. 25:10). To Hebrews enslaved in debt, these words promised the freedom and the land necessary to earn a living. Today, poverty enslaves billions. The God of the Bible still demands institutionalised mechanisms which will enable everyone to earn a just living. The jubilee inscription on the Liberty Bell issues a ringing call for international economic justice.

Do Christians have the courage to demand and implement the structural changes needed to make that ancient inscription a contemporary reality?

Study Questions

1. Chapter 9 starts with a parable. Which character in the parable do most Christians you know most identify with and imitate?

2. Chapters 7 and 8 discuss how we can respond as individuals and churches. Are these two responses enough? If not, why not?

3. Do biblical norms apply to modern secular societies? If so, how?

4. What are the strengths and weaknesses of the structural changes suggested in this chapter?

5. How much difference would it make if we ended trade barriers to goods from poor nations? Why don't we?

6. How can we reduce the debt crisis? And environmental pollution?

7. How does this chapter underline chapter 7's call for living more simply?

8. Should foreign aid be given to poor nations? If so, how could it be more effective?

9. Should we redirect money from military expenditures to reducing poverty? What typical objections do people raise to this suggestion? How would you respond?

10. How do you sense God calling you to work for structural change in our world?

EPILOGUE

We live at one of the great turning-points in history. The present division of the world's resources dare not continue. And it will not. Either courageous pioneers will persuade reluctant nations to share the good earth's bounty, or we will enter an era of catastrophic conflict.

Christians should be in the vanguard. The church of Jesus Christ is the most universal body in the world today. All we need to do is truly obey the One we rightly worship. But to obey will mean to follow. And he lives among the poor and oppressed, seeking justice for those in agony. In our time, following in his steps will mean simple personal lifestyles. It will mean transformed churches with a corporate lifestyle consistent with worship of the God of the poor. It will mean costly commitment to structural change in secular society.

Do Christians today have that kind of faith and courage? Will we pioneer new models of sharing for our interdependent world? Will we dare to become the vanguard in the struggle for structural change?

I must confess my fear that the majority of affluent 'Christians' of all theological labels have bowed the knee to Mammon. If forced to choose between defending their luxuries and following Jesus among the oppressed, I am afraid they will imitate the rich young ruler.

But I am not pessimistic. God regularly accomplishes his will through faithful remnants.[1] Even in affluent nations, there are millions of Christians who love their Lord Jesus more than houses and lands. More and more Christians are coming to realise that their Lord calls them to feed the hungry and seek justice for the oppressed.

If at this moment in history a few million Christians in

affluent nations dare to join hands with the poor around the world, we will decisively influence the course of world history. Together we must strive to be a biblical people ready to follow wherever Scripture leads. We must pray for the courage to bear any cross, suffer any loss and joyfully embrace any sacrifice that biblical faith requires in an Age of Hunger.

We know that our Lord Jesus is alive! We know that the decisive victory over sin and death has occurred. We know that the Sovereign of the universe wills an end to hunger, injustice and oppression. The resurrection of Jesus is our guarantee that, in spite of the massive evil that sometimes almost overwhelms us, the final victory will surely come.[2] Secure on that solid rock, we will plunge into this unjust world, changing now all we can and knowing that the Risen King will complete the victory at his glorious return.

Appendix A: Resource Materials

General Works

Barnet, Richard J., *The Lean Years: Politics in the Age of Scarcity*. New York: Simon and Schuster, 1980.

Bauer, P. T., *Equality, the Third World, and Economic Delusion*. London: Methuen, 1982.

Benne, Robert, *The Ethic of Democratic Capitalism: A Moral Reassessment*. Philadelphia: Fortress Press, 1981.

Berger, Peter, *Pyramids of Sacrifice*. New York: Basic Books, 1975. A sociological analysis.

Birch, Bruce C., and Rasmussen, Larry L., *The Predicament of the Prosperous*. Philadelphia: Westminster Press, 1978.

Borgstrom, Georg, *The Food and People Dilemma*. Belmont, Calif.: Duxbury Press, 1973.

Brandt, Willy, et. al., *North-South: A Program for Survival*. Cambridge, Mass.: MIT Press, 1980.

Bread for the World Institute on Hunger & Development, *Report on Global Hunger*. Washington: The Institute, 1990.

Brown, J. Larry, and H. F. Pizer, *Living Hungry in America*. New York: Macmillan, 1987.

Brown, Lester R., et. al., *State of the World 1990*. New York: Norton, 1990. (This annual publication is an excellent guide on the relationship between environmental issues and global poverty.)

Byron, William, ed., *The Causes of World Hunger*. New York: Paulist Press, 1982.

Cahill, Kevin M., ed., *Famine*. Maryknoll, N.Y.: Orbis Books, 1982.

Camara, Dom Helder, *Revolution Through Peace*. New York: Harper and Row, 1971.

Chinweizu, *The West and the Rest of Us*. New York: Random House, 1975.

Christian Aid, *Banking on the Poor: The Ethics of Third World Debt*. London: Christian Aid, 1988.

Connelly, Philip, and Robert Perlman, *The Politics of Scarcity: Resource Conflicts in International Relations*. New York: Oxford Univ. Press, 1975.

Corson-Finnerty, Adam D., *World Citizen: Action for Global Justice*. Maryknoll, N.Y.: Orbis Books, 1982.

Davis, Shelton H., *Victims of the Miracle: Development and the Indians of Brazil*. Cambridge University Press, 1977.

De Jesús, Carolina María, *Child of the Dark*, trans. David St. Clair. New York: Signet Books, 1962. An explosive personal account of urban Brazilian poverty.

Duchrow, Ulrich, *Global Economy: A Confessional Issue for the Churches?* Geneva: WCC Publications, 1987.

Ensminger, Douglas, and Bomani Paul, *Conquest of World Hunger and Poverty*. Ames, Iowa: Iowa State Univ. Press, 1980.

Fenton, Thomas P., and Mary J. Heffron, comps. and eds, *Food, Hunger, Agribusiness: A Directory of Resources*. New York: Orbis Books, 1987.

Freudenberger, C. Dean, and Paul M. Minus, Jr., *Christian Responsibility in a Hungry World*. Nashville: Abingdon Press, 1976.

Fryer, Jonathan, *Food for Thought: The Use and Abuse of Food Aid in the Fight against World Hunger*. Geneva: WCC Publications, 1981.

George, Susan, *Debt and Hunger*. Minneapolis: American Lutheran Church Hunger Program, 1987. Available from Augsburg Publishing, 800–328–4648.

George, Susan and Nigel Paige, *Food for Beginners*. New York: Norton, 1983.

Gheddo, Piero, *Why Is the Third World Poor?* Maryknoll, N.Y.: Orbis Books, 1973.

Gilder, George, *Wealth and Poverty*. Surrey: Buchan & Enright, 1982.

Goudzwaard, Bob, *Aid for the Overdeveloped West*. Toronto: Wedge, 1975.

——, *Capitalism and Progress: A Diagnosis of Western Society*, trans. Josina Van Nuis Zylstra. Grand Rapids, Mich.: Eerdmans, 1979.

Griffiths, Brian, *Morality and the Market Place: Christian Alternatives to Capitalism and Socialism*. London: Hodder & Stoughton, 1982.

Griffiths, *The Creation of Wealth: A Christian's Case for Capitalism*. Downers Grove, Ill.: Inter Varsity, 1984.

Hay, Donald, *Economics Today: A Christian Critique*. Leeds: Apollos, 1989.

Jegen, Mary Evelyn, and Charles K. Wilbur, eds, *Growth with Equity*. New York: Paulist Press, 1979.

Lappé, Frances Moore, and Joseph Collins, *Food First: Beyond the Myth of Scarcity*. Kent: Abacus Books, 1982.

Lappé, Frances Moore, Joseph Collins, and David Kinley, *Aid as Obstacle: Twenty Questions About Our Foreign Aid and the Hungry*. San Francisco: Institute for Food and Development Policy, 1980.

Lutz, Charles P., ed., *Farming the Lord's Land*: Christian Perspectives on American Agriculture. Minneapolis: Augsburg, 1980.

McGinnis, James B., *Bread and Justice: Toward a New International Economic Order*. New York: Paulist Press, 1979.

Miller, G. Tyler, Jr., *Living in the Environment*. Belmont, Calif.: Wadsworth, 1988.

Millett, Richard, *Guardians of the Dynasty: A History of the U.S. Created* Guardia Nacional de Nicaragua *and the Somoza Family*. Maryknoll, N.Y.: Orbis Books, 1977.

Mische, Gerald, and Patricia Mische, *Toward a Human World Order: Beyond the National Security Straitjacket*. New York: Paulist, 1977.

Morgan, Elizabeth, Van Weigel, and Eric DeBaufre, *Global Poverty and Personal Responsibility*. New York: Paulist, 1989.

Myrdal, Gunnar, *The Challenge of World Poverty*. New York: Random House, 1971. A classic.

Nelson, Jack A., *Hunger for Justice: The Politics of Food and Faith*. Maryknoll, N.Y.: Orbis Books, 1981.

Physician Task Force on Hunger in America, *Hunger in America: The Growing Epidemic*. Wesleyan U.P., 1986.

Rau, Bill, *Feast to Famine: The Course of Africa's Underdevelopment*. Washington: Africa Faith and Justice Network, 1985.

Rich, William, *Smaller Families Through Social and Economic Progress*. Washington: Overseas Development Council, 1973.

Rodney, Walter, *How Europe Underdeveloped Africa*. London: Bogle-L'Ouverture, 1988.

Sachs, Jeffrey D., ed., *Developing Country Debt and the World Economy*. Chicago: University of Chicago Press, 1989.

Schiller, John A., ed., *The American Poor*. Minneapolis: Augsburg, 1982.

Schumacher, E. F., *Small Is Beautiful: Economics As If People Mattered*. Blond and Briggs, 1973.

Schwartz-Noble, Loretta, *Starving in the Shadow of Plenty*. New York: Putnam's, 1981.

Simon, Arthur, *Bread for the World*. Grand Rapids, Mich.: Eerdmans; New York: Paulist Press, 1975. Superb overview of public policy issues. Rev. edn 1984.

Sivard, Ruth Leger, *World Military and Social Expenditures 1990*. Leesburg, Va.: World Priorities. 1989. An annual collection of useful data.

Skillen, James W., *International Politics and the Demand for Global Justice*. Sioux Center, Iowa: Dordt College Press, 1981.

Spykman, Gordon, et. al., *Let My People Live: Faith and Struggle in Central America*. Grand Rapids, Mich.: Eerdmans, 1988.

Taylor, John V., *Enough Is Enough*. London: SCM Press, 1975. An excellent overview with considerable biblical analysis.

Todaro, Michael P., *Economic Development in the Third World*, 4th edn. New York: Longman, 1989.

United Nations Children's Fund, *The State of the World's Children 1990*. Oxford: Oxford University Press (Annual).

U.S. Foreign Policy and the Third World. An annual volume written by the Overseas Development Council and published by Praeger.

Wilkinson, Loren, ed., *Earthkeeping: Christian Stewardship of Natural Resources*. Grand Rapids, Mich.: Eerdmans, 1980.

Williams, Robert G., *Export Agriculture and the Crisis in Central America*. Chapel Hill: University of North Carolina Press, 1986.

Wilson, Francis, and Mamphela Ramphele, *Uprooting Poverty: The South African Challenge*. New York: W. W. Norton, 1989.

Withers, Leslie, and Tom Peterson, eds, *Hunger and Action Handbook*. Decatur, Ga: Seeds Magazine, 1987.

World Bank, *World Development Report 1989*. New York: Oxford Univ. Press, 1989, Annual.

World Hunger Program, Brown University, *Hunger in History: Food Shortage, Poverty, and Deprivation*. New York: Basil Blackwell, 1990.

Lifestyle

Alexander, John, *Your Money or Your Life*. New York: Harper, 1986.

Beckmann, David M., and Elizabeth A. Donnelly, *The Overseas List: Opportunities for Living and Working in Developing Countries*. Minneapolis: Augsburg, 1979.

Eller, Vernard, *The Simple Life: The Christian Stance Toward Possessions*. Grand Rapids, Mich.: Eerdmans, 1973. It is important to read Eller's warning against legalism, but the overall effect is to give aid and comfort to our carnal inclination to rationalise our sinful affluence.

Ewald, Ellen Buchman, *Recipes for a Small Planet*. New York: Ballantine Books, 1973. Recipes for delicious meatless dishes.

Foster, Richard J., *Freedom of Simplicity*. London: Triangle, 1981.

Kerr, Graham, *The Graham Kerr Step-by-Step Cookbook*. Elgin, Ill.: David C. Cook, 1982.

Lappé, Frances Moore, *Diet for a Small Planet*, rev. edn. New York: Ballantine, 1975. 'How to' book on simple, nutritious diet.

Longacre, Doris Janzen, *More-with-Less Cookbook*. Oxford: Lion, 1987. Commissioned by the Mennonite Central Committee; simple lifestyle recipes of Pennsylvania Dutch quality!

——, *Living More with Less*. Scottdale, Pa.: Herald Press, 1980.

Macmanus, Sheila, *Community Action Sourcebook: Empowerment of People*. New York: Paulist Press, 1982.

McGinnis, James, and Kathleen McGinnis, *Parenting for Peace and Justice*. Maryknoll, N.Y.: Orbis Books, 1981.

Shannon-Thornberry, Milo, *Alternate Celebrations Catalogue*. Washington, D.C.: Alternatives, 1982.

Sider, Ronald J., ed., *Lifestyle in the Eighties: An Evangelical Commitment to Simple Lifestyle*. Exeter: Paternoster Press, 1981.

——, *Living More Simply: Biblical Principles and Practical Models*. Downers Grove, Ill.: InterVarsity Press, 1980.

Sine, Tom, *Why Settle for More and Miss the Best?* Waco: Word, 1989.

Theology, Biblical Studies and the Church

Armerding, Carl E., ed., *Evangelicals and Liberation*. Nutley, N.J.: Presbyterian and Reformed, 1977.

Banks, Robert J., *Paul's Idea of Community*. Grand Rapids, Mich.: Eerdmans, 1980.

Batey, Richard, *Jesus and the Poor: The Poverty Program of the First Christians*. New York: Harper and Row, 1972.

Baum, Gregory, *The Priority of Labor: A Commentary on Laborem Exercens; Encyclical Letter of Pope John Paul II*. New York: Paulist, 1982.

Beisner, E. Calvin, *Prosperity and Poverty: The Compassionate Use of Resources in a World of Scarcity*. Westchester, Ill.: Crossway, 1988.

Boerma, Conrad, *The Rich, the Poor – and the Bible*. Philadelphia: Westminster, 1979.

Brueggemann, Walter, *The Land*. Philadelphia: Fortress Press, 1986.

Byron, William J., *Toward Stewardship: An Interim Ethic of Poverty, Pollution and Power*. New York: Paulist Press, 1975.

Cassidy, Richard J., *Jesus, Politics and Society: A Study of Luke's Gospel*. Maryknoll, N.Y.: Orbis Books, 1978.

Catherwood, Sir Frederick, *The Christian in Industrial Society*. London: Tyndale Press, 1964.

Cesaretti, C. A., and Stephen Cummins, eds, *Let the Earth Bless the Lord: A Christian Perspective on Land Use*. New York: Seabury Press, 1981.

Cosby, Gordon, *Handbook for Mission Groups*. Waco, Tex.: Word Books, 1975.

Cone, James H., *God of the Oppressed*. New York: Seabury Press, 1975.

Dayton, Donald W., *Discovering an Evangelical Heritage*. New York: Harper and Row, 1976.

De Santa Ana, Julio., *Good News to the Poor: The Challenge of the Poor in the History of the Church*. Geneva: WCC Publications, 1977.

Dickinson, Richard D. N., *To Set at Liberty the Oppressed*. Geneva: CCPD, 1975.

Economic Justice for All: Pastoral Letter on Catholic Social Teaching and the US Economy. Washington: National Conference of Catholic Bishops, 1986.

Escobar, Samuel, and John Driver, *Christian Mission and Social Justice*. Scottdale, Pa.: Herald Press, 1978.

Gill, Athol, *Life on the Road: The Gospel Basis for a Messianic Lifestyle*. Homebush West (Australia): Anzea Publishers, 1989.

Gollwitzer, Helmut, *The Rich Christians and Poor Lazarus*, trans. David Cairns. New York: Macmillan, 1970.

Gremillion, John, ed., *The Gospel of Peace and Justice: Catholic Social Teaching Since Pope John*. Maryknoll, N.Y.: Orbis Books, 1978.

Hengel, Martin, *Poverty and Riches in the Early Church: Aspects of a Social History of Early Christianity*. Philadelphia: Fortress Press, 1974.

Johnson, Luke T., *Sharing Possessions*. London: SCM Press, 1986.

Keith-Lucas, Alan, *The Poor You Have Always With You: Concepts of Aid to the Poor in the Western World from Biblical Times to the Present*. St. Davids, Penn.: North American Association of Christians in Social Work, 1989. (Box S-90, St. Davids, PA 19087.)

Kerans, Patrick, *Sinful Social Structures*. New York: Paulist Press, 1974.

Kirk, Andrew, *Liberation Theology: An Evangelical View from the Third World*. Atlanta: John Knox Press, 1979. A useful introduction to the voluminous, important literature on 'liberation theology'.

——, *Theology and the Third World Church*. Downers Grove, Ill.: InterVarsity Press, 1983.

——, *Theology Encounters Revolution*. Downers Grove, Ill.: InterVarsity Press, 1983.

Kraybill, Donald B., *The Upside Down Kingdom*. Scottdale, Pa.: Herald Press, 1978.

Lernoux, Penny, *Cry of the People*. Garden City, N.Y.: Doubleday, 1980.

Ludwig, Thomas E., et. al. *Inflation, Poortalk and the Gospel*. Valley Forge, Penn.: Judson Press, 1981.

Meeks, M. Douglas, *God the Economist: The Doctrine of God and Political Economy*. Minneapolis: Fortress, 1989.

Mott, Stephen C., *Biblical Ethics and Social Change*. New York: Oxford, 1982.

Novak, Michael, *Will It Liberate? Questions About Liberation Theology*. New York: Paulist, 1986.

Perkins, John, *With Justice for All*. Glendale, Calif.: Regal, 1982.

Pilgrim, Walter E., *Good News to the Poor: Wealth and Poverty in Luke-Acts*. Minneapolis: Augsburg, 1981.

Presbyterian Eco-Justice Task Force, *Keeping and Healing the Creation*. Louisville: Committee on Social Witness, Presbyterian Church (USA), 1989.

Samuel, Vinay. *The Meaning and Cost of Discipleship*. Bombay: Bombay Urban Industrial League for Development, 1981.

Samuel, Vinay and Albrecht Hauser, eds, *Proclaiming Christ in Christ's Way: Studies in Integral Evangelism*. Oxford: Regnum Books, 1989.

Scott, Waldron, *Bring Forth Justice*. Basingstoke: M & S Marshall, 1982.

Seccombe, David Peter, *Possessions and the Poor in Luke-Acts*. *Studien zum Neuen Testament und seiner Umwelt*, 1982.

Sider, Ronald J., ed., *Cry Justice: The Bible Speaks on Hunger and Poverty*. Downers Grove, Ill.: InterVarsity Press; New York: Paulist Press, 1980.

Sine, Tom, *The Mustard Seed Conspiracy*. Kent: MARC Europe, 1985.

Speiser, Stuart M., *Ethical Economics and the Faith Community*. Bloomington, Ind.: Meyer-Stove, 1989.

Taylor, Richard K., *Economics and the Gospel*. Philadelphia: United Church Press, 1973.

Wallis, James, *Agenda for Biblical People*. New York: Harper and Row, 1984.

——, *The Call to Conversion: Recovering the Gospel for These Times*. Oxford: Lion, 1982.

Westphal, Carol, 'Covenant Parenting for Peace and Justice'. Office of Family Life, Reformed Church of America. (Write RCA Distribution Center, 18525 Torrence Avenue, Lansing, IL 60438.)

White, John, *The Golden Cow: Materialism in the Twentieth-Century Church*. Downers Grove, Ill.: InterVarsity Press, 1979.

Wright, Christopher J. H., *An Eye for An Eye: The Place of Old Testament Ethics Today*. Downers Grove, Ill.: InterVarsity, 1983.

Ziesler, J. A., *Christian Asceticism*. Grand Rapids, Mich.: Eerdmans, 1973.

Development

Batchelor, Peter, *People in Rural Development*. Exeter: Paternoster, 1981.

Freire, Paulo, *Pedagogy of the Oppressed*, trans. Myra B. Ramos. New York: Herder and Herder, 1970. A revolutionary educational philosophy.

Elliston, Edgar J., ed., *Christian Relief and Development: Developing Workers for Effective Ministry*. Dallas: Word, 1989.

Goulet, Denis, *A New Moral Order*. Maryknoll, N.Y.: Orbis Books, 1974.

Sider, Ronald J., ed., *Evangelicals and Development: Toward a Theology of Social Change*. Exeter: Paternoster, 1981.

Sinclair, Maurice, *Green Finger of God*. Exeter: Paternoster, 1981.

Sine, Tom, ed., *The Church in Response to Human Need*. Monrovia, Calif.: Missions Advanced Research Communication Center, 1983.

Periodicals

The New Internationalist, 113 Atlantic Avenue, Brooklyn, NY 11201. An influential development periodical with a radical analysis of the relationship of the developing and developed worlds.

The Other Side, Box 12236, Philadelphia, PA 19144. A journal of radical discipleship; frequent articles on hunger, justice.

Seeds, 222 East Lake Drive, Decatur, GA 30030. An excellent magazine on world hunger published by Southern Baptists.

Sojourners, Box 29272, Washington, DC 20017. A biblical magazine with regular articles on economic justice, discipleship and community (202–636–3637).

Transformation: An International Dialogue on Evangelical Social Ethics, 312 W. Logan Street, Philadelphia, PA 19144. One of the best places to listen to all parts of the worldwide evangelical community.

U.N. Development Forum, A monthly tabloid *free* from Center for Economic and Social Information, United Nations, New York, NY 10017.

World Christian, PO Box 400010, Pasadena, CA 91114. Monthly.

World Watch, 1776 Massachusetts Avenue, N.W., Washington, DC 20036. Bi-monthly.

Numerous other religious journals regularly carry related items: *Christian Century, Christianity and Crisis, Christianity Today, Commonweal, Engage/Social Action, Worldview*.

Audiovisuals

Many excellent audiovisuals are available. For lists write to almost any of the organisations listed in Appendix B. Especially helpful are the lists from Bread for the World, Mennonite Central Committee, and World Hunger Education Service.

Appendix B: British Organisations

ActionAid, Hamlyn House, Archway, London N19 5PG. ActionAid enables individuals, families and groups in the UK to give direct, practical help to children and communities fighting poverty in some of the world's poorest countries. ActionAid helps poor people to identify the causes of poverty and to plan long-term development programmes involving education, health, water supply, savings and credit, agricultural assistance and rural industries.

Amnesty International, 99–119 Rosebery Avenue, London EC1R 4RE and International Secretariat, 1 Easton Street, London WC1X 0DW. Amnesty International works for the relief of Prisoners of Conscience and campaigns against torture, the death penalty and other serious violations of human rights. A wide range of information available on request.

The Catholic Fund for Overseas Development (CAFOD), 2 Romero Close, Stockwell Road, London SW9 9TY. Official aid agency of the Catholic bishops of England and Wales. Speakers, posters, material and information can be provided.

Catholic Institute for International Relations (CIIR), 22 Coleman Fields, London N1 7AF. Independent Catholic organisation which promotes within the UK on international relations, particularly overseas development. It publishes material suitable for use with adult groups, and produces a regular newsbrief, *Comment*, on issues of current international importance, and *CIIR News Quarterly*.

Centre for World Development Education (CWDE). Regent's College, Inner Circle, Regent's Park, London NW1 4NS. Independent educational organisation whose main aim is to increase knowledge and understanding in Britain of world development and the developing countries. CWDE publishes a wide range of written and visual materials.

Christian Aid, 35 Lower Marsh, London SE1 7RL. Official development and relief agency of the British Council of Churches. It offers free and sale publications, posters, simulation games, filmstrips and films; catalogues free.

Christian Impact, St Peter's Church, Vere Street, London W1M

9HP. A lay institute which aims to promote a more biblical approach to today's world, encouraging active Christian involvement in all levels of society. It organises courses and publishes resource material for churches and individuals.

Commonwealth Secretariat, Marlborough House, London SW1Y 5HX. The Secretariat is responsible to and financed by the fifty independent nations of the Commonwealth, and is the main instrument of multilateral co-operation between them. It provides technical assistance, advisers, experts and training to Commonwealth developing countries. Free publications list, information office.

Friends of the Earth, 26–28 Underwood Street, London N1 7JQ. One of the leading environmental pressure groups in the UK, addressing those who destroy the environment and those who have power to protect it.

Help the Aged, 16 St James's Walk, London EC1R 0BE. Help the Aged seeks to promote the welfare of the elderly in Britain and the Third World, both by fund-raising and by public campaigning. Posters, wall-charts, booklets and other publications, films and slides. Callers welcome.

The Institute of Development Studies (IDS), University of Sussex, Brighton BN1 9RE. The Institute of Development Studies was set up by ODM in 1966 as a national centre concerned with Third World Development and with the relationships between rich and poor countries. The library, which is open to individual researchers, contains publications from most Third World countries and is an official UN depository. The Annual Report and an IDS publications catalogue available.

Intermediate Technology Development Group Ltd (ITDG), 103 Southampton Row, WC1B 4HH. Non-profit organisation concerned with the publication and dissemination of information on low-cost small-scale equipment and processes appropriate to the needs and resources of developing countries. Leaflet describing its work and publication list available.

Overseas Development Administration (ODA), Information Department, ODM, Eland House, Stag Place, London SW1E 5DH. ODA is responsible for the management of the British Government's aid programme to developing countries. Official reports and annual statistics are available from HMSO. A list of publications and other material, and a film catalogue, are available free, and the library is open weekdays.

Overseas Development Institute (ODI), Regent's College, Inner Circle, Regent's Park, London NW1 4NS. Independent research organisation set up to provide a centre for research in development problems. Free publication list available. Library open on weekdays: enquiries and visitors welcome.

Oxfam, 274 Banbury Road, Oxford OX2 7DZ. Independent voluntary organisation campaigning to involve as many people as possible in the cause of world development and to raise funds for relief and development projects. Free and sale publications, posters and films. Catalogue.

Returned Volunteer Action (RVA), 1 Amwell Street, London EC1R 1UL. Independent UK association of ex-overseas volunteers, together with those who support its aims. Access is offered through its clearing house to people who have worked in the Third World – for consultation, seminars and involvement with development issues; critical information on volunteering; and the distribution of some relevant publications.

The Save the Children Fund, Mary Datchelor House, 17 Grove Lane, London SE5 8RD. Independent voluntary organisation concerned with the welfare of children throughout the world, particularly in the developing countries. Publications and posters about its organisation, the health and education of children in developing countries and its work in disaster areas, slides and films.

TEAR Fund (The Evangelical Alliance Relief Fund), 100 Church Road, Teddington, Middlesex TW11 8QE. An interdenominational evangelical relief and development agency working through missionaries and national Christian leaders. In addition to the support of projects and personnel overseas, it runs a child-sponsorship programme. Educational literature for all ages is published, together with audio-visual aids and publicity material. Free catalogue.

Tearcraft, 100 Church Road, Teddington, Middlesex TW11 8QE. Tearcraft is a Christian organisation importing handicrafts and cottage industry products from Third World producers. They are sold through a mail order catalogue, and by selling direct to shops, other groups and societies at wholesale rates. Further information and a free catalogue available.

Third World First (3W1), 100 Pilgrim Street, Newcastle NE1 6QF. Independent voluntary movement of students and other young people, encouraging action and understanding on the causes of poverty and underdevelopment. Publications include catalogues of Third World music and films available in the UK, posters, a fund-raising pack and an activists' handbook. Catalogue free, SAE if possible.

Third World Publications Ltd (TWP), 25 Horsell Road, London

N5. TWP, a non-profit-making company, distributes books from and about the Third World. It has stocks of development literature published both in Britain and overseas, as well as imports of African, Indian and Caribbean books, and books on theology. Free catalogue.

Traidcraft plc, Kingsway, Team Valley Trading Estate, Gateshead NE11 0NE. The company, which is a Christian initiative, aims to enable poor communities in the Third World to improve their quality of life and retain a fairer share of the wealth they help to create. It does this by selling crafts, clothing, jewellery, foodstuffs, teas and coffees. It pays a fair price for what it buys and provides support services to the producers. It also sells a range of environment-friendly paper products mainly sourced in the UK. The company sells by mail order, through a country-wide network of representatives and through retail outlets.

United Nations Children's Fund (UNICEF), UK Committee for UNICEF, 55 Lincolns Inn Fields, London WC2A 3NB. UNICEF is financed entirely by voluntary contributions. It is now mainly concerned with long-term development programmes meeting the basic needs of children. It has free and sale publications, posters, slide sets and films. Free catalogue.

United Nations Information Centre (UNIC), Ship House, 20 Buckingham Gate, London SW1E 6LB. A Secretariat office of the United Nations Headquarters in New York, provides materials on the work of the United Nations and its specialised agencies. Free publications available in limited quantities to teachers; sale publications may be purchased through HMSO. Reference library open on Mondays, Wednesdays and Thursdays.

War on Want, 37–39 Great Guildford Street, London SE1 0ES. Independent voluntary organisation to inform the British public about poverty, aid and development in the Third World. Free and sale publications, posters and films. Publications list.

World Development Movement (WDM), 26 Bedford Chambers, Covent Garden, London WC2 8HA. Independent voluntary organisation of local action groups concerned to campaign on the political issues of aid and development. Catalogue of free and sale publications.

World Vision, Dychurch House, 8 Abington Street, Northampton NN1 2AJ. An interdenominational relief and development agency offering practical Christian caring in more than 60 countries.

Notes

Chapter 1: A Billion Hungry Neighbours

1. 'Iracema's Story', *Christian Century*, November 12th, 1975, p. 1030.

2. Michael P. Todaro, *Economic Development in the Third World*, 4th ed. (New York: Longman, 1989), pp. 31–2.

3. Robert L. Heilbroner, *The Great Ascent: The Struggle for Economic Development in Our Time* (New York: Harper and Row, 1963), pp. 33–6.

4. The Chinese government claims to have abolished absolute poverty. If true, this would lower the number of people living in absolute poverty to 800 million. (See Todaro, *Economic Development*, 1989, p. 31.)

5. Todaro, *Economic Development*, 1989, pp. 30–1.

6. World Bank, *World Development Report 1988* (New York: Oxford University Press), p. 4.

7. World Bank, *World Development Report 1989* (New York: Oxford University Press), pp. 164–5.

8. *Ibid.*

9. Todaro, *Economic Development*, 1989, pp. 48–61.

10. These population and income statistics come from the World Bank's *World Development Report 1989*, pp. 164–5. Per capita GNP is in 1987 dollars.

11. *Ibid.*, p. 166.

12. James Brooke, 'Brazilians Vote Today for President in a Free and Unpredictable Election', *New York Times*, November 15th, 1989, A10.

13. Arthur Simon, *Bread for the World* (Grand Rapids, Mich.: Eerdmans; Paramus, N.J.: Paulist Press, 1975), pp. 64–5. The *New York Times* reported on July 11th, 1976, p. 3 'According to [Brazilian] government statistics, wages for unskilled workers, after taking inflation into account, have fallen almost 40 per cent since the right-wing military government took power 12 years ago. Meanwhile the Gross National Product rose more than 150 per cent in the period. . . . There has been a radical distribution of income in favor of wealthier economic sectors.' Also: 'Brazil's

agriculture expands fast, but mostly for benefit of well-to-do', *New York Times*, August 16th, 1976, p. 2. For the statistic on malnutrition see the World Bank Country Study, *Brazil: Human Resources Special Report* (Washington, D.C.: The World Bank, 1979), p. 61 of Annex 3.

14. 'Trade with Justice', BFW Background Paper, no. 67 (August 1983): 4.

15. James P. Grant, *State of the World's Children 1990* (Oxford: Oxford University Press, 1990), pp. 78–9.

16. Brooke, *New York Times*, November 15th, 1989, A10.

17. This data comes from the *World Development Report 1980*, pp. 111, 143, 157. Distribution data, population data, and GNP data are used to derive the average income figures for the respective classes.

18. W. Stanley Mooneyham, *What Do You Say to a Hungry World?* (Waco, Tex.: Word Books, 1975), pp. 38–9.

19. Lester Brown, *State of the World 1990* (New York: Norton, 1990), pp. 4, 10–12.

20. Lester R. Brown, *In the Human Interest* (New York: Norton, 1974), pp. 55–6.

21. Grant, *The State of the World's Children 1990*, pp. 4, 16, 31.

22. *Child of the Dark: The Diary of Carolina Maria de Jesus* (New York: Dutton, 1962), p. 42.

23. Mooneyham, *Hungry World*, p. 191.

24. Donald A. Hay, *Economics Today* (Leicester: Inter-Varsity, 1989), p. 257.

25. Todaro, *Economic Development* (1989), pp. 48–53, 335.

26. Ruth L. Sivard, *World Military and Social Expenditures 1989* (Washington, DC: World Priorities, 1989), p. 11.

27. Brown, *State of the World 1990*, pp. 135, 143.

28. Grant, *State of the World's Children 1989*, pp. 2–3 and *State of the World's Children 1990*, pp. 16–17.

29. *Ibid*.

30. Grant, *State of the World's Children 1990*, pp. 27, 30. This statistic excludes China.

31. World Health Organization, *Health Conditions in the Americas* (Pan American Health Organization, Scientific Publications Series, no. 427, 1982), p. 102.

32. Mooneyham, *Hungry World*, p. 191.

33. Grant, *State of the World's Children 1990*, p. 30.

34. Population Reference Bureau, *1989 World Population Data Sheet* (Washington, DC: Population Reference Bureau, Inc.).

35. Quoted in BFW *Newsletter*, July 1976. This issue has an excellent refutation of Hardin and Paddock's call for triage and lifeboat ethics.

36. Population Reference Bureau, *1989 World Population Data Sheet*.

37. Robert L. Heilbroner, *An Inquiry into the Human Prospect* (London: Calder, 1975).

38. Brown, *State of the World 1990*, p. 3.

39. Heilbroner, *Human Prospect*, p. 39.

40. Sivard, *World Military and Social Expenditures 1989*, pp. 16–17.

41. Arms Control and Foreign Policy Caucus of the US Congress, *The Developing World: Danger Point for U.S. Security* (Washington, DC: August 1st, 1989), p. 3.

42. Mooneyham, *Hungry World*, p. 50.

43. Mark Hatfield, 'World Hunger', *World Vision 19* (February 1975): 5.

44. Quoted in Stephen Coats, 'Hunger, Security and U.S. Foreign Policy', BFW Background Paper, no. 53 (May 1981).

45. *Philadelphia Inquirer*, October 13th, 1974, p. 9b.

46. Supplement to *Radar News*, January 1975, pp. 3–4.

47. Compare Ronald J. Sider, 'Where Have All the Liberals Gone?' *The Other Side* 12, No. 3 (May–June 1976): 42–4.

Chapter 2: The Affluent Minority

1. *Revolution Through Peace* (New York: Harper and Row, 1971), p. 142.

2. Sivard, *World Military and Social Expenditures 1990*, p. 5.

3. Minus the profit and interest payments that leave the country to pay foreign owners of capital, and plus similar payments that are made to local businessfolk who own capital in foreign countries.

4. There are, however, several serious problems with using GNP as a standard for comparison:

a. GNP and GNP per capita say nothing about the distribution of income. A country with a certain GNP per capita that is evenly distributed may be much better off than a country with a much higher GNP per capita, but in which a small proportion of the population controls a disproportionately high share of the GNP.

b. Less developed economies are usually largely rural and may trade goods and services without using money. Although World

Bank figures attempt to account for such contingencies, there is no doubt a wide margin of error in their statistics.

c. Since we are really interested in what each person can buy with his income, international comparisons can be quite difficult. Prices of similar goods and services are different in different countries. Haircuts, for example, may cost a lot in Britain, but they do not cost much in Kenya.

d. GNP figures may not be all that closely correlated with measures of welfare. If, for example, the government of Iran decides to produce a great stock of military equipment, the GNP may rise significantly, but it would be hard to argue that the people in Iran are better off.

5. *Global 2000*, p. 13.

6. Todaro, *Economic Development* (1989), pp. 28–9.

7. James W. Howe et. al., *The U.S. and World Development: Agenda for Action, 1975* (New York: Praeger, 1975), p. 166.

8. *Newsweek*, August 18th, 1975, p. 66. Irving B. Kravis et. al., *A System of International Comparisons of Gross Product and Purchasing Power* (Baltimore: Johns Hopkins Univ. Press, 1975), esp. pp. 8–9.

9. Brown, *State of the World 1990*, p. 137.

10. US Bureau of the Census *Statistical Abstract of the United States 1989* 109th edn (Washington, DC, 1989), pp. 833–4.

11. Telephone conversation, July 21st, 1983.

12. Conversation between John Ginzel, Economic Research Service of the USDA, and Mary Beekley-Peacock, February 21st, 1990.

13. Hollender, Jeffrey. *How to Make the World a Better Place* (New York: Morrow, 1990), p. 124.

14. At the same time we must remember that ruminants (cattle, sheep) unlike pigs can convert grass, hay, and silage into protein. Marginal land unsuited for growing grain should certainly continue to be used to raise cattle.

15. 'Facts of Food', supplement to *Development Forum*, November 1974.

16. Quoted in Mooneyham, *Hungry World*, p. 184. For excellent suggestions towards more healthy eating patterns, see Doris Longacre, *More with Less Cookbook* (Scottdale, Pa: Herald Press, 1976) and Frances Moore Lappé, *Diet for a Small Planet*, rev. edn (New York: Ballantine, 1975).

17. For the earlier figures, see Brown, *In the Human Interest*, p. 44; 1982 figures come from George Allen, agricultural economist, USDA; telephone conversation, July 21st, 1983. Figures for 1987 are from US Bureau of the Census, *Statistical Abstract of the*

United States 1989, p. 120. British figures from The Meat and Livestock Commission Statistics.

18. Unpublished data from the National Health and Nutrition Examination survey (1976–80) of the National Center for Health Statistics: 32 per cent of all men and 36 per cent of all women are 10 per cent overweight; 16 per cent of all men and 24 per cent of all women are 20 per cent overweight. (Telephone conversation, August 9th, 1983, with Sidney Abraham, Chief, Nutrition Statistics Branch, National Center for Health Statistics.) See further 'Overweight Adults in the United States', advance data, No. 51, August 30th, 1979.

19. The Consumer Price Index in 1974 was 49.3; in 1989, 124.0 (based on 1982–4 as 100). From Department of Labor, Bureau of Labor Statistics.

20. 'Middle Class? Not on $15,000 a Year', *Philadelphia Inquirer*, October 28th, 1974, p. 9a.

21. *Newsweek*, September 21st, 1977, pp. 30–1. The 1977 dollar figures used in the article were $15,000, $18,000 and $25,000, which convert to the 1989 equivalents in the text. The CPI in 1977 was 60.6.

22. *New York Times*, July 12th, 1949. Quoted in Jules Henry, *Culture Against Man* (New York: Random House, 1963), p. 19.

23. Calculated on the basis of average television viewing of about 20 hours per week, of which half is ITV and half BBC (1 + 2). Commercial time is limited to a maximum of six minutes per hour, so about 10–20 commercials per hour on average may be watched.

24. Richard K. Taylor, 'The Imperative of Economic De-Development', *The Other Side* 10, no. 4 (July–August 1974): 17. For the figures on advertising and education, see US Bureau of Commerce, *Statistical Abstract of the United States 1989*, pp. 126, 550.

25. Bellah, *The Broken Covenant*, p. 134.

26. *Newsweek*, October 28th, 1974, p. 69; my emphasis.

27. John V. Taylor, *Enough is Enough* (London: SCM Press, 1975), p. 71.

28. *Mad* (New York: E.C. Publications).

29. Patrick Kerans, *Sinful Social Structures* (New York: Paulist Press, 1974), pp. 80–1.

30. See the helpful comments on this in Art Gish, *Beyond the Rat Race* (Scottdale, Pa: Herald Press, 1973), pp. 122–6.

31. BFW *Newsletter*, May 1976, p. 1; Howe, *Agenda for Action, 1975*, p. 258.

32. Paul A. Laudicina, *World Poverty and Development: A*

Survey of American Opinion (Washington, DC: Overseas Development Council, 1973), p. 21.

33. US Bureau of the Census, *Statistical Abstract of the United States 1989*, p. 424.

34. These statistics are obtained by adapting data on population and GNP per capita found in *US Statistical Abstracts 1982*, p. 421, and from foreign aid data found in *World Development Report 1982*, pp. 140–1.

35. Earlier percentages are from Lewis and Kallab, eds, *U.S. Foreign Policy and the Third World: Agenda 1983*, p. 273; 1980–7 percentages are from *World Development Report 1989*, pp. 167, 200.

36. Sivard, *World Military and Social Expenditures 1989*, pp. 5, 21.

37. Triage is any system used to allocate a scarce commodity, such as medical help or food, only to those whom it may help to survive and not to those who have no chance of surviving or who will survive without assistance.

38. Garrett Hardin, 'Lifeboat Ethics: The Case against Helping the Poor': *Psychology Today* 8, no. 4 (September 1974): 38ff. See also William and Paul Paddock, *Famine 1975!* (Boston: Little, Brown, 1967), reprinted in 1976 under the title *Time of Famines: America and the World Food Crisis*.

39. Brown, *In the Human Interest*, pp. 113–14; my emphasis.

40. Labour-intensive development uses people rather than machines (for example, dams can be built by five thousand people carrying ground and stones just as well as by two bulldozers and three earthmovers). Advocates of intermediate technology urge developing nations to move from, for example, the hoe to the ox-drawn plough rather than from the hoe to the huge tractor. See E. F. Schumacher, *Small is Beautiful* (New York: Harper Torchbooks, 1973), esp. pp. 161–79.

41. For short critiques of triage and lifeboat ethics, see Lester Brown, *The Politics and Responsibility of the North American Breadbasket*, Worldwatch Paper, No. 2 (October 1975), p. 36; and BFW *Newsletter*, July 1976.

42. Robert H. Schuller, *Your Church Has Real Possibilities!* (Glendale, Calif: Regal Books, 1974), p. 117.

Part Two: A Biblical Perspective on the Poor and Possessions

1. Quoted in *Post-American* 1, No. 4 (Summer 1972), p. 1.

 2. Laudicina, *World Poverty and Development*, p. 21.

 3. Ronald J. Sider, ed., *Cry Justice: The Bible Speaks on Hunger and Poverty* (New York: Paulist Press; Downers Grove, Ill.: InterVarsity Press, 1980).

Chapter 3: God and the Poor

 1. See, for instance, Enzo Gatti, *Rich Church–Poor Church?* (Maryknoll, NY: Orbis Books, 1974), p. 43. Liberation theology in general leans in this direction. For excellent evaluations of liberation theology, see J. Andrew Kirk, *Liberation Theology: An Evangelical View from the Third World* (Atlanta, Ga.: John Knox Press, 1980); and Harvie Conn's two excellent chapters (8 and 9) on liberation theology in Stanley N. Gundry and Alan F. Johnson, eds, *Tensions in Contemporary Theology* (Chicago: Moody Press, 1976).

 2. Ernst Bammel, 'πτωχός', in Gerhard Kittell and Gerhard Friedrich, eds. *Theological Dictionary of the New Testament*, trans. Geoffrey W. Bromiley, 10 vols (Grand Rapids, Mich.: Eerdmans, 1968), 6:888. Hereafter called *TDNT*.

 3. A. Gelin, *The Poor of Yahweh* (Collegeville, Minn.: Liturgical Press, 1964), pp. 19–20.

 4. See the helpful distinctions among those who are poor because of (1) sloth, (2) calamity, (3) exploitation, and (4) voluntary choice in R. C. Sproul, 'Who Are the Poor?' *Tabletalk* 3, No. 6 (July 1979). See also the discussion of the 'spiritual poor' below, n. 26.

 5. Unlike some liberation theologians who take the exodus merely as an inspirational device, I assert that in the exodus God was *both* liberating oppressed persons and *also* calling out a special people to be the recipients of his special revelation. Yahweh called forth a special people so that through them he could reveal his will and salvation for all people. But his will included, as he revealed even more clearly to his covenant people, that his people should follow him and be on the side of the poor and oppressed. The fact that Yahweh did not liberate all poor Egyptians at the exodus does not mean that he was not concerned for the poor everywhere any more than the fact that he did not give the Ten Commandments to everyone in the Near East means that he did not intend them to have universal application. Because God chose to reveal himself in history, he disclosed to particular people at particular points in time what he willed for all people everywhere.

6. John Bright, *A History of Israel* (London: SCM Press, 1972).

7. *Ibid.*

8. Roland de Vaux, *Ancient Israel* (London: Darton, Longman & Todd, 1973), 2:72–3.

9. So also in the case of Judah; compare Ezek. 20, Jer. 11:9–10.

10. Preaching the gospel and seeking justice for the poor are *distinct, equally important* dimensions of the total mission of the church; see my 'Evangelism, Salvation and Social Justice: Definitions and Interrelationships', *International Review of Mission*, July 1975, pp. 251ff. (esp. p. 258), and my 'Evangelism or Social Justice: Eliminating the Options', *Christianity Today*, October 8th, 1976, pp. 26–29.

11. This is not to deny that a 'spiritual' usage of the term *the poor* emerged in the inter-testamental period. But even then, the material, economic foundation was never absent. See my 'An Evangelical Theology of Liberation', in Kenneth S. Kantzer and Stanley N. Gundry, eds, *Perspectives on Evangelical Theology* (Grand Rapids, Mich.: Baker, 1979), pp. 122–4.

12. See also Rev. 7:16.

13. Richard Batey, *Jesus and the Poor* (New York: Harper & Row, 1972), p. 7.

14. Martin Hengel, *Property and Riches in the Early Church: Aspects of a Social History of Early Christianity* (London: SCM Press, 1974).

15. Batey, *Jesus and the Poor*, p. 6.

16. See also Ps. 107:35–41. See chapter 5, pp. 99–100, for a discussion of the different versions of the beatitudes in Matthew 5 and Luke 6.

17. One dare not overlook, of course, the biblical teaching that obedience brings prosperity. See chapter 5, pp. 113–15, for a discussion of this theme.

18. Bright, *History of Israel*, p. 306. For a similar event, see Dan. 4 (esp. v. 27).

19. See also Mic. 2:1–3.

20. Joachim Jeremias, *The Parables of Jesus* (London: SCM Press, 1954), pp. 128–30, and others have argued that Jesus's point was an entirely different one. But I am still inclined to follow the usual interpretation; see, for instance, *The Interpreter's Bible*, 8:288–92.

21. *Ibid.*, p. 290.

22. Clark H. Pinnock, 'An Evangelical Theology of Human Liberation', *Sojourners*, February 1976, p. 31.

23. 'The Bible and the Other Side', *The Other Side* 11, No. 5 (September–October 1975): 57.

24. See J. A. Motyer, *The Day of the Lion: The Message of Amos* (London: Inter Varsity Press, 1974), for a good exegesis of these verses. See also Mic. 6:6–8; Jas 2:14–17.

25. That is not to say that God is unconcerned with true worship. Nor does Amos 5:21–4 mean that God is saying, 'I do not want you to defend my rights, real or imaginary; I want you to struggle and expend your energies in advancing the rights of the poor and oppressed' (Gatti, *Rich Church–Poor Church?* p. 17). Such a dichotomy ignores the central prophetic attack on idolatry. God wants both worship and justice. Tragically, some people today concentrate on one, some on the other. Few seek both simultaneously.

26. G. E. Ladd, *A Theology of the New Testament* (Guildford: Lutterworth Press, 1975), p. 133. For this whole topic of whether Matt. 25, 1 John 3 and so on, must be limited in their application to Christians, see the superb discussion of Stephen C. Mott, *Biblical Ethics and Social Change* (New York: Oxford Univ. Press, 1982), pp. 34–6.

27. God does not desire the salvation of the poor more than the salvation of the rich. I disagree strongly with Gatti's assertion: 'They [the poor and oppressed] are the ones that have the best right to that word [of salvation]; they are the privileged recipients of the Gospel' (*Rich Church–Poor Church?* p. 43). God desires all people – oppressors and oppressed alike – to be saved. No one has any 'right' to hear God's Word. We all deserve death. It is only by contrast with the sinful perversity of Christians who prefer to preach in the suburbs rather than the slums that Jesus and Paul seem to be biased in favour of preaching to the poor.

28. For a more elaborate development of these points, see my 'An Evangelical Theology of Liberation', pp. 117–20.

29. See chap. 6, pp. 84–9.

30. See my several articles on the resurrection listed in n. 2 of the epilogue.

Chapter 4: Economic Relationships Among the People of God

1. Also Ezek. 47:14. See the discussion and the literature cited in Mott, *Biblical Ethics and Social Change*, pp. 65–6; and

Stephen Charles Mott, 'Egalitarian Aspects of the Biblical Theory of Justice', in the *American Society of Christian Ethics, Selected Papers 1978*, ed. Max Stackhouse (Newton, Mass.: American Society of Christian Ethics, 1978), pp. 8–26.

2. See the excellent book edited by Loren Wilkinson, *Earthkeeping: Christian Stewardship of Natural Resources*, 2nd edn (Grand Rapids, Mich.: Eerdmans, 1980), esp. pp. 232–7.

3. See in this connection the fine article by Paul G. Schrotenboer, 'The Return of Jubilee', *International Reformed Bulletin*, Fall 1973, pp. 19ff. (esp. pp. 23–4).

4. See also Eph. 2:13–18. Marc H. Tanenbaum points out the significance of the day of atonement in 'Holy Year 1975 and Its Origins in the Jewish Jubilee Year', *Jubilaeum* (1974), p. 64.

5. For the meaning of the word *liberty* in Lev. 25:10, see Martin Noth, *Leviticus* (Philadelphia: Westminster, 1965), p. 187: 'Derōr, a "liberation" . . . is a feudal word from the Accadian (an)durāru = "freeing from burdens".'

6. Roland de Vaux reflects the scholarly consensus that Leviticus 25 'was a Utopian law and it remained a dead letter' (*Ancient Israel*, 1:177). Tanenbaum ('Holy Year 1975', pp. 75–6), on the other hand, thinks it was practised. The only other certain references to it are in Lev. 27:16–25, Num. 36:4 and Ezek. 46:17. It would be exceedingly significant if one could show that Isa. 61:1–2 (which Jesus cited to outline his mission in Luke 4:18–19) also refers to the year of jubilee. De Vaux doubts that Isa. 61:1 refers to the jubilee (*Ancient Israel*, 1:176). The same word, however, is used in Isa. 61:1 and Lev. 25:10. See John H. Yoder's argument in *Politics of Jesus* (Grand Rapids, Mich.: Eerdmans, 1972), pp. 64–77; see also Robert Sloan, *The Acceptable Year of the Lord* (Austin, Tex.: Scholar Press, 1977); and Donald W. Blosser, 'Jesus and the Jubilee' (Ph.D. diss., Univ. of St Andrews, 1979).

7. De Vaux, *Ancient Israel*, 1:173–5.

8. Leviticus 25 seems to provide for emancipation of slaves only every fiftieth year. But the purpose is the same: prevention of ever greater inequality among God's people.

9. See Jer. 34 for a fascinating account of God's anger at Israel for their failure to obey this command.

10. Some modern commentators think that Deuteronomy 15:1–11 provides for a one-year suspension of repayment of loans rather than an outright remission of them. See S. R. Driver, *Deuteronomy*, International Critical Commentary, 3rd edn (Edinburgh: T. and T. Clark, 1895), pp. 179–80. But Driver's

argument is basically that remission would have been *impractical*. He admits that v. 9 seems to point towards remission of loans. So too Gerhard von Rad, *Deuteronomy* (London: SCM Press, 1966).

11. See de Vaux, *Ancient Israel*, 1:174–5, for discussion of the law's implementation. In the Hellenistic period, there is clear evidence that it was put into effect.

12. See also de Vaux, *Ancient Israel*, 1:165.

13. This is an extremely complicated problem which has been debated throughout church history. The long dispute among Lutherans over the 'third use of the law' is one example of the perennial debate.

14. De Vaux, *Ancient Israel*, 1:171.

15. See, *ibid.*, p. 170; and Taylor, *Enough Is Enough*, pp. 56–60.

16. Driver, *Deuteronomy*, p. 178.

17. For a highly fascinating, scholarly account of the entire history, see Benjamin Nelson, *The Idea of Usury: From Tribal Brotherhood to Universal Otherhood*, 2nd edn (Chicago: Univ. of Chicago Press, 1969).

18. See the excellent discussion by Bob Goudzwaard, *Capitalism and Progress: A Diagnosis of Western Society* (Grand Rapids, Mich.: Eerdmans, 1979).

19. See Matt. 4:23; 24:14; Mark 1:14–15; Luke 4:43; 16:16; and my 'Evangelism, Salvation and Social Justice', pp. 251–67. Also, my 'Words and Deeds', *Journal of Theology for Southern Africa*, Fall 1979, pp. 31–50.

20. For this common interpretation, see Batey, *Jesus and the Poor*, pp. 3, 9, 100, n. 8; J. A. Ziesler, *Christian Asceticism* (Grand Rapids, Mich.: Eerdmans, 1973), p. 45; *TDNT*, 3:796; *Interpreter's Bible*, 8:655, 690; Carl Henry, 'Christian Perspective on Private Property', in *God and the Good*, ed. C. Orlebeke and L. Smedes (Grand Rapids, Mich.: Eerdmans, 1975), p. 98.

21. See also Batey, *Jesus and the Poor*, p. 8.

22. Taylor, *Economics and the Gospel*, p. 21.

23. See D. Guthrie et. al., eds, *The New Bible Commentary Revised* (Leicester: Inter Varsity Press, 1970); Batey, *Jesus and the Poor*, p. 38.

24. *TDNT*, 3:796.

25. The key verbs are *epipraskon* and *diemerizon* (Acts 2:45) and *epheron* (Acts 4:34). See *Interpreter's Bible*, 9:52; Batey, *Jesus and the Poor*, pp. 33, 103, n. 9.

26. Ziesler, *Christian Asceticism*, p. 110.

27. Batey, *Jesus and the Poor*, pp. 36, 96–7.

28. See Keith F. Nickle, *The Collection: A Study of Paul's Strategy*, Studies in Biblical Theology, No. 48 (Naperville, Ill.: Allenson, 1966), p. 29; and *Interpreter's Bible*, 9:153.

29. See Diane MacDonald, 'The Shared Life of the Acts Community', *Post-American*, July 1975, p. 28.

30. See *Interpreter's Bible*, 9:150–2, for a summary of the reasons for accepting the reliability of this account.

31. See Nickle, *The Collection*, pp. 68–9.

32. See *TDNT*, 3:804ff.

33. In fact, Paul was probably at Jerusalem to deliver the gift mentioned in Acts 11:27–30. See *Interpreter's Bible*, 9:151.

34. See *TDNT*, 3:807–8.

35. See also the striking use of *koinōnos* in Philemon 17–20. As fellow Christians, the slave Onesimus, his master Philemon and Paul are all partners (*koinōnoi*). This common fellowship means that Paul can ask Philemon to charge Onesimus' debt to his own account. But Paul and Philemon are also partners in Christ. Furthermore, Philemon owes Paul his very soul. Therefore, Paul suggests there is no need for anyone to reimburse Philemon. Their fellowship in Christ cancels any debt that Onesimus might otherwise owe. See *TDNT*, 3:807.

36. (The italics are mine.) Not all translations are accurate. But the Greek word *isotēs* clearly means 'equality'. So Charles Hodge: 'The word *isotēs* means here neither reciprocity nor equity, but equality, as the illustration in verse 15 shows.' *An Exposition of the Second Epistle to the Corinthians* (Edinburgh: Banner of Truth Trust, 1974). So too C. K. Barrett, *The Second Epistle to the Corinthians* (London: A. & C. Black, 1973); and the Tyndale commentary by R. V. G. Tasker, *The Second Epistle of Paul to the Corinthians* (London: Tyndale Press, 1971).

37. Quoted in Hengel, *Property and Riches in the Early Church*, pp. 42–3.

38. *Ibid.*, pp. 42–4.

39. Quoted *ibid.*, p. 45.

40. On December 5th, 1975, the *Wall Street Journal* reported that since 1971 a professional archaeologist had been measuring the amount of food thrown away in Tucson, Arizona. He discovered that the average family discards $100 worth of food each year (and that does not count food fed to pets or ground up in the rubbish disposal). Assuming a family size of five, 236 million North Americans discard $4.7 billions-worth of food each year. Using the figures on per capita GNP (1973) in Roger D. Hansen, *Agenda*

for Action, 1976 (New York: Praeger, 1976), p. 146, I estimated (in 1976) that 120 million African Christians earned $25 billion annually. (I assumed 74 million at $150 per year; 45 million at $300; and 1 million at $1,000.)

41. C. H. Jacquet, Jr., ed., *Yearbook of American and Canadian Churches: 1974* (New York: National Council of Churches, 1974), p. 263.

42. See Helmut Gollwitzer, *The Rich Christians and Poor Lazarus*, trans. David Cairns (Edinburgh: St Andrew Press, 1970); and Arthur C. Cochrane, *Eating and Drinking with Jesus* (Philadelphia: Westminster Press, 1974).

Chapter 5: A Biblical Attitude Towards Property and Wealth

1. So, correctly, Carl F. H. Henry, 'Christian Perspective on Private Property', p. 97; Hengel, *Property and Riches in the Early Church*, p. 15.

2. See further Emil Brunner, *Justice and the Social Order*, trans. Mary Hottinger (London: Lutterworth Press, 1945), pp. 42ff., 133ff.; and E. Clinton Gardner, *Biblical Faith and Social Ethics* (New York: Harper & Row, 1960), pp. 285–91.

3. Adam Smith, *The Wealth of Nations* (Oxford: Oxford University Press, 1976).

4. See, for example, Gary North, 'Free Market Capitalism', in *Wealth and Poverty: Four Christian Views of Economics*, ed. Robert G. Clouse (Downers Grove, Ill.: InterVarsity Press, 1984).

5. See Goudzwaard, *Capitalism and Progress*.

6. Henry, 'Christian Perspective on Private Property', p. 97.

7. Hengel, *Property and Riches in the Early Church*, p. 12.

8. See Tony Cramp, 'Cutting the Cake', *Third Way*, July 28th, 1977, pp. 3–6.

9. Walther Eichrodt, 'The Question of Property in the Light of the Old Testament', in *Biblical Authority for Today*, eds Alan Richardson and W. Schweitzer (London: SCM Press, 1951), p. 261.

10. *Ibid.*, p. 271.

11. See further Gardner, *Biblical Faith and Social Ethics*, pp. 276–7.

12. *Interpreter's Bible*, 7:320; see also 1 Tim. 6:17–19.

13. A. W. Argyle, *Matthew*, The Cambridge Bible Commentary (Cambridge: Cambridge Univ. Press, 1963), p. 58. So too *Interpreter's Bible*, 7:318.

14. Camara, *Revolution through Peace*, pp. 142–3.

15. *TDNT*, 6:271. Taylor (*Enough Is Enough*, p. 45) suggests that the word connotes 'excess' or 'wanting more and more'.

16. For a discussion of church discipline, see my 'Watching Over One Another in Love', *The Other Side* 11, No. 3 (May–June 1975): 13–20, 58–60 (esp. p. 59).

17. For a good discussion of this issue, see Ziesler, *Christian Asceticism.*

18. See the biblical texts in Sider, *Cry Justice*, pp. 175–87 for the former and pp. 148–53 for the latter.

19. See Gordon D. Fee, 'The New Testament View of Wealth and Possessions', *New Oxford Review* (May 1981): 9: 'It is only as one is righteous – i.e., walks in accordance with God's law – that one is promised the blessing of abundance and family. But to be righteous meant especially that one cared for or pleaded the cause of the poor and the oppressed.'

20. Taylor, *Enough Is Enough*, chap. 3.

21. See further the twenty references in Batey, *Jesus and the Poor*, p. 92.

22. Ziesler, *Christian Asceticism*, p. 52. See further my 'An Evangelical Theology of Liberation', pp. 122–5.

23. See chap. 1, p. 3, on Heilbroner's predictions.

Chapter 6: Structural Evil and World Hunger

1. 'Edison High School – A History of Benign and Malevolent Neglect', *Oakes Newsletter* 5, No. 4 (December 14th, 1973): 1–4; and 'Northeast High Took the Glory Away', *Sunday Bulletin*, January 27th, 1974, sect. 1, p. 3.

2. Rodney Stark et. al., 'Sounds of Silence', *Psychology Today*, April 1970, pp. 38–41, 60–7.

3. Bright, *History of Israel* (London: SCM Press, 1972).

4. Compare Isaiah 3:13–17.

5. This is not to deny that the degree of responsibility and guilt has some relationship to the degree of one's awareness, understanding, and conscious choice. See my more extended comments in 'Racism', *United Evangelical Action* 36 (Spring 1977): 11–12. At the same time, it is important to remember that we regularly *choose* not to learn more about topics that we know would challenge and demand a change in our current thinking and living. For an excellent, extended treatment of systemic evil (including a discussion of the Pauline concept of the 'principalities and powers'), see Mott, *Biblical Ethics and Social Change*, chap. 1.

6. Mooneyham, *Hungry World*, pp. 117, 128.

7. See especially Piero Gheddo, *Why Is the Third World Poor?* (Maryknoll, NY: Orbis Books, 1973). But see also Laurence Harrison, *Underdevelopment Is a State of Mind* (Lanham, Md.: The Center of International Affairs, Harvard University and University Press of America, 1985). Michael Novak is surely correct in insisting that religio-cultural values in Latin America itself are one major cause of its poverty. Unfortunately he grossly understates the extent to which US political and economic power is also at fault. See his *The Spirit of Democratic Capitalism* (New York: Simon and Schuster, 1982).

8. Mahbub ul Haq, *The Poverty Curtain* (New York: Columbia Univ. Press, 1976), p. 162. For more on the impact of colonialism on the Third World, see Walter Rodney, *How Europe Undeveloped Africa* (London: Bogle-L'Ouverture Pub., 1972). Rodney explains how European nations found culturally sophisticated African nations and under colonial practices gradually stripped them of their cultural, social, and economic vitality. In a shorter but succinct case study, Cristobal Kay points out the injustices that prevailed during the first years of European contact in South America ('Comparative Development of the European Manorial System and the Latin American Hacienda System', *Journal of Peasant Studies* 2, No. 2 [January 1975]). It would be silly, of course, to accept uncritically Marxist scholars who explain all history in terms of class struggle, but there is equal danger in denying the importance of history as a crucial explanatory factor. P. T. Bauer, for example, in *Equality, the Third World, and Economic Delusion* (Cambridge, Mass.: Harvard Univ. Press, 1981), disregards history and argues instead that current economic inequalities are almost totally due to differences in ingenuity, effort, and resource distribution rather than to historical misuses of political and economic power. But Bauer's extremism on the one side is just as wrong as the Marxist extremism on the other. For a balanced criticism of Bauer from a rather traditional economist, see Amartya Sen, 'Just Desserts', a review of Bauer's book in the *New York Review of Books*, March 4th, 1982. It is also interesting to note that David Beckmann, a Christian economist working at the World Bank and author of *Where Faith and Economics Meet* (Minneapolis: Augsburg Press, 1981), attributes much of Third World poverty to colonial and other exploitative practices.

9. Gunnar Myrdal, *Asian Drama: An Inquiry into the*

Poverty of Nations, 3 vols (New York: Twentieth Century Fund, 1968), 1:455. See pp. 447–62 for a more extended analysis.

10. For two divergent views about the origin and validity of the mercantilist spirit, see William Cunningham, 'Medieval and Modern Economic Ideas Contrasted', *Growth of English Industry and Commerce*, 3 vols (London: John Murray, 1910), 1:457–72; and G. Schmoller, *The Mercantile System and Its Historical Significance* (New York: Macmillan, 1895).

11. James B. McGinnis, *Bread and Justice* (New York: Paulist Press, 1979), pp. 29–31.

12. June Kronholz, 'Gabon's Been Working on Its New Railroad, But Pay Day Is Far Off', *Wall Street Journal*, July 30th, 1981, pp. 1ff.

13. Joan Robinson, *Aspects of Development and Underdevelopment* (Cambridge: At the University Press, 1979).

14. For a balanced summary, see Gheddo, *Why is the Third World Poor?*, pp. 69–100.

15. For a careful discussion of how US tariff structures discriminate against the exports of poor countries, see Guy F. Erb, 'U.S. Trade Policies Toward Developing Areas', *Columbia Journal of World Business* 8, No. 3 (Fall 1973): 59–67.

16. Brown, *State of the World 1990*, p. 144.

17. James P. Grant, 'Can the Churches Promote Development?', *Ecumenical Review* 26 (January 1974): 26.

18. McGinnis, *Bread and Justice*, p. 72.

19. World Bank, *World Development Report 1987* (Washington, DC: Oxford University Press, 1987), Table 8.3, p. 142.

20. Donald Hay, *Economics Today* (London: InterVarsity Press, 1989), pp. 259–60.

21. 'Brazil vs. the U.S.', *New York Times*, January 7th, 1968; 'Brazil Agrees to Accept Terms', *Wall Street Journal*, February 20th, 1968.

22. Theodore Morgan, *Economic Development: Concept and Strategy* (New York: Harper and Row, 1975), p. 316.

23. See, for example, W. Arthur Lewis, *The Evolution of the International Economic Order* (Princeton: Princeton Univ. Press, 1978), pp. 23–4.

24. Gheddo, *Why Is the Third World Poor?*, p. 83.

25. *New Internationalist*, August 1975, p. 1.

26. Barbara Segal, 'The Debt Crisis', BFW Background Paper, 1990.

27. *World Development Report 1982*, p. 28.

28. Todaro, *Economic Development* (1989), p. 376.

29. See the chart showing the trend over the last thirty years, *ibid.*, pp. 26–30. For a summary of other views, see John Spraos, 'The Statistical Debate on the Net Barter Terms of Trade Between Primary Commodities and Manufacturers', *Economic Journal* 90 (March 1980): 107–28.

30. Donald Hay, 'The International Socio-Economic Political Order and Our Lifestyles', in *Lifestyle in the Eighties: An Evangelical Commitment to Simple Lifestyle*, ed. Ronald Sider (Philadelphia: Westminster Press, 1982), p. 104.

31. Hans W. Singer, *International Development: Growth and Change* (New York: McGraw-Hill, 1964), p. 165.

32. Brown, *State of the World 1990*, p. 144.

33. UNCTAD *Handbook of International Trade and Development Statistics*, 1988.

34. Jeffrey Sachs, 'Making the Brady Plan Work', *Foreign Affairs* (1989), p. 92.

35. Sachs, 'Debt Crisis', *Challenge*, p. 20.

36. Todaro, *Economic Development* (1989), p. 421.

37. James Grant, *State of the World's Children* (1989), p. 30.

38. George Ann Potter, *Dialogue on Debt: Alternative Analyses and Solutions*, p. 102. See also the study of malnourished children in a rural hospital, Albina Patino, in Kenneth Jameson and Peter Henriot, 'International Debt, Austerity and the Poor', Lee Travis, ed., *Rekindling Development: Multinational Firms and World Debt* (Notre Dame: Univ. of Notre Dame Press, 1988) pp. 31–2.

39. John Cavanagh and Robin Broad, 'Repaying RP Debt Kills a Filipino Child Per Hour', *Philippine Daily Inquirer*, March 30th, 1989, pp. 1, 10.

40. Giovanni Andrea Cornia, Richard Jolly, and Frances Stewart, *Adjustment With a Human Face*, vol. I, pp. 29, 34.

41. Quoted in James P. Grant, *State of the World's Children 1990* (UNESCO), pp. 45, 47.

42. Potter, *Dialogue on Debt* (1989), pp. 98–100.

43. Rudiger Dornbusch, 'Dealing With Debt in the 1980s', *Third World Quarterly*, July 1985, p. 547.

44. Potter, *Dialogue on Debt* (1989), pp. 98–9.

45. Jeffrey Sachs in *Foreign Affairs* (Summer 1989), p. 91.

46. Jameson and Henriot, 'International Debt, Austerity and the Poor', Lee Travis, ed., *Rekindling Development*; pp. 15–56.

47. Todaro, *Economic Development* (1989), p. 419.

48. Jeffrey Sachs, *Developing Country Debt and the World Economy* (Chicago: University Press, 1989), pp. 8–9; see also

Anthony Sampson, *The Money Lenders* (London: Hodder & Stoughton, 1981).

49. Sachs, *Developing Country Debt*, p. 8.

50. Todaro, *Economic Development* (1989), p. 423.

51. William R. Cline, *International Debt and the Stability of the World Economy* (1983: Institute for International Economics, Washington, DC: See also Todaro, *Economic Development*, 1989, p. 423).

52. 'Appointments in Santiago (I): Rough Sledding Ahead', *Journal of Commerce*, March 27th, 1972, editorial.

53. See United Nations, *A Study of the Problems of Raw Materials and Development* (A/9556, pt. 2), May 1st, 1974; and *Newsweek*, September 15th, 1975, pp. 38–40.

54. See, for example, W. M. Corden, *The NIEO Proposals: A Cool Look*, Thames Essay, No. 21 (London: Trade Policy Research Centre, 1979); and Herbert G. Grubel, 'The Case Against the New International Economic Order', *The Contemporary International Economy*, ed. John Adams (New York: St Martin's Press, 1979). Grubel argues that while the NIEO may be politically appealing to small, poor countries, it would be economically harmful to them. He does not believe that either the developed, wealthy countries or multinational corporations possess any inordinate market power. His suggestion is that instead of setting up some huge bureaucratic system, the poor countries ought to encourage, with their own internal pricing policies or collective action in the UN, a more competitive international economic environment.

55. Hay, 'The International Socio-Economic Political Order', pp. 116–22, and Donald Hay, 'North and South: The Economic Debate', in *The Year 2000*, ed. John R. W. Stott (Downers Grove, Ill.: InterVarsity Press, 1984).

56. It is interesting to note that, in 1975, then-Secretary of State Henry Kissinger proposed nine new international agencies to aid the poorer nations. Further, he promised to give poor nations preferential import tariffs for their goods. But in reporting the substance behind the proposals, *Newsweek* noted that 'Kissinger's expectations . . . *in fact his hope* . . . is that negotiations will stretch out over months and perhaps years' (*Newsweek*, September 15th, 1975, p. 45; my emphasis).

57. For a summary of the details of the nearly finalised treaty, see S. P. Jagota, 'Developments in the UN Conference on the Law of the Sea', *Third World Quarterly* 3, No. 2 (April 1981): 286–319. See also 'Sea-Law Conference Begins Final Phase',

UN Chronicle 18 (May 1981); and *Newsweek*, March 23rd, 1981.

58. Willy Brandt, *North-South: A Program for Survival* (London: Pan Books, 1980). For a review of the report and its initial impact, see Miguel S. Wionczek, 'The Brandt Report', *Third World Quarterly* 3, No. 1 (January 1981): 104–18; or John P. Lewis, 'Shaking Loose from Difficult Year', *OECD Observer*, No. 107 (November, 1980): 6–13.

59. Mooneyham, *Hungry World*, pp. 117–18.

60. Lester R. Brown, et. al., *State of the World 1990* (New York: Norton, 1990), p. 3.

61. *Ibid.*, p. 21.

62. *Ibid.*, p. 19.

63. E. F. Schumacher, 'Implications of the Limits to Growth Debate – Small is Beautiful', *Anticipation*, No. 13 (December 1972), p. 14.

64. Brown, *State of the World 1989*, pp. 1, 8.

65. Brown, *State of the World 1990*, p. 17.

66. Brown, *State of the World 1989*, pp. 10, 15.

67. *Ibid.*, p. 10.

68. *Ibid.*, p. 11.

69. *Ibid.*, p. 1.

70. Brown, *State of the World 1990*, pp. 36, 174.

71. *Ibid.*, p. 36.

72. Brown, *State of the World 1989*, p. 80.

73. *Ibid.*, p. 26, 180–3.

74. The Presbyterian Eco-Justice Task Force, *Keeping and Healing the Creation* (Louisville: Committee on Social Witness, 1989), p. 10.

75. Quoted from Susan George, *A Fate Worse Than Debt* (New York: Grove Press, 1988), pp. 164–5.

76. Brown, *The State of the World 1988*, p. 87.

77. Presbyterian Eco-Justice Task Force, *Keeping and Healing the Creation*, p. 10.

78. Robert C. Williams, *Export Agriculture and the Crisis in Central America* (Chapel Hill: University of North Carolina Press, 1986), pp. 116–17.

79. Brown, *State of the World 1988*, p. 86.

80. Brown, *State of the World 1989*, pp. 31–2.

81. Brown, *State of the World 1988*, p. 94.

82. *The Developing World: Danger Point for US Security*, released on August 1st, 1989 by the Arms Control and Foreign Policy Caucus in the US Congress (p. 32).

83. G. Tyler Miller, Jr., *Living in the Environment* (Belmont, Calif.: Wadsworth, 1988), p. 197.

84. Brown, *State of the World 1989*, p. 21.

85. Brown, *State of the World 1990*, p. 3.

86. *Ibid.*, pp. 10–12.

87. Brown, *State of the World 1989*, p. 46.

88. Charles H. Southwick, ed. *Global Ecology* (Sunderland, Mass.: Sinauer Associates Inc., 1983), pp. 166, 169.

89. Quoted in Southwick, *Global Ecology*, p. 169.

90. Presbyterian Eco-Justice Task Force, *Keeping and Healing*, p. 7.

91. Brown, *State of the World 1990*, p. 185.

92. See the documentation cited in *ibid.*, p. 231, n. 48.

93. *Ibid.*, p. 148.

94. Georg Borgstrom, *The Hungry Planet* (New York: Collier-Macmillan, 1967), esp. chap. 1; and 'Present Food Production and the World Food Crisis', mimeographed paper presented September 2nd, 1974.

95. Borgstrom, 'Present Food Production', p. 3.

96. Simon, *Bread for the World*, pp. 19–20.

97. Borgstrom, 'Present Food Production', p. 12.

98. For a summary of this entire process, see part 3 of Frances Moore Lappé and Joseph Collins, *Food First* (Boston: Houghton Mifflin, 1977).

99. Quoted in *ibid.*, p. 77.

100. J. Jeffrey Leonard, *Natural Resources and Economic Development in Central America: A Regional Environment Profile* (Washington: International Institute for Environment and Development, 1987), pp. 179–80.

101. See the careful study by Robert G. Williams, *Export Agriculture and the Crisis in Central America* (Chapel Hill: University of North Carolina Press, 1986).

102. *Ibid.*, p. 109.

103. Beverly Keene, 'Export Cropping in Central America', BFW Background Paper, No. 43 (January 1980).

104. Williams, *Export Agriculture*, p. 170.

105. *Ibid.*, p. 160.

106. Keene, 'Export Cropping'. For the infant mortality rates, see James P. Grant, *The State of the World's Children 1990* (New York: Oxford, 1990), pp. 92–93.

107. Grant, *The State of the World's Children 1990*, pp. 76–7, 86–7.

108. Ricki Ross, 'Land and Hunger: Philippines', BFW Background Paper, No. 55 (July 1981).

109. See chap. 3 in Ronald J. Sider, *Non-violence: The Invincible Weapon?* (Dallas: Word, 1989). Published in Great Britain under the title, *Exploring the Limits of Non-violence* (London: Hodder & Stoughton).

110. Michael P. Todaro, *Economic Development in the Third World* (New York: Longman, 1977), p. 326.

111. Todaro, *Economic Development* (1989), p. 469.

112. Joseph La Palombara and Stephen Blank, *Multinational Corporations and Developing Countries*, report No. 767 (New York: The Conference Board, 1979), p. 5.

113. Todaro, *Economic Development* (1977), pp. 328–9.

114. Todaro, *Economic Development* (1989), p. 474.

115. See my 'Towards a Political Philosophy', *ESA/Advocate*, October 1988, p. 1ff.

116. Richard J. Barnet, 'Multinationals and Development', *New Catholic Worker* 222, No. 1325 (September–October 1978): 222. See also Richard J. Barnet and Ronald Muller, *Global Reach: The Power of the Multinational Corporations* (New York: Simon and Schuster, 1974).

117. Streeten and Lall (as noted in Hay, 'International Socio-Economic Political Order', p. 113) found in their sampling of MNC investments in LDCs that only 12 per cent of new capital investment represented an inflow of funds from outside the LDCs. See also Hay's more recent discussion of MNCs in *Economics Today* (1989), pp. 264–6.

118. Hay, 'International Socio-Economic Political Order', p. 84.

119. Barnet, 'Multinationals and Development', p. 225.

120. *Ibid.*, p. 224; also mentioned by Hay, 'International Socio-Economic Political Order', p. 113.

121. Ivan Illich ('Outwitting the "Developed" Countries', in *The Political Economy of Development and Underdevelopment*, ed. Charles K. Wilber [New York: Random House, 1979], pp. 436–44) is a development ethicist who is particularly galled by the proliferation of soft drinks in the LDCs.

122. Danny Collum, 'Nestlé Boycott', *Sojourners* (October 1989), p. 8.

123. Grant, *State of the World's Children 1990*, p. 26.

124. Grant, *State of the World's Children 1982–83*, pp. 3–4.

125. Letter from James P. Grant, Executive Director of UNICEF, to Regional Directors Representatives, August 16th, 1989.

126. Collum, 'Nestlé Boycott'. For more information about the boycott, see chapter 9, n. 12.

127. H. W. Walter, 'Marketing in Developing Countries', *Columbia Journal of World Business* (Winter, 1974), quoted in Lappé and Collins, *Food First*, p. 309.

128. Todaro, *Economic Development* (1977), p. 330; Todaro's emphasis.

129. Hay, 'International Socio-Economic Political Order', p. 123.

130. *Markings* (New York: Knopf, 1964), p. xxi.

131. *Philadelphia Inquirer*, April 10th, 1975, pp. 1–2.

132. See 'Bananas', *New Internationalist*, August 1975, p. 2.

133. 'Action', *New Internationalist*, August 1975, p. 32.

134. Carl Oglesby and Richard Schaull, *Containment and Change* (New York: Macmillan, 1967), p. 104; and Stephen Schlesinger and Stephen Kinzer, *Bitter Fruit: The Untold Story of the American Coup in Guatemala* (Garden City, NY: Doubleday, 1982).

135. See, for instance, Ronald J. Sider, 'Love, Freedom, Justice? Nicaragua', *Report from the Capitol*, March 1983, pp. 10–12. For a superb historical overview of the way the United States has frequently interfered and supported repressive dictatorship in Nicaragua, see the book by evangelical historian Richard Millet, *Guardians of the Dynasty: A History of the U.S. Created Guardia Nacional De Nicaragua and the Somoza Family* (Maryknoll, NY: Orbis Books, 1977).

136. See further, Sider, *Non-Violence*, pp. 36–54.

137. See, for instance, Schlesinger and Kinzer, *Bitter Fruit*.

138. For the infant mortality rates, see James P. Grant, *The State of the World's Children 1990*. (New York: Oxford, 1990), pp. 92–3.

139. 'America's World Role: Should We Feel Guilty?' *Philadelphia Inquirer*, July 18th, 1974, p. 7a.

140. See the helpful comments on this in Patrick Kerans, *Sinful Social Structures* (New York: Paulist Press, 1974), pp. 47–51.

Chapter 7: The Graduated Tithe and Other Modest Proposals: Towards a Simpler Lifestyle

1. Ronald J. Sider, ed., *The Chicago Declaration* (Carol Stream, Ill.: Creation House, 1974), p. 2.

2. J. D. Douglas, ed., *Let the Earth Hear His Voice: International Congress on World Evangelization, Lausanne, Switzerland* (Minneapolis: World Wide Publ., 1975), p. 6, sect. 9.

3. 'Creation, Technology, and Human Survival', Plenary

Address, WCC's Fifth Assembly, December 1st, 1975. This is a recent rendering of Elizabeth Seton's statement 'Live simply that others may simply live.'

4. *New York Times*, June 14th, 1973.

5. This sermon was one of the series of sermons which constituted the standard doctrines of the early Methodists. See *The Works of John Wesley*, 14 vols. (1872; reprint edn, Grand Rapids, Mich.: Zondervan, n.d.), 5:361–77.

6. *Ibid.*, pp. 365–8.

7. J. Wesley Bready, *England: Before and After Wesley* (London: Hodder & Stoughton, n.d.), p. 238.

8. A good UK equivalent would be the Income Support Allowances, the figures for which can be found in the Social Security Statistics published each year by HMSO and available at reference libraries.

9. Michael Harper, *A New Way of Living* (London: Hodder & Stoughton, 1974).

10. Doris Longacre, *Living More with Less* (Scottdale, Penn.: Herald Press, 1980). See also the personal testimonies in Ronald J. Sider, ed., *Living More Simply: Biblical Principles and Practical Models* (Downers Grove, Ill.: InterVarsity Press, 1980), pp. 59–159.

11. See Gene M. Daffern, 'One Man Can Make a Difference', *These Times*, September 1982, pp. 6–11.

12. See his moving testimony, 'From Galloping Gourmet to Serving the Poor', in Sider, *Lifestyles in the Eighties*, pp. 174–82. For his programme write to: The Creative Lifestyle Center, PO Box 504, Tacoma, Washington 98401 (206–752–0065).

13. Ginny Hearn and Walter Hearn, 'The Price is Right', *Right On*, May 1973, pp. 1, 11.

14. See my suggestions on this in 'Living More Simply for Evangelism and Justice', in Sider, *Lifestyles in the Eighties*, pp. 32–5.

15. Lester R. Brown with Erick P. Eckholm, *By Bread Alone* (New York: Praeger, 1974), p. 198.

16. The figure for grain used (September 1988–August 1989) in making alcoholic beverages is from a telephone call (March 28th, 1990) with Larry Van Meir, ERS, the US Department of Agriculture. One ton of grain will feed five people in India for a year.

17. See Ron W. Jones, Julia Cheever and Ferry Ficklin, *Finding Community* (Palo Alto, Calif.: James E. Freel and Associates, 1971), pp. 48–50. Or visit the local welfare office!

18. *Transformation* magazine publishes a series of holistic

models of evangelism and social concern (e.g., October–December 1988, pp. 32–46).

19. I owe much to John F. Alexander in the development of these criteria.

20. Criteria a, c, d, and f are adapted from Edward R. Dayton, 'Where to Go from Here', Fuller Seminary's *Theology News and Notes*, October 1975, p. 19.

21. Quoted from a fund-raising piece written by John F. Alexander.

22. See Joe Remenyi's article on credit-based income generation projects (a summary of a forthcoming book) in *Transformation*, April–June 1990 and the statement on Income Generation in the same issue.

23. Maranatha Trust's address is PO Box 886, Bondi Junction 2022, NSW, Australia. US tax-deductible donations can be given through Opportunity International, 360 W. Butterfield Rd, Elmhurst, Ill. 60126 (708–279–9300).

24. *Christianity Today*, May 10th, 1974, pp. 32–3.

25. All OECD countries. See Stephen Hellinger, Douglas Hellinger and Fred M. O'Regan, *Aid for Just Development: Report on the Future of Foreign Assistance* (Boulder: Lynne Rienner Publishers, 1988), pp. 99–100.

26. Minear, *New Hope for the Hungry*, p. 79.

Chapter 8: Watching Over One Another in Love

1. Dave Jackson and Neta Jackson, *Living Together in a World Falling Apart* (Carol Stream, Ill.: Creation House, 1974), p. 15.

2. See above, chap. 4, pp. 86–98.

3. See my 'Spare the Rod and Spoil the Church', *Eternity*, October 1976.

4. From John Wesley's account (1748) of the origin of the class meetings (*The Works of John Wesley*, 8:269).

5. Peter Berger, *A Rumour of Angels* (Harmondsworth: A. Lane, 1976). See also Peter Berger and Thomas Luckman, *The Social Construction of Reality* (Harmondsworth: A. Lane, 1967).

6. Berger, *A Rumor of Angels*, p. 17. See further pp. 41ff for Berger's rejection of the common idea that the sociology of knowledge leads inexorably to thoroughgoing relativism.

7. See Floyd Filson, 'The Significance of the Early House Churches', *Journal of Biblical Literature* 58 (1939: 105–12). See also the brief overview in John W. Miller's (mimeographed)

'House Church Handbook'. For a copy, write to John Miller, Conrad Grebel College, University of Waterloo, Waterloo, Ont., Canada.

8. Personal conversations with John Poole. For further information or cassette tapes, write to Living Word Community, 142 N. 17th St., Philadelphia, Pa. 19143.

9. I have relied largely on Gordon Cosby's *Handbook for Mission Groups* (Waco, Tex Word Books, 1975 for this discussion. See also Elizabeth O'Connor's several books about or for Church of the Savior, including: *Call to Commitment* (New York: Harper & Row, 1963): *Journey Inward, Journey Outward* (New York: Harper & Row, 1968). For further information, write to: Church of the Savior, 2025 Massachusetts Ave., NW, Washington, DC 20036.

10. Cosby, *Handbook for Mission Groups*, p. 63.

11. *Ibid.*, p. 140.

12. For further information about Dunamis, write to Dunamis Vocation Church, 2025 Massachusetts Ave., NW, Washington, DC 20035 [(202) 387–1234].

13. Howard A. Snyder, *New Wineskins: Church Structure in a Technological Age* (London: Marshall, Morgan & Scott, 1977). See also his more recent *Liberating the Church: The Ecology of Church and Kingdom* (Downers Grove, Ill.: Inter Varsity Press, 1983).

14. For a discussion of Reba Place, see Jackson and Jackson, *Living Together in a World Falling Apart*, esp. pp. 36–9, 230–3. For the names and addresses of 24 communities, see pp. 287–97.

15. *Ibid.*, p. 183.

16. *Ibid.*, p. 65.

17. For a good historical perspective on Christian communes and an excellent bibliography, see Donald G. Bloesch, *Wellsprings of Renewal: Promise in Christian Communal Life* (Grand Rapids, Mich.: Eerdmans, 1974). For a handbook by a Catholic charismatic, see Stephen B. Clark, *Building Christian Communities* (Notre Dame, Ind.: Ave Maria Press, 1972).

Chapter 9: Structural Change

1. From an article in *Our Hope* 10, No. 2 (August 1903): 76–7.

2. For my preliminary thoughts, see my 'Toward a Biblical Perspective on Equality: Steps on the Way Toward Christian Political Engagement', *Interpretation*, April 1989, pp. 156–69; 'A

Plea for Conserving Radicals and Radical Conservatives', *Christian Century*, October 1st, 1987, pp. 834–8; 'An Evangelical Vision for Public Life', *Transformation*, July–September 1985, pp. 1–9, 13–14.

3. See, for example, Clouse, ed., *Wealth and Poverty: Four Christian Views*. See my plea for tolerance and understanding of the specific reasons for disagreement in 'A Plea for Conservative Radicals and Radical Conservatives', *Christian Century*.

4. See most recently my *Non-Violence: The Invincible Weapon?; Nuclear Holocaust and Christian Hope* (Downers Grove, Ill.: InterVarsity Press, 1982), co-authored with Richard K. Taylor; and earlier my *Christ and Violence* (Scottdale, Penn.: Herald Press, 1978).

5. See my further comments on this in 'Towards a Political Philosophy', *ESA/Advocate*, October 1988, pp. 1–2.

6. See, for instance, Ogelsby and Shaull, *Containment and Change*, pp. 72–111, and the books on Nicaragua and Guatemala cited in chapter 6, notes 134 and 135.

7. See Amnesty International, *Report on Torture* (New York: Farrar, Straus and Giroux, 1975), especially the special report on Chile on pp. 243ff. See also Fred B. Morris, 'Sustained by Faith under Brazilian Torture', *Christian Century*, January 22nd, 1975, pp. 56–60; *Latin America and Empire Report* 10, No. 1 (January 1976); and Bread For the World 'Military Aid, the World's Poor and U.S. Security'.

8. Penny Lernoux, *Cry of the People* (New York: Penguin, 1982).

9. Todaro, *Economic Development*, 1989, pp. 470, 474.

10. See Grant, *The State of the World's Children 1982–83*, pp. 3–4.

11. 'The Breast vs. the Bottle', *Newsweek*, June 1st, 1981, p. 54.

12. This is not to argue that the total impact of MNCs is negative. For information on the Nestlé boycott and the analyses of its impact, write to the Interfaith Centre on Corporate Responsibility (475 Riverside Drive, New York, NY 10027) and Action for Corporate Accountability (3255 Hennepin Avenue South, Suite 230, Minneapolis, MN 55408).

13. Robert E. Frykenberg, ed., *Land Tenure and the Peasant in South Asia: An Anthology of Recent Research* (Madison, Wis.: Land Tenure Center, 1976), p. 14.

14. See the interesting Indian case study, Saral K. Chatterji, *Religious Values and Economic Development: A Case Study*,

Social Research Series, No. 5 (Bangalore: Christian Institute for the Study of Religion and Society, 1967).

15. See, for example, page 7 in chapter 1 and corresponding notes 13 and 14.

16. See, for example, Normal Faramelli, 'Trade Barriers to Development in Poor Nations', in *The Causes of World Hunger*, ed. William Byron (New York: Paulist Press, 1982), chap. 9.

17. Quoted in Ernest Levinsohn, 'Getting Aid to the Poor', BFW Background Paper, No. 59 (April 1982): 2.

18. See Denis Goulet, *The Cruel Choice* (New York: Atheneum, 1971), pp. 123–52.

19. Paul Streeten, 'A Basic-Needs Approach to Economic Development', in *Directions in Economic Development*, ed. Kenneth P. Jameson and Charles K. Wilber (Notre Dame, Ind.: University of Notre Dame Press, 1979), p. 74.

20. McGinnis, *Bread and Justice*, p. 261. Of course, to the extent that a nation's traditional values hinder development, Christians will share biblical values in a non-paternalistic but forthright fashion.

21. Examples of successful Basic Needs Programmes are the health programme in the state of Kerala, India, as discussed by Streeten, 'Basic-Needs Approach', pp. 109–14; the village of Patti Kalyana's comprehensive programme as reported in McGinnis, *Bread and Justice*, pp. 265–77; and the Sarvodaya Shramadana movement in Sri Lanka as discussed in *World Development Report 1980*, p. 75.

22. Guy F. Erb, 'U.S. Trade Policies toward Developing Areas', *Columbia Journal of World Business*, No. 3 (Fall 1973): 60.

23. World Bank, *World Development Report 1987* (New York: Oxford University Press, 1987), p. 150.

24. Anne O. Krueger et. al., eds, *Trade and Employment in Developing Economies* (Chicago: University of Chicago Press, 1981), argue that the poor would benefit because LDC exports would be labour-intensive.

25. Brandt, *North-South*, p. 186. For some alternatives to trade adjustment assistance, see chapter 11 by George R. Neumann in *International Trade and Finance: Readings*, eds Robert E. Baldwin and David J. Richardson, 2nd edn (Boston, Mass.: Little, Brown, 1981).

26. Donald Hay, *Economics Today*, p. 262.

27. Don Reeves, BFW Background Paper, No. 110 (March, 1989), p. 4.

28. 'Textiles and the Multi-Fiber Agreement', in David B. Yoffie, *International Trade and Competition* (New York: McGraw-Hill, 1990), pp. 223–38.

29. Morgan, *Economic Development* (2nd edn) p. 320.

30. Loinger, 'Trade with Justice', p. 3.

31. These criteria are taken, in part, from the USCC's 'Relieving Third World Debt: A Call for Co-Responsibility, Justice, and Solidarity', a booklet published by the USCC (September 27th, 1989), pp. 30–1.

32. See *Bread for the World Newsletter*, October 1989, p. 3.

33. Sachs in *Challenge*, May–June, 1988, p. 23. See also his article in *Foreign Affairs*, Summer 1989, p. 95.

34. See Sachs, *ibid* and the proposal of American Express's James Robinson in testimony before the US Senate's Subcommittee on International Finance and Monetary Policy (August 2nd, 1988).

35. Sachs does not think the economic cost to taxpayers would be excessive (*Challenge*, May–June, 1988).

36. Todaro, *Economic Development* (1989), pp. 597–8.

37. See World Bank figures in *State of the World's Children* (1988), p. 18.

38. See the paper delivered by Walter Lamp, vice-president, taxes, Chase Manhattan Bank at the May 23rd, 1988 Seminar for PVOs sponsored by USAID. Debt equity swaps also occur but there is vigorous debate about whether further foreign purchase of local businesses should be encouraged.

39. For further information, write to World Development Movement, Bedford Chambers, Covent Garden, London WC2, England.

40. Brown, *State of the World 1990*, p. 17.

41. *Ibid.*, pp. 177–8.

42. *Ibid.*, p. 24.

43. *Ibid.*, p. 25.

44. *Ibid.*, p. 122.

45. *Air Quality Management Plan: South Coast Air Basin* (El Monte, Calif: March 1989).

46. Brown, *State of the World 1990*, pp. 115–34.

47. *Ibid.*, p. 131.

48. *Ibid.*, p. 179.

49. *Ibid.*, p. 180.

50. *Ibid.*, p. 29.

51. *Ibid.*, p. 182.

52. *Ibid.*, p. 30.

53. See the suggestion *ibid.*, p. 30.

54. *Ibid.*, p. 27–8.

55. Thurow, *Zero-Sum Society*, pp. 103–7.

56. Bob Goudzwaard in *Capitalism and Progress* carefully traces the development of the corrupted notion of progress from its inception in the Enlightenment to the present.

57. Richard A. Easterlin, 'Does Money Buy Happiness?' *The Public Interest*, No. 3 (Winter 1973): 10. See also Martin Bolt and David G. Myers, 'Why Do the Rich Feel So Poor?' in *The Human Connection* (Downers Grove, Ill.: InterVarsity Press, 1984); and Paul L. Wachtel, *The Poverty of Affluence: A Psychological Portrait of the American Way of Life* (New York: Macmillan, 1983).

58. See the emphasis on increasing personal services in Robert L. Stivers, *The Sustainable Society: Ethics and Economic Growth* (Philadelphia: Westminster, 1976). For a different view, see Simon Webley, 'Can Christians Support Economic Growth as a Policy Objective?' *Christian Graduate*, March 1977, pp. 1–5. Roland Hoksbergen disagrees with Webley: 'The Morality of Economic Growth', *Reformed Journal* 32, No. 12 (December 1982): 10–13.

59. Wilkinson, ed., *Earthkeeping*.

60. See, for instance, Frances Moore Lappé, *Aid as Obstacle: Twenty Questions about Our Foreign Aid and the Hungry* (San Francisco: Institute for Food and Development Policy, 1980). See also James A. Cogswell's excellent summary of both views in his 'Crisis of Confidence in U.S. Aid to Poor Nations', in *The Causes of World Hunger*, ed. William Byron (New York: Paulist Press, 1982), pp. 141–5. A recent, important book calls for radical changes in aid: Stephen Hellinger, Douglas Hellinger, and Fred M. O'Regan, *Aid for Just Development: Report on the Future of Foreign Assistance* (Boulder: Lynne Rienner, 1988).

61. Ernest Loevinsohn, 'Making Foreign Aid More Effective', BFW Background Paper, No. 49 (March 1981).

62. See chap. 1, pp. 10–17.

63. Timothy King, ed., *Population Policies and Economic Development*, published for the World Bank (Baltimore: Johns Hopkins Univ. Press, 1974), p. 54. See also William Rich, *Smaller Families Through Social and Economic Progress*, monograph, No. 7 (Washington, DC: Overseas Development Council, 1973), esp. p. 76.

64. Hellinger et. al., *Aid for Just Development*, pp. 162, 180.

65. See *ibid.*, pp. 171–80 and Bread for the World's rec-

ommendations on US aid in Elmira Nazombe, 'Foreign Aid' (BFW Background Paper No. 11, May 1989).

66. See Hellinger et. al., *Aid for Just Development*, p. 4.

67. See World Bank testimony before the Committee on Banking, Finance and Urban Affairs of the US House of Representatives, June 15th, 1988.

68. Mahbub Hossain, *Credit for Alleviation of Rural Poverty: The Grameen Bank in Bangladesh*, Research Report 65 (Washington, DC: IFPRI, 1988); Kristin Helmore, 'Banking on a Better Life', *Christian Science Monitor*, March 15th, 1989.

69. Danielle Yariv, *Where Credit is Due: Report on AID's Compliance with 1988 Microenterprise Earmark* (Results Educational Fund, 236 Mass. Ave., NE, Suite 110, Washington, DC), November 19th, 1989.

70. See the 'Statement on Income Generation Programs Among the Poor in Developing Countries', *Transformation*, April–June, 1990; also the detailed study by Professor Joe Remenyi, *Income Generation By the Poor: A Study of Credit-Based Income and Employment Generation Programs in Developing Countries* (a manuscript being prepared for publication by Professor Remenyi, Center for Applied Social Research, Deakin University, Geelong 3217, Australia).

71. An excellent introduction to US foreign aid is in Bread for the World's pamphlet 'Foreign Aid: A Primer' (c. 1987).

72. For an excellent discussion of US food aid, see the letter of Larry Hollar, Bread for the World's Director of Issues, to Senator Patrick Leahy, chairman of the Senate Agricultural Committee, on February 6th, 1990.

73. Simon, *Bread for the World*, p. 113. (The figure in Simon's text was in 1975 dollars; 1989 dollars calculated based on 1975 Consumer Price Index of 53.8.)

74. See Tables 12 and 13 in chapter 2.

75. The data for this and the preceding paragraph comes from Stephen Coats, 'Military Spending and World Hunger'.

76. See their excellent material, especially the booklet, *Share the Harvest of Peace* (see address under organisations).

77. *Congressional Record* (Vol. 135, No. 107), August 2nd, 1989.

78. Quoted in Simon, *Bread for the World*, p. 170.

79. Cited from the report of the Presidential Commission on World Hunger in 'Hunger and Global Security', p. 1.

80. *Ibid.*

81. For example, Donald A. Hay, *A Christian Critique of*

Capitalism, Grove Booklet on Ethics, No. 5 (Bramcote, Nottingham: Grove Books, 1975); and Gouzwaard, *Capitalism and Progress*.

82. Many liberation theologians advocate some form of socialism. See for instance José Miguez-Bonino, *Christians and Marxists* (Grand Rapids, Mich.: Eerdmans, 1976), and John Eagleson, ed., *Christians and Socialism: Documentation of the Christians for Socialism Movement in Latin America* (Maryknoll, NY: Orbis Books, 1975).

83. Robert Benne, *The Ethic of Democratic Capitalism: A Moral Reassessment* (Philadelphia: Fortress Press, 1981); Michael Novak, *The Spirit of Democratic Capitalism* (New York: Simon and Schuster, 1982); and Michael Novak, 'The Economic System: The Evangelical Basis of a Social Market Economy', *The Review of Politics* 43, No. 3 (July 1981): 355–80.

84. My own view is that the right direction to grope for new solutions lies in some modification of the market economy and private 'ownership'. It is clear that centrally planned economies and collective agriculture do not work. Even more important, centralising the ownership of property and the means of production in the state leads to such centralised power that totalitarianism is almost guaranteed. At the same time, 'capitalist' MNCs have also centralised power to such a degree that political democracy is fundamentally threatened and workers have little participation in the decisions that affect their lives.

The jubilee and other biblical material point in the direction of decentralised ownership (or better stewardship under God, the only absolute owner). Farmers should normally own their own land. Smaller business enterprises should be encouraged. Industrial workers should be able to participate in the decisions affecting their own lives. (This can happen in a variety of ways: management-employee committees, co-operatives, and so on.) In order for persons to be co-shapers of history with God in responsible freedom, decentralised stewardship of the earth's resources, not highly centralised state or MNC ownership, is necessary.

85. The Oxford Declaration is printed in *Transformation*, April–June, 1990. For the ongoing process of The Oxford Conference, write to the Executive Director, Oxford Conference, Lancaster and City Avenue, Philadelphia, PA 19151.

Epilogue

1. Robert Bellah says that 'the quality of a culture may be changed when two per cent of its people have a new vision' ('Civil Religion', *Psychology Today*, January 1976, p. 64).

2. See my 'A Case for Easter', *HIS*, April 1972, pp. 27–31. For a more extensive discussion, see also my 'The Historian, the Miraculous and Post-Newtonian Man', *Scottish Journal of Theology* 25 (1972): 309–19; 'The Pauline Conception of the Resurrection Body in 1 Cor 15:35–54', *New Testament Studies* 21 (1975): 428–39; 'St. Paul's Understanding of the Nature and Significance of the Resurrection in 1 Cor. 15:1–19', *Novum Testamentum* 19 (1977): 1–18; and 'Jesus' Resurrection and the Search for Peace and Justice', *Christian Century*, November 3rd, 1982, pp. 1103–8.

WHAT READERS SAY

I profoundly believe that *this book contains the most vital challenge which faces the church of today*. It is one of the most searching and disquieting books I have ever read. It requires not only careful study, and, perhaps, some adaptation to the society in which we may live; it calls, above all, for immediate and sacrificial *action*, if we know anything of God's love in our hearts. It is useless calling Jesus 'Lord, Lord', if we do not do what he tells us. It will not be easy. It will often be painful. But I am convinced that this practical expression of God's love for people, especially for the afflicted and oppressed, will bring about the greatest impact for Christ that the church could ever make in this present world.

'He who has an ear, let him hear what the Spirit says to the churches.'

David Watson
St Michael-le-Belfry, York, 1978

There is no doubt that this book has become one of the most influential books of the past decade. It has served as a manifesto for those who believe that the Bible calls us to a simple lifestyle. It has been the inspiration for redesigning the structure and function of the church so that it might better serve the poor. And it has encouraged Christians everywhere to consider how God identifies with the oppressed in their struggle for justice. Some have called this book subversive, while others have called it prophetic. What better evidence is there of its importance?

Tony Campolo
Professor of Sociology
Eastern College

Like the Lausanne Covenant, drafted in 1974 by like-minded evangelicals from the six continents, Ron Sider's thought is prompted by the Spirit of Christian compassion, rooted in biblical revelation, and presented in a way conducive to action. The biblical approach to economic issues developed in *Rich Christians in an Age of Hunger* has been especially meaningful to Latin American evangelicals in their dialogue with Liberation theologies. Sider's approach has the thrust and the promise of a vision that is deeper and more realistic than the pervasive materialism of both European Marxism and American Functionalism.

> *Samuel Escobar*
> *Thornley B. Wood Professor of Missiology*
> *Eastern Baptist Theological Seminary*

Rich Christians in an Age of Hunger is a landmark book. In it Ron Sider calls Christians to a clear understanding of the social implications of the gospel they affirm. Love of God and love of neighbour are not two commands but one. Ron Sider clearly understands this and helps us all to understand it more clearly. We are the better for this seminal book.

> *Richard J. Foster*
> *Author*, Celebration of Discipline

Rich Christians in an Age of Hunger literally fell on me after having read Susan Graham's book *How the Other Half Die*. Synergistically the texts exploded in my life.

I knew, for the first time, the impact of revelation and the call to obedience. It seemed to me, as a result, that the gospel should be presented with both hands, the hand of the preached Word, and the hand of the supplied resource (that was the whole gospel needed by the whole world!).

Both my wife, Treena, and I have committed our lives to better understand how to 'give ourselves, first to God and *then* to works that are in the will of God' (2 Cor. 8:5).

Ron Sider's writing, example and commitment have

helped to provide us with fifteen years of truly creative Christianity, which we hope to continue with increasing celebration in this less hedonistic decade (?) of the 'nineties.

Graham Kerr
Tacoma, Washington

Ron Sider's *Rich Christians in an Age of Hunger* pricked the conscience of a generation of Christians, both in the U.S. and elsewhere, who were beginning to be concerned about world hunger. The strength of the book is its combination of biblical roots and practical application. The book continues to be useful because it shows what kingdom lifestyle really means in today's world.

Howard A. Snyder
Dayton, Ohio

Transformation can help readers explore further and implement the concerns of this book.

Transformation is an international journal dealing with Christian social ethics, edited by Vinay Samuel of India, Tokunboh Adeyemo of Africa, and Ronald J. Sider from North America. Probably the only evangelical, international periodical on social ethics, **Transformation** publishes authors from every continent and every ideological perspective. The debate flows fast, but not furious – because we have a common commitment to the authority of the Scriptures.

In the issues of **Transformation** you will find probing analyses of tough current topics, scholarly studies of how to apply the Bible to social issues, and exciting descriptions of holistic models of evangelism and social concern.

For further information and a subscription form, write to me at:

Transformation
The Oxford Centre for Mission Studies
PO Box 70
Oxford, ENGLAND OX2 6HB

Ronald J. Sider
Co-Editor
Transformation